The
Golden Age
of Enduros

D1379671

"There is something about a motorcycle and a man that once you have had one, you will always want one"

Ted Webster (Ron's father)

The
Golden Age
Of Enduros

By

Piet W. Boonstra

Another Adventure Touring Publication
Buchanan, New York

Acknowledgements

Many of my friends helped to compile the research material that I used to write this book. I am particularly grateful to Bob Hicks for searched through years of his *Cycle Sport* and *Trail Rider* magazine archives for write-ups, photos and results of enduros that I rode. He copied and sent a great deal of that material to me; including many photos that were scanned and sent via email by his daughter, Roberta. I used some of that material verbatim, and some I incorporated into my own writing.

I am also grateful to Boyd Reynolds, retired Action Sports photographer, who pored over many hundreds of photos that he took at national championships during that period, and he sent a great deal of that material to me to choose from. Boyd also took the cover photo of this book at the 150-mile national championship in Schuyler County, NY in 1965.

I wish to thank Marjorie "Pete" Kieburg for contributing several professional photographs taken by her late father, Grant Whidden.

I would also like to thank Marcia MacDonald, Jake Herzog, Ron Webster, Drew Smith and several other friends who contributed remembrances, bios, and photos of that great era that began for me in the late 1940s, when I rode my first enduro, and continued through the 1960s and beyond.

I am grateful to Tom Smith for having been an invaluable sounding board for me on the overall structure and content of the book.

To my Family

Left to right, Donna, Tom, Jim, Oma (a Friesian name for Grandma), John (in front), Kathy and Lillian. This photo was taken on Christmas Day, 1967, at the height of my glory days.

In Loving Memory of
Lillian, Kathy and Oma

CONTENTS

Introduction

Those who know Piet Boonstra from having read his "Motorcycling Stories" will think of him as the consummate adventure tourer, compiling a million miles in the saddle of a road bike from the Yucatan Peninsula to the Arctic Circle, including seven trips from his home in New York to Alaska. And they wouldn't be wrong, because Boonstra's exploits on the tarmac earned him the title of AMA Road Rider of the Year in 2002. Those who knew Boonstra before he launched his epic touring career in 1977 are more likely to think of him as an accomplished off-road endurance rider.

When Piet Boonstra began riding motorcycles, there wasn't all that much difference between road and off-road motorcycles. In fact, he bought a big 1947 Harley Knucklehead for the road, then immediately stripped it down to compete in an enduro. To riders of modern off-road machines, this seems incredible, but it really wasn't so unusual at the time. In fact, like Boonstra, off-road champion John Penton also entered his first enduro aboard a Harley. Big Indians and Harleys were what was available at the time, prior to the arrival of the so-called "lightweights" from Great Britain, and later the really lightweights from Europe and Japan.

After sharpening his off-road riding skills and wearing out several motorcycles (most were already well-used when he bought them), Boonstra won the New England Enduro Grand Championship in 1966 aboard a 500cc Triumph. The following year he won the heavyweight championship at the famed Canadian National Corduroy Enduro, and over his career he has collected more than 200 awards, many times as high-point rider. By Boonstra's reckoning, he has lived through the greatest era of American off-road riding, what he calls "a golden age of enduros."

His book about this golden age is not just one man's trip down memory lane. The era Boonstra writes about was indeed a period of technological and cultural revolution in the history of American motorcycling. It was a time of opportunity and diversity, when enthusiasts could take their choice from many brands made in America, England, Europe, and finally Japan. It was a time of transition when two-strokes vied with four-strokes for technological supremacy. It was a time when off-road motorcycles changed from modified road machines to purpose-built sport bikes designed to tackle the toughest trails and hold up under the most punishing conditions.

Boonstra experienced every aspect of this evolving technology. From the big road Harley he moved to a lightweight two-stroke Harley, then to a Villiers-powered DMW; but eventually he settled for the 500cc Triumph, like that ridden by seven-time Grand National Enduro Champion Bill Baird. It was not the lightest bike on the trail, but it proved the perfect partner for Boonstra's strength and imposing six foot, four inch frame.

This golden age of off-roading also benefited from the fact that the new environmental consciousness of the 1970s had not yet arrived. Sure, clubs had to work to be good neighbors, but for the most part they could go their merry way through the woods, so long as they cleaned up afterward. In fact, whole communities rolled out the red carpet at annual events such as the Jack Pine and the Corduroy. They found the off-roaders novel, entertaining, and generous contributors to the local economy. Later, a triple assault of institutionalized environmentalism, government regulation, and suburban sprawl began to challenge the rights of clubs to host events and riders to enjoy the woods.

And there were changes within the sport that dulled the shine for the true endurance time keepers who looked for a challenge as much in their head as on the trail. First, a largely level playing field was upset by professionalism. What had previously been a friendly amateur sport was invaded by factory teams and sponsored riders who didn't come to have fun or make friends. Then computers changed the basic nature of enduro competition, virtually eliminating the aspects of quick wit and mental discipline that had been fundamental qualities of championship riders. A new generation of riders and organizers looked for simpler rules that would eliminate the need to keep time.

Piet Boonstra lived through this era, and he rode shoulder-to-shoulder with the greats of his day: Bill Baird, John Penton, Sal Scirpo, and others, and he describes it expertly and convincingly in this book. Boonstra has told me that writing does not come easy, and that he has to work at every page. I could respond with two observations. First, the long suffering does not show in his prose, for which in 1998 he won the American Motorcyclist Association's Joe Christian Award for outstanding freelance writing. Secondly, some of our greatest writers – Hemingway, for example – complained that writing didn't come easy. Beyond his straightforward and unembellished style, Boonstra – again, like Hemingway – addresses the themes of competition, camaraderie, fellowship, conflict, and man's struggle with external forces, and ultimately with the self within.

Ed Youngblood

Preface

Having been raised in the 1930s, in the midst of the Great Depression, I was programmed to pinch every penny, and the only way we ever got our hands on a penny in those days was to work for it. That frugality carried over to my motorcycling. We often rode motorcycles back then, not just for fun, but because we couldn't afford a car. Whenever we were lucky enough to earn a few dollars, most of that was given to Mom for food; and later, after starting our own families, we'd bring it home for them to live on.

A teenager was often better able to find work in the late 1930s than his father; and our mothers, who worked at home without the help of automatic dishwashers, clothes washer/driers, and all of the other modern conveniences that many mothers enjoy today, didn't bring home any extra income.

Our motorcycles were bought with money we earned with no help from our families. There were, however, even at that time, a few that had fathers who could and would buy their motorcycles for them, or at least help to buy them; as well as laying out money to maintain and fix them when they were broken. Usually the fathers who did that were either rich or in the motorcycle business. My father was neither.

Most of my adult life was shaped by the frugal way that my family lived in the thirties after my father died. Except for my first motorcycle, which I bought with my World War II mustering-out pay, most of my motorcycles through the years, especially those for competition, were selected on the basis of what I felt I could afford to lay out for what I considered to be my personal enjoyment, as opposed to the needs of my family. I have always considered my competition to be a personal thing, which had a much lower priority than my transportation for commuting or for the needs of my family.

It makes me wonder sometimes what my competitive career might have been, had I been able to rearrange those priorities and spend as much time and money on my hobby as I would have liked, or as many others with lesser family obligations and greater resources were able to spend. I might have been able to mount a fresh tire, or put on a new chain prior to a national championship, which my bikes were usually in dire need of; or I might even have been able to lay out the money to have the bike set up and maintained by professionals whenever the demands of my job were such that I couldn't find time to do it myself.

But I have no regrets. I had a wonderful family, a lot of fun with them, as well as with my hobby; and I enjoyed many great friendships, all of which were, and still are, much more important to me than any of my trophies. And I carry a warm feeling of satisfaction and pride that whatever I did accomplish was derived through a fervent determination to be all I could be, stopping short of sacrificing my family, my friends, my job, or any amount of enjoyment for that fame.

Piet W. Boonstra
March 2005

Chapter One

Getting Started

I first became interested in motorcycles in 1946, during the time I was attending school in Detroit. I made friends out there with a guy named Bob Armstrong, who owned a 1946 Harley Davidson 74 UL. One day he let me take a ride on his sporty-looking "Flathead" in a quiet park in Dearborn. I made out fine with it, although I only rode it for about a half-mile or so, on a straight and relatively deserted park road. Turning it around was also quite easy, because I did that in an empty parking lot.

Not long after that first ride I quit school altogether. I'm not really sure if I eventually quit because I got the motorcycle bug or if I just didn't relish going to school in the first place; especially after having spent three-and-a-half years in the U.S. Navy during World War II. It's possible that the exciting Navy life totally spoiled me for sitting still in a classroom.

I had been taking post-graduate courses at Cass Technical High School in Detroit, funded by my post-WWII GI Bill. I was picking up extra credits I needed to enter an engineering college. I originally began studying business earlier that year at the Detroit Institute of Technology, working toward an accounting degree, but after learning through some aptitude tests that I was more inclined toward engineering than business, I promptly quit the business course and went back to high school to pick up those necessary academic credits. Though I had originally graduated from high school in New York State in 1942, I chose to remain in Detroit to get the credits. I was living in the Detroit YMCA at the time.

I returned home in May of 1947 and bought a new 1947 Harley Davidson 74 FL "Overhead" from Jack Tracey in Yonkers, which I crashed right out in front of his bike shop moments after laying out $785 of my mustering out pay for it. I've already published a brief account of that incident in my earlier book *Motorcycling Stories*, but here's the whole story:

When I arrived at Tracey's to pick up my new bike, it was already out front facing north on Broadway. I had to make a U-turn with it because I intended to go home a different way, a move I had never practiced with Bob Armstrong's Flathead. This U-turn involved crossing four lanes of city traffic and two sets of streetcar tracks, with rough bricks on both sides and in between.

I remembered what Bob had told me about the power of the overhead-valve engine. He suggested that when I take it out for the first time, I should probably start out in second gear, so that the power wouldn't come on so strong all of a sudden. I thought about those words as I threw my leg over the machine in front of Tracey's that day, although Bill Tracey was standing right there next to me at the time, and he saw me slip the shifter lever into second.

He said, "Hey wait a minute! You're supposed to start this motorcycle in first gear." I thought about giving him my reasons, but not wanting to show how little I actually knew about it, or to make more of a scene than I already had, I simply pulled the shifter into first and let it pass. I was already a little nervous and rattled, and after getting "yelled at," I totally lost my concentration. I then applied far too much throttle and let the clutch out much too fast, which caused the powerful machine to lurch forward and literally ROAR across Broadway! As my weight got thrown backward, my hand seemed to roll the throttle open even more. The bike flew across those streetcar tracks like a screaming banshee, with me hanging on for dear life.

Leaning hard to the left, I had almost completed my turn and regained control when the right crash bar hooked the front bumper of a new Nash, parked on the other side of Broadway. The bike came to a sudden stop, jamming itself between the Nash and a '37 Packard coupe. It threw me clear over the handlebars onto the roof of the Packard. I continued to roll off the roof, across the hood, and into the gutter.

Bill Tracey came running across Broadway yelling, "I thought you could ride that thing." With great embarrassment I said, "So did I." After visiting the local Nash dealer with the car's owner, and after Bill Tracey replaced a few bent and broken parts on my new Harley, I was ready to go again. There was still a good-sized dent on the roof of the Packard, but I never did find the owner to make the proper reparations. I hoped he was short and would never notice it.

My first motorcycle – a beautiful 1947 Harley Davidson 74 OHV, known nowadays as a "knucklehead." Note the Mack bulldog on the front fender.

Before they would let me leave, they wanted me to go out with Gene Baron, one the mechanics, so that he could give me a brief lesson on making U-turns. This was quite humiliating to me, but I agreed. The whole scene of picking up my motorcycle was becoming an embarrassment and laying the groundwork for my future reputation.

"Barrie" came out of the shop smiling and wiping oil from his hands, and he got on my bike. He told me to get on the back. More humiliation! But I got on anyway and we rode over to a relatively quiet spot on McLean Avenue, where he said to get off and stand by the curb while he demonstrated, "the right way to make a U-turn." He went through the motions two or three times, until I thought I had enough. I finally said, "OK. I see. I really have to go. I'm leaving for Detroit in the morning and I haven't packed my bags yet."

He got off, put one hand on his forehead in a gesture of disbelief and repeated most of what I had said, like he wanted to make sure he heard me right. Then after a brief pause he said, (like my mother might), "Don't you think it would be better to get a little practice before you leave on a trip like that?"

I don't remember exactly how I answered that question, but as I got on the bike I said, "Would you like me to ride you back to the store?"

By this time he was shaking his head and laughing like, "I don't believe this guy!" He answered, "No thanks, I'll walk back." It was about a half-mile. As I pulled away, I held on a little extra tight, leaned forward a little, and I gave the throttle a healthy twist. I was sure he was standing there shaking his head as he watched me disappear down McLean Avenue, in one big, continuous roar – in first gear! He was probably saying to himself, "I'll never see that poor idiot again."

I took my second spill the very next morning on my way to Detroit. During the first few hundred miles of riding my new Harley, I had learned what a terrific thrill it was to lay the bike into a turn and have the floorboard gently scrape the pavement. By this time I was really hooked, but I owned the bike for less than 24 hours and I was already pushing the envelope.

That morning I laid it deep into a turn near Saugerties, NY, until the floorboard scraped the tarmac. But then I had to lay it down a little farther because the turn was tighter than I had anticipated. It made a long, loud scraping sound as both wheels were gently lifted off the pavement. My new bike slid on its "crash bars" clear across the oncoming lane and came to rest on the far shoulder. I was lucky there were no cars coming the other way. I picked it up and continued on to Detroit.

While there I showed off my new Harley to my friends, I picked up some things I had left behind the last time I was there, as much as I could carry, and then I headed back. I had originally planned to head for home in the morning, but I learned that there would be no gas stations open in Canada on Sunday, so I left sometime Saturday afternoon, figuring on possibly stopping for the night after crossing Canada.

There weren't many lines painted on the roads along my route, which didn't bother me much during the day, but nightfall descended before I was halfway across Canada. It became much more difficult to follow the road in the darkness without those lines. I rounded one curve doing about sixty-five and was blinded by bright headlights from an oncoming car. I left the road at speed, and the wheels immediately got into some soft sand, causing the front wheel to dig in. The bike then did a complete somersault, as I went sailing over the handlebars.

I flew through the air for quite a long distance, and tumbled at least three times before finally coming to rest. I remember thinking after the first bounce that I was still conscious, and I felt pretty good about that. The second and third tumbles were a piece of cake, but the wind got totally knocked out of me and I couldn't utter a sound, as I lie there quite still. A couple saw the accident and stopped to offer assistance. They insisted on taking me to a doctor, who lived nearby. After being examined by the doctor, and after he confirmed that there were no serious injuries, they took me back to where my motorcycle was still lying on its side.

When the guy picked it up, we could see that all three lights on the front were smashed – the headlight and both spotlights. The handlebars were also bent a little, and the front fender was damaged, as well as having a few scrapes and dents in other areas. The guy got on and drove it for a short distance up the road and back. When he came back he said it handled a little strange because of the bent handlebar, and there wasn't much light coming from the bare bulbs, as the lenses were broken and the reflectors were crushed. I got on, thanked them very much for their help and headed for Niagara Falls in the darkness.

It gave me a problem about an hour or so later, when it seemed as though the generator wasn't putting out enough to power all three lights at the slower speeds that I was forced to travel. When I noticed that the light intensity was fluctuating with the throttle, I turned off the spotlights, giving me even less light. I struggled to make my way across Canada.

I remember finding a big old house in Lackawanna, NY, with a small, lighted sign on the front lawn that said, "Rooms." It was around 2 AM when I knocked at the door. A woman finally answered, but she would only open the door a crack as she peeked out. I had obviously gotten her out of bed. "What do you want?" she said. I must have been quite a sight! Some of my clothes were torn, my face had dried blood on it, and I really looked like a bum. I pleaded with her to rent me a room. I gave her a sob story through the slightly open door about my accident, and she finally opened it all the way to let me in.

If I recall correctly, the room cost only about three or four dollars, which included breakfast. It was like a "bed & breakfast" of the forties, long before they started using that name. In those days it was known as a tourist home. After a hearty breakfast of bacon and eggs in the kitchen the next morning, I rode the final 400 miles to get home.

One of the reasons I needed to be back by Monday was because that was the day I signed for my weekly $20 check, which I received through the "52-20 Club," a GI Bill benefit that paid unemployed veterans $20 a week for 52 weeks. I milked mine to the very end! Twenty dollars bought a lot of gasoline for the motorcycle when it cost only about 33 cents a gallon. I remember it being as low as seven gallons for a dollar during a "price war" in the late 1930s, but after the war it settled in at around three gallons for a dollar.

Since the bike had about 2,300 miles on it when I got back, I figured I should take it in for its thousand-mile checkup. I had been gone from Tracey's for less than a week when I pulled up and parked in front of the shop. Bill met me with a big smile as I entered, saying, "You made it!" sarcastically implying that he was surprised. I was sure Barrie had told him that they'd never see me again. I said yes, I've come for my thousand-mile check. "Thousand-mile check?" he replied, repeating my words in disbelief and grinning broadly, "You have that many miles on it already?"

As I was explaining to him that the mileage was from my trip to Detroit, someone yelled, "Hey Bill. Come here. You gotta see this!" The guy had apparently been looking out through the front window and was of course referring to the dramatic change in appearance of my motorcycle. I suspected they had probably been discussing the earlier incident ever since I left. Then of course everyone had to pile out of the shop and stand by the curb to have his big laugh.

It was with this background a few months later that I inquired about the upcoming competitive event for which I had seen a poster on their bulletin board. The Yonkers Motorcycle Club was promoting the event. It was an endurance run called the Yonkers Turkey Run. I got more laughs when I announced that I planned to ride my big Harley in their turkey run.

I learned that an endurance run involved riding one's motorcycle through a series of wooded trails for a distance of nearly two hundred miles, while maintaining a precise 24-mile-per-hour average speed. It sounded like fun to me. It seemed that 24 miles per hour wasn't very fast; although they made a point of saying that it wasn't a race, and if I were to arrive early at any of the "secret checkpoints" that the club sets up along the way, I would be penalized double for the infraction.

My bike was no longer new and shiny when I decided to take it for a ride in the woods the first time. I have never been one for washing and polishing my motorcycles anyway, or for fixing cosmetic damage for that matter. I had thought from the beginning that motorcycles are made for riding, and certainly not for washing, polishing and looking at. I had already ridden it on a few trails and dirt roads for months before I decided to try off-road competition with it. I had seen the event posters a few times on the bulletin board at Tracey's and I wondered what these "turkey runs" were all about.

Apparently the trick was to keep an eye on the odometer, the speedometer, and also on a watch, to ensure maintaining the prescribed average speed. Aside from riding over and through many obstacles, the object seemed also to be based on the reliability of the machine, and making sure you don't break something on it while continuing to stay on time.

1947 was long before the age of the computers, exotic GPS instruments or other clever electronic time-keeping devices, and it was also before manufacturers made special motorcycles or special clothing for this type of competition. It was even before we wore helmets. Helmets were only worn in professional track races. Very few wore them in endurance runs. Contestants would modify their standard street motorcycles for the event using their own ingenuity, and they'd wear tough outer clothing that would not only protect them, but wouldn't tear easily if the clothes got hooked on a branch.

I had no idea at first what to do to my Harley to get it ready for the event, but I started out by taking off most of the things that I didn't think I would need, like the windshield, the spotlights, the saddlebags, the front fender, and the back half of the rear fender. It's a good thing it didn't rain, with no front fender! There was something mentioned about possibly getting stuck in the mud, so I searched around and found a used 6.00 X 16 knobby snow tire from a car to mount onto the back wheel. Tire manufacturers didn't make special knobby tires for motorcycles at that time, nor could I have afforded one. The tire I found barely cleared the inside of the back fender of my Harley. I still had to trim some rubber from the corners of the tread to keep it from rubbing.

There was no room at all for mud buildup under the fender, which meant that whenever I got into a muddy section I'd have to depend on the power of the engine to keep the back end from clogging up with mud. I planned to carry an old watch, but I suspected that I probably wouldn't need it on that first run. I had learned that the club awarded medals to riders who rode the entire distance, even though they didn't win or place, so my primary objective was to go the distance and finish. I think the total length of that first run was around 175 miles. I worked on the bike for a couple of days to get the weight down to a little over 600 pounds.

There was a special meeting for all contestants at the clubhouse in Yonkers the night before the event, the purpose of which was to draw numbers to determine starting positions. The contestants would start one minute apart from each other. They said it would be to my advantage to draw an early number so that the trails would still be in fairly good shape, and not crowded with other riders. Riders with the higher starting numbers would have to struggle through much deeper mud holes, possibly crowded with other motorcycles already stuck in the mud.

I rode my stripped-down Harley the 27 miles to Yonkers for the meeting. Most riders came by car for that meeting, but I didn't own a car. Each rider's name was called, one at a time, and they would come forward to draw their starting positions from a huge bowl. Route sheets were given out at the same time. I decided to tape mine onto the gas tank when I got home. The route sheet held the details about the run, like the cumulative mileage to each turn on the planned course.

Bill Tracey was the master of ceremonies at the dinner and when he called my name to come forward and draw a number, it was not without fanfare, especially after he made a point of announcing (while laughing) that everyone should take a good look at this guy, because "He's the dark horse in this run." I learned that the winner would take home a 15-pound turkey along with the largest trophy. The drawing and the run were held shortly before Thanksgiving.

I got to see several of the local favorites at the dinner, including Don Pink, Phil Phillips, Warren "Specky" Sherwood, Rod Coates, and others. Occasionally riders would come from great distances to compete in the Yonkers endurance runs. I remember seeing the names Al and Julie Kroeger from upstate New York on the result sheets of that and other Yonkers runs. I learned that they were well-known national endurance run riders. Having a dinner like that was a really great way to get acquainted and to develop lifelong friendships with many of the other riders. I learned many years later that a similar pre-event dinner was held every year on the eve of the famous two-day, 500-mile National Jack Pine Endurance Run in Michigan.

The start of a Yonkers Turkey Run in the mid 1940s, directly across Broadway from Jack Tracey's shop. The starter was AMA Hall of Fame's Reggie Pink. The rider checking out was Aldo Otto on a Harley 61 OHV. Piloting the sidecar outfit behind Otto is Ignacious Charboneau.

Photo courtesy of Jim Moroney.

On the morning of the run I again rode my Harley the 27 miles to Yonkers, which was a chilly ride without a windshield. I had drawn a starting position that was just about in the middle of the pack. I think there was a total of 30 riders that started across Broadway from Tracey's shop that morning. The route sheet took us over a few miles of paved roads to get out of the city and into the first trail section, which was called Ardsley Woods.

Luckily there were relatively smooth trails in the woods, so I made it all the way through without incident. There were a few other similar trail sections with various size rocks and occasionally some mud, but nothing too difficult to get through; that is, until we got to the infamous waterhole about 40 miles from the start. After descending Turkey Mountain along a steep, rocky downhill trail, beneath some high-tension power lines near Yorktown Heights, the trail led directly into a huge, muddy patch of water and mud that someone had given the ominous name, "The Yorktown Swamp."

There were more than a half-dozen contestants on much smaller motorcycles than mine already stuck in the mud. A few of them were buried to beyond their axles in deep muddy water.

At least one had drowned out his engine. I paused for a few moments, contemplating the possible routes through it. As I sat mesmerized, watching the excitement, I saw Phil Phillips ride up to the edge of the mud with his 350 cc Panther. He hesitated only briefly to choose his route before making it non-stop all the way across, using both his feet for paddles in the muddy water. He seemed to make the crossing with a minimum of effort.

It didn't look that difficult to me, so from my position about 10 feet from the edge, I grabbed a big handful of throttle, braced myself and headed straight for the same track that Phil took. With the momentum I had built up, I managed to get almost halfway across the swamp; but the 600+ pounds of iron simply buried itself in the mud as the engine stalled. There must have been 20 or more spectators standing around cheering – and a few laughing. A couple of them jumped in to try and help me to get the big Harley out, but it was almost to a point where you might say, "forget it!" It wouldn't budge an inch.

Even getting it restarted was a chore because I couldn't get full travel out of the kick-starter. Spinning the back wheel didn't help at all because the center was hung up on something. While I was in the mud hole I saw Don Pink come through with his Harley 45 WLDR. His movements were smooth as silk as he made the crossing look far easier than it was – to me, anyway.

After spending the better part of an hour struggling with it, several other spectators jumped in to help get my Harley out. It took about five people pulling and pushing with all of their might, with help from the engine. I was well "over my hour" when I reached the checkpoint on the far side of the swamp, which meant that I was disqualified from the event for having reached that point more than an hour late. So from there I simply went home, which was a short 10-mile ride from Yorktown over paved roads. I got the results in the mail a week or so later and I don't recall now who finally took home the turkey.

There were no Japanese motorcycles being imported at that time and the best bikes for endurance runs seemed to be the comparatively lightweight English motorcycles like the AJS, BSA, Matchless, Velocette or Triumph. There were not many riders around who could ride a Harley through the woods, or anywhere for that matter, quite like Don Pink rode his 45. My overall opinion of endurance runs after that first ride was that I could probably make it through most of the trails with my big Harley as long as they didn't use that Yorktown Swamp.

Drew Smith wrote the following account of that same event:

As I reflect back to November 1947, at age 19, having ridden motorcycles for just a year and a half, and living in the very heart of New York City, I realize I had been "chickened" into riding my first enduro, the Yonkers M.C. Turkey Run. Back then, most of the bike riders had Harleys and Indians. I had recently bought a used 1938 80 cu. in. flathead.

It was with this bike that I'd ride the enduro, and as I surveyed my spotlights, crash-bars, bald tires and saddlebags, I wondered how my first enduro would go. I heard there would be mud, plenty of woods, and water crossings, so I prepared by putting galoshes in the saddlebags. What did I know?

On Saturday night the Yonkers Club held a drawing for riding positions. When I went home that night I could hardly sleep, anticipating what would be in store for me the next morning. Well, on Sunday we contestants took off from South Broadway in Yonkers, one minute apart, and headed north on a 24 mph schedule. Before long we reached Ardsley and turned into some secondary roads, then into some dirt trails. Oh boy, so far, so good! Then the ruts got rougher with plenty of mud holes, adverse cambers, and me slipping and sliding with bald tires. Riders that I considered to be "pros" (wearing leathers) started to zoom by me on stripped down Indians and lighter Harley 45s. They seemed to know how to cover the rough stuff with very little effort, passing me while sending rooster tails of mud in the air behind them. Wow, I had plenty to learn! I got stuck up to the frame in some mud holes while still on the trail, but finally made my way to the first stream crossing.

I stopped and surveyed the situation and watched some riders hit the water, blast through and up the bank on the other side. Then cleverly (I thought) I put on my galoshes from the saddlebags, and I prepared to enter the stream. Half an hour later my bike was on the other bank with the help of some other riders, still laughing at my galoshes filled with water.

They pointed me to the top of a muddy hill ahead of us, where the checkpoint workers were signing the riders in. After more slipping and sliding and wheel spinning (and with more help) I signed in more than an hour late and was disqualified! I was disillusioned and exhausted, and the steam from my body heat was fogging my glasses. It was tougher than I thought it would be, and I knew I'd have to take a lot of ribbing over those galoshes.

The two greatest loves of my life, Lilli and my bike, circa spring of 1948

I met Lillian in the fall of 1947 around the same time I rode that Yonkers Turkey Run for the first time. A group of about 14 of us were out one night on a ride similar to the horde of bikers depicted in the movie *The Wild One*, which was released seven years later in 1954. Several of the motorcycles in our group, including mine, had very loud exhaust pipes. I had made a set of "straight pipes" from thin brass bedposts, which produced an extremely loud and very distinctive rattling blast of sound that could be heard for miles, especially at night.

We were out tearing around through the local towns making far too much noise and creating a nuisance. The police had run us out of White Plains, a good-sized city, and later we passed through Ossining the same way, headed for Yorktown Heights. We were riding quite fast along NY Route 129, when one of the guys in our group named Rusty slid his bike on some sand in a turn and crashed hard against a bridge abutment. Several of us stood around while someone rushed to a nearby house to use the telephone and call an ambulance.

Lillian had been riding with my friend, Sammy Bell, who owned a beautiful and ultra-fast 1947 Indian Chief. Sammy and I traveled together quite a bit. That night, as we stood around waiting for the ambulance to arrive, I talked with Lillian, who struck me as being a really fine person. When I learned later that she and Sammy weren't actually "going together," I got his OK to ask her out. His first answer was, "Go ahead, she's too rich for me." I said, "What do you mean, 'too rich'?"

He said they had stopped at a diner a few nights earlier while out on a ride, where he had apparently intended to order only a coffee. Not realizing this, Lillian ordered a hamburger, which Sammy didn't seem to appreciate.

Actually I was quite happy with the way it turned out, and we began seeing each other soon after that. We eloped on the motorcycle in May of 1948, and were married by a justice of the peace just up the river in Cornwall, followed by a brief impromptu honeymoon in the Catskills. I would sometimes kid her later about having gotten her at bargain prices – the price of a hamburger, which then was only around 30¢.

Two days before Thanksgiving 1947, I decided to take one final trip to Detroit to pick up the last of what I had left there. I had to make it to Detroit in a day, and back in a day, so I wouldn't miss my mother's Thanksgiving dinner at home. I had much more riding experience by then and I was able to make the 765-mile ride to Detroit easily in a day, using the most direct route across Canada.

Unfortunately I hadn't checked the weather forecast before leaving. It began to snow the evening I arrived in Detroit. So I revised my return route and headed south early the next morning, to take the longer southern route back to New York. Soon after stepping out of the YMCA around 5 a.m., I witnessed a mugging in the alley near the secluded spot where I had parked the bike. Detroit always was a tough neighborhood! I went back in and reported it to the desk clerk at the YMCA, but I left before the police arrived. I had more than 800 miles to travel that day, and it was already snowing.

By mid-morning I was entering Ashland, Ohio, where the snow was beginning to accumulate on the road surface. I approached the main part of town moving about 60 to 65 mph, when the surface underneath the thin layer of snow turned to a sheet of ice. The bike went down and slid for more than 200 feet, with me holding on and sliding with it. When it stopped, I tried to pick it up, but I could barely stand on the icy surface. With considerable effort I managed to get it over to the sidewalk, which appeared to be sanded. I rode for a block or more on the sidewalk before I heard a police whistle. The cop was yelling for me to get off the sidewalk. As soon as I turned and entered the road, I dumped it hard on the icy pavement – even harder than the first time when I went down at speed.

The snow got progressively deeper and I had a miserable time getting over Allegany Mountain in Pennsylvania; but I finally arrived home around 10 a.m. the following day, having traveled all night. I had to stop several times for coffee. My mother was happy because I arrived home safely, and in the nick of time for our Thanksgiving Dinner.

By the end of 1947, I had crashed the bike at least a half-dozen times and ridden it in an endurance run, so it certainly wasn't new and shiny any more. I had taken on and beaten several of the "hot" local riders on the street as well as on back roads, and the word being passed around was "Don't mess with 'Petey,' – you'll kill yourself." I had ridden more than 25,000 miles during those first six months, and I had built a reputation for being fast, wild, and fearless – and maybe a little crazy!

A few weeks after Lillian and I were married, we heard about an annual Gypsy Tour that took place in Laconia, New Hampshire. We both thought it would be ideal for a second honeymoon, to ride the bike to the Gypsy Tour for the weekend. It was a few miles short of 300 miles each way for us.

We stayed at the Chanticleer Inn on Lake Winnepesauki, not far from Weirs Beach. We had a great time! We danced at the inn, and took a boat excursion on the lake; and of course we attended the motorcycle races and the bike show. We had never seen so many motorcycles in one place in our lives. I became a member of the American Motorcyclist Association (AMA) there at the Gypsy Tour in Laconia in 1948, and have been a member ever since.

I remember that Joe Weatherly won the 100-mile national championship road race at the Belknap Recreation Area track that year on a Harley Davidson. The track consisted of a hairpin curve at the bottom of a long hill, followed by a long, sweeping, uphill curve. Most of the track was paved, although there was one short straight stretch of sugary sand that was part of the racecourse.

We missed very few years between then and the year of the riots at Weirs Beach, many years later, sparked by the Hells Angels, which I believe was in 1963. I came that year with our oldest daughter Kathy, who was 14 at that time. We saw Jody

Taken in 1948, around the time Lillian and I eloped on the bike. I was a little too wild for my own good at the time, but I outgrew it and calmed down in my later years. We had a club in 1948 called the Westchester Cavaliers, of which I was the president. We often went on picnics and club rides together.

Earl's Diner was a popular meeting place in Laconia

Nicholas drop his 500 cc BSA in the hairpin with one lap to go. After being passed by an unbelieving George Roeder on a KR Harley Davidson, Jody picked up his bike, turned up the throttle without even being fully on the machine, and with his feet barely back on the pegs he passed Roeder on the long uphill curve on that very last lap and won the race before a huge cheering crowd.

Lillian and I took a trip in 1948 to Washington, DC to visit the Smithsonian Institution. We also visited and stayed overnight with my stepbrother Leonard in Alexandria, Virginia.

My visits to Yonkers became less frequent during the summer of 1948, as they would inspire much laughter and friendly teasing. Someone would invariably look outside to check on the latest condition of my motorcycle and make remarks about its shabby appearance. I began to frequent the small Harley shop in Somers, NY, where a whole different group of riders hung out, and many of them became lifelong friends.

William B. "Wild Bill" Johnson in the early 1950s

Bill Johnson, the owner, was a black man, known during the 1920s and '30s throughout the northeast hill-climbing circuit as "Wild Bill." For more than 60 years he owned and operated a Harley Davidson dealership in Somers, where the local people knew him as Mr. Johnson. His many customers and friends knew him affectionately as "Willie."

William B. Johnson was a Harley Davidson dealer and a member of the AMA long before membership was open to black riders. He was not only the first black person ever to hold a valid AMA card, but he ranks high among the great hill climbers of the past. He was well known for his courage and his natural ability to charge fearlessly up the most famous hills in the east, and for consistently winning his class. Bill Johnson loved the sport, he loved motorcycles, and he loved people. He was a genuine motorcyclist through every fiber of his being.

When representatives of the AMA came to Somers in the 1920s to negotiate with local landowners for the use of their hill for sanctioned events, a deal was struck: They were welcome to use the property under one condition – that their neighbor, Mr. Johnson, would be allowed to compete. The terms were gladly accepted and he was promptly issued an AMA card in appreciation of his help in securing the property.

With it, "Wild Bill" went on to compete in up to 20 hill climb events a year in New England, New York, and as far west as Pittsburgh. The Somers hill, his "home turf," became known as one of the toughest hills around, and he consistently excelled there, to the joy of the local crowd.

In 1932, while in the pits preparing his machine for a shot at a national championship hill-climb event near Albany, he was approached unknowingly by a prominent official of the AMA, who informed him that he was very sorry, but "coloreds" were not allowed to compete in an AMA-sanctioned event. Willie whipped out his cherished AMA card with a smile and displayed it proudly, whereupon the official reluctantly backed off. Encouraged by the outcome of this confrontation with the AMA official, Wild Bill Johnson went on to win the championship that very same day.

In a hotly contested hill climb in Connecticut in the late 1930s, his bike reared up fiercely near the top of the hill and the handlebars struck him square in the mouth, knocking out six teeth, and tearing a big gash on his face. It was the kind of spill that would discourage most competitors pushing forty, but Johnson was right back on the hill three weeks later, as fearless as ever.

At the age of eighty he would service a bike at his shop and then take it out for a thorough test ride. He'd have a big smile on his face and a distinct twinkle in his eye as he rode out. It was not uncommon to see "Wild Bill" come by the shop a few minutes later at a speed to match his age, with a grin from ear to ear and his legs stretched out in glee, like he was riding a bronco. He would then usually unleash a yell like he often did when he topped a challenging hill fifty years earlier.

There wasn't a motorcyclist for miles around who didn't know him and like him. For people who really got to know him well, as I did, he was one of the kindest, most generous human beings ever to sit astride a motorcycle. He often loaned a demo bike right off his showroom floor to a friend to ride to a race meet on Sunday, or even to take it to Laconia for the Gypsy Tour. As might be expected, he was often taken advantage of, but he never spoke an unkind word about anyone.

Johnson was a native of Maryland who emigrated to Somers soon after the turn of the century. His motorcycle shop became a landmark in the village. He often spoke of having met James A. Bailey, of Barnum and Bailey fame, who was almost a next-door neighbor to Bill. Bailey had brought the first elephant to this country, which he housed in Somers for several years. For new riders who needed directions to Bill's shop, they would be told that it was near the elephant statue.

Willie retired from riding at the age of 82, after having received serious injuries in a fall on a patch of ice while walking across his driveway. That fall and a later botched operation left him paralyzed in both arms.

He continued to maintain his dealership for many years in spite of his disability, although others ran it for him in the later years. The sport lost one of its great riders in 1985 and I lost a close personal friend, when he died quietly in the back room of his shop at the age of 95.

I was determined to return in the fall of 1948 to ride the Yonkers Turkey Run at least one more time, and to do better than I had on my first try. I worked on the bike for more than a month before the event, getting it ready and test riding it. I picked up an old 18" front wheel from a 1930-something Harley. I figured that the larger wheel would raise it farther off the ground and improve the ground clearance, especially going through the mud or over big rocks. I located a huge 4.50 X 18 car tire from a 1920-something Chevy, which I mounted onto that 18-inch front wheel. It barely fit between the fork legs.

The tire was slightly rounded on its face, which allowed, at least at a minimum, for leaning into turns. I remounted the same huge 16" snowcapped tire from the previous year onto the rear wheel. I was determined to finish the run this time. I made a route sheet holder from a board that I mounted above the center of the handlebars. By the time the Yonkers Turkey Run rolled around, I was ready to give it my best shot.

As many clubs often did in those days, they used basically the same route, but ran it backwards from the previous year, which meant, thank goodness, that the Yorktown Swamp would be considerably more than 100 miles into the event. I got a real taste of enduros (short for endurance runs) this time. I managed to get my big Harley over and through all kinds of obstacles, and I was encouraged to press on every time I came to one of their secret checkpoints. Many of the guys who frequented Tracey's would man the checks, and at more than one I would be offered a swig from some kind of bottle to "keep me going."

Arriving at the Noon Control at Yorktown Heights with my Harley 74 in the 1948 Yonkers Turkey Run. I wore a leather jacket, lineman's boots, and an aviator's helmet, and since it was late November, I wore the big Harley sheepskin-lined mittens with gauntlets.

I pulled into one check where two of the guys, who I often referred to as "Mutt and Jeff," were working. I called them that because one was tall and slim and the other was short and stocky, like the well-known comic strip characters of that era. They would always seem to be "three sheets to the wind" when I got to their check, and they were always very friendly. I could usually count on being offered a sip of whiskey, brandy or something, whenever they were manning one of the checks. They also checked at modified road runs that I rode in later years, and I would always look forward to their checkpoint.

The greatest obstacle I met in the first 100 miles was the infamous hill on Bullet Hole Road in Putnam County, called Tompkins Corners Hill. It was a very steep hill in the woods

Drew Smith (left) and Wink Butz in the infamous Yorktown swamp, circa 1952.
Photo complements of Drew Smith

with rocks of all sizes and shapes strewn all over it. There were a few rock ledges to get over and a few big, half-buried, concrete drainpipes that ran across the abandoned road, which were probably once underground but years of erosion from the rain had uncovered them. I actually passed a few other riders on that hill, as the awesome power of my big Harley pulled me over the top with the greatest of ease. Of course I was strong like a bull.

The "noon control," which was a scheduled stopover for lunch and refueling, was at Yorktown Heights, a short distance before the course would take us into that dreadful swamp. I got to the noon control about 40 minutes late, but still within the hour I was allowed. The noon control usually gave us a half-hour layover, but since I was already running 40 minutes late when I got there, I would also be late leaving.

Lillian was there, as were a few of my other friends to offer encouragement and refreshments. They said that the swamp was in even worse condition than it had been the previous year – meaning deeper! They convinced me that I would never get the Harley through it without the help of many spectators, and that would almost certainly be after my one-hour grace period would have been used up. I decided against continuing. I had a really enjoyable ride up to that point, so I decided to "quit while I was

Don Pink riding a hand-shift Harley Davidson 45 cu. in. WLDR – feet up.

ahead." I concluded that if I were to ride any more enduros, it would have to be on a smaller motorcycle. Meanwhile, I would stick to the timed road runs and field meets.

I rode several "modified" road runs over rough dirt roads with Lillian as a passenger. At least one of those was with a sidecar that I bought and attached to our next road motorcycle, a 1949 Harley 74 OHV. That machine was equipped with the newly designed Hydra Glide front forks that left a lot to be desired in handling; and the "Panhead" engine wasn't nearly as fast as my old "Knucklehead." I bought the sidecar "used" with the idea of possibly taking trips with our family. Our first child, Kathleen, was born in June 1949; although we never did travel much with it because I didn't care for the awkward way the bike handled with the sidecar attached.

I rode the sidecar in one event sponsored by the Yonkers Motorcycle Club, which was laid out on both gravel and paved roads not far from our home. With my "auxiliary time keeper" in the sidecar and I at the controls, I figured it would be an easy win for us. I had already begun to master some of the time keeping essentials, where I was able to use my watch as a

Popular BSA rider of the 1940s Rod Coates being checked in by Phil Phillips on crutches, soon after Phil broke his leg in an earlier enduro.

simple computer and play tricks with numbers so that I could figure my time easily in my head.

In events where Lillian rode in the sidecar, she would handle the seconds, using her own watch. Whenever we would approach an Emergency Check, signified by a green flag, she would call out the seconds, so that I could arrive at the check at exactly 30 seconds into the correct minute. The exact middle of the minute is the time that one is supposed to pass by the green flag at an Emergency Check. There was usually just one Emergency Check in an enduro, although occasionally there would be a need for two, in order to ensure against tie scores.

We were "zeroing" all of the checks until we got to a narrow dirt road on East Mountain near Fishkill, where we came upon a forest fire. Many firemen were there with a tank truck, and they had laid out some 4-inch hoses across the dirt road with which to fight the fire. I had to stop because there was no way to get around the truck or over the hoses. All of the solo bikes were

At a checkpoint soon after the forest fire. Lillian was even managing to smile at the checker while I signed in. There would be times during that road run when she wasn't smiling! The route sheet I was following was taped to the inside of the windshield of my 1949 Harley Davidson 74 OHV, with Hydra Glide forks.

squeezing by on the side where there were no hoses, but the space was far too narrow to get a sidecar through.

Knowing many of the roads in the area, I turned the rig around and took a detour, losing several minutes of valuable time in the process. It's a good thing that Lillian put up with my antics, because we got sliding on the gravel on several of the left-hand turns, and raising the sidecar clear off the ground on a few of the right-hand turns, as I tried desperately to stay on time. We had quite an exciting ride! Lillian never said a word. She always trusted me. By the time we got to the next checkpoint though, we were several minutes late, removing any possibility for the High Score trophy.

Chapter Two

Turning Over a New Leaf

I had become pretty wild and somewhat of an outlaw on the public roads during my first five years of riding. A steady accumulation of traffic tickets had gradually become a problem for my getting to and from work, and consequently for making a living. I recall one afternoon in particular when Lilli and I were headed north on US Route 9 (the old Albany Post Road) on my 1947 Harley. We were traveling at our usual speed, which was far above the posted limit. I was in the process of passing a string of cars on a twisty two-lane section of road just north of the village of Croton-on-Hudson, straddling the double-yellow line all the way when I noticed that one of the cars in the string was a NY State Trooper's cruiser. A steady stream of cars was also coming from the opposite direction.

I figured it was far too late at that point to do anything but pass the cruiser and keep going. I was traveling quite fast already, and there was very little room between the cars. I didn't worry too much about the sudden predicament I had gotten myself into, because I was usually able to outrun most of the troopers, especially one that was blocked in like that, as it afforded me a pretty comfortable head start.

I stepped up my speed to ensure building up a safe distance between us before he could get free of all the traffic, and I thought he probably wouldn't even bother to chase me. My arrogant mind had concluded that I would be long gone before he could even get started on a chase, and I was sure he had more important things to do than trying to catch a motorcyclist. I covered the next few miles of twisty road at speeds up to 85 and 90 mph, passing many cars, until I was fairly confident that he probably didn't even bother to take up the chase, since I could have easily ducked into any of the side roads along the way.

As I approached my hometown of Buchanan, I rounded the bend near Meyers' Sunoco Station still doing well over 80. I noticed that three of the "regulars" from the garage were out near the shoulder of the road looking in my direction as I rounded the bend. Unbeknownst to me, they had heard the scream of the siren, which I couldn't hear because of the wind in my ears. They had apparently come out to see what was coming. As I passed, I threw a big wave and smiled, as I usually did, and continued on my merry way.

They said later that the trooper was less than 100 yards behind me at the time and that he almost lost control as he came around the curve on two wheels. I passed through the center of Montrose and into Buchanan running smoothly at about 75, but when the traffic began to get heavier, I chopped the throttle, thinking he was far behind. But almost simultaneously the cruiser flew by and cut me off onto the shoulder.

It turned out that it wasn't a trooper driving the car, but a special investigator from the NYS Bureau of Criminal Investigation driving one of the state police cruisers. I noticed when he got out that his hands were trembling, so I asked if he was OK. He took my friendly question of concern as a wise crack, and he asked if I thought I could get away from him; to which I calmly replied that I would have if I had known he was there. My overall arrogance didn't set well with him at all. He didn't have a ticket book with him, so he took my license and registration and said, "Follow me." He then led me back over the same route that we had just come, probably to show everyone that he "got his man."

I had already acquired a somewhat undesirable reputation with the police and the local judges, and after that incident they were determined to take my license forever. That's about the gist of what the judge said to me a week later. I rode around without a license for years after that, getting to and from work, but I got nailed a few more times; and of course then the charge would be driving without a license in addition to what I might have been originally stopped for.

It got to a point by early 1953 that I simply couldn't get to and from work anymore without being constantly harassed. It became like a cat-and-mouse game. I was 27 years old, and I finally realized that it was time for me to clean up my act. Not only had I begun to develop a bad reputation, but I finally realized that I had been living the wild life for far too long for my own good, as well as my family's, not to mention other problems I had gotten myself into.

I was working full-time for the NY Air National Guard at Westchester County Airport at the time, servicing radios on F51-H Mustang fighters based there. I asked the colonel in charge of the National Guard outfit if it would be possible for me to "activate" myself, which meant to be individually deployed into the regular Air Force for two years with the rank I held at the time. I was a Tech Sergeant in the guard, which was the equivalent of Petty Officer First Class in the Navy, the rank I held when I was discharged seven years earlier in 1946.

He arranged it by pulling a few strings, but no sooner I got into the Air Force, they wanted to ship me off to Saudi Arabia for a year, where I wouldn't be able to take my family. That was not at all what I had in mind. Being an old hand at wangling things in the service, I managed to wangle out of that shipment, but found myself in Newfoundland a short time later, working on trying to get Lillian and Kathy to join me there.

It took several weeks of additional wangling, but I was able to make that happen too. I arranged for a hop back home aboard a military air transport to pick up my family. We bought a house trailer and we moved the whole kit and caboodle to Newfoundland for two years.

I hoped that things would cool down at home in the meantime, as I served my time in the Air Force. It wasn't really hard time, in that our little family enjoyed a very memorable two years in Newfoundland, hunting, fishing and participating in many of the social activities at the base. I even "bagged" a moose on one of my hunting trips, and we got to eat lots of codfish that we caught while they were spawning just offshore.

F-89 Scorpions were based at Ernest Harmon Air Force Base

Lillian and Kathy in Newfoundland. This photo was taken while we were on a cod-fishing trip together. Lilli was pregnant with Donna at the time.

   Before we left Newfoundland two years later, I was named "Non-Commissioned Officer of the Month" for my squadron, and later for the entire Ernest Harmon Air Force Base, for designing and building a small mobile control unit to be used by the pilots for special runway service. I built it on an old Army K-1 wagon-type trailer body. It was above and beyond my regular assignment as NCO-in-Charge of the radio/radar shop of 61st Fighter-Interceptor Squadron. Our squadron flew the two-seater, twin-engine F89 Scorpions, which were loaded with exotic electronic sensing equipment, and assigned as part of the Northeast Air Command's defenses of our northern borders on what was known as the Distant Early Warning (DEW) Line.

Here I'm working inside the hanger on the mobile control unit that I designed.

Receiving the award from Colonel Fellows, which included money and time off from duty.

The finished product fully equipped with UHF radio equipment and towing an auxiliary power unit is shown next to the old Army truck that it replaced.

16 November 1954

Subject: NCO-of-the-Month
To: T/Sgt Piet W. Boonstra

It is with great pleasure that I extend to you my appreciation for your outstanding performance of duty as Non-Commissioned-Officer-in-Charge of the Communications Section of the 61st Fighter Interceptor Squadron. It is only with the type of support you are rendering in solving the problems pertaining to your job and your innate ability to coordinate and cooperate with your fellow workers that this base is able to accomplish its mission. Because of your confidence, forcefulness, and understanding of human nature and your ability in your specialty, you were selected as Non-Commissioned-Officer-of-the-Month for October 1954 at Ernest Harmon Air Force Base.

You may well be proud or this distinction. You were selected above all other nominees of all other organizations at this base. The selection was based on standards of allegiance to duty, military appearance, self-improvement and moral character.

(signed)
Richard W. Fellows
Colonel, USAF
Commander

Chapter Three

The New Beginning

When we returned from my self-imposed exile two years later with two children, (Donna was born there), the first thing I thought about was buying another motorcycle. I found a used 1947 Harley 74 OHV, similar to the one I had owned years before, although not nearly as fast. I bought it for getting around and for competing in field meets. Around that same time I landed a job as electronic technician working on the final test of the giant computers at IBM's manufacturing plant in Poughkeepsie.

I had a tough time getting my license back, but I managed to do so with a good lawyer and letters from a few influential people. The lawyer was good but he wasn't cheap, as none are! I rode that second 74 Overhead through a few field trials and road runs and did well with it, but it wasn't long before I got the real bug again – I wanted to ride those endurance runs.

With two children in the family I felt that I couldn't afford to spend as much of the family's money as a BSA or an AJS might cost, although I had always loved the looks, the sound and the performance of English single-cylinder motorcycles.

I wasn't totally sure that was the way I wanted to go anyway, but I was convinced that I wanted something a lot lighter than my Harley 74 for riding in the woods. I was also thinking that I should probably stick with an American-made motorcycle, having served in two wars.

The lightweight machines that seemed to be doing most of the winning at the time were the 200 cc Triumph Cub with a 4-cycle engine, and the Harley 165, which was a 2-stroke. I thought the Harley 165 would be ideal for me, even though it had a slightly smaller engine than the Cub; but then I thought that a new Harley 165 might hang a little heavy on my family's budget, especially when I noticed that it cost a hundred dollars more than a very similar machine sitting right next to it on the showroom floor – the 125 cc Hummer.

1956 Harley Davidson Hummer

Being the frugal Frisian that I have always been, I chose the Hummer and a deal was struck.

My 6'4" frame made me appear like a giant riding a child's tricycle! A week or so later I took it down to Tracey's to show off my new acquisition to the "regulars" there. They all had their usual big laugh, especially when I announced that I was ready to take on their very next Yonkers Turkey Run in November of that year, 1956. I'm sure they thought, "He's back. That big, crazy Dutchman is back!"

Gene Baron suggested that he could make it better by installing rear suspension for a nominal charge, which he did, and the little machine was ready for the challenge.

One of the first competitive events I entered with it was that Yonkers Turkey Run. I didn't do another thing to it to get it ready for the run, except break it in and readjust the chain after the break-in period. I even used the standard road tires that came with it. I teamed up with a good friend Ralph Spencer, who I had met while working briefly on the railroad back in 1947. Ralph owned a Triumph T15 Terrier at the time, which had a 150 cc 4-stroke engine, and was similar in appearance to the Cub, except that it was smaller and had less power than the Cub.

When it came to deciding whether to ride our bikes to Yonkers or to carry them, we decided on the latter. But since we didn't have a trailer at the time, a problem arose how to get two motorcycles into one car. I had recently acquired a 1937 Hudson four-door "straight-eight," which we affectionately called "The Lunger," short for "Eight-lunger," which in turn was derived

Note the shocks on the rear, which was a modification made to my stock Hummer by Gene Baron from Jack Tracey's shop, before I started riding it in the enduros. Otherwise the bike is stock, road tires and all.

from single-cylinder motorcycles often being called "one-lungers."

I removed the rear doors from the Lunger, took out the seat, and we lifted the Hummer inside, with its wheels protruding from both sides of the car. We then lifted Ralph's Terrier into the trunk on its side, shoving the rear wheel far inside and leaving the front wheel to hang out the back of the car, over the bumper. Of course we had to leave the trunk lid open as I drove the car to Yonkers, and we had to carry the gas in a separate can, as it would have spilled from the tank. We carefully lifted them out when we got to the start, which was across from Tracey's shop; and which of course caused another spectacle.

The route sheet we were given when we signed in had us leaving Yonkers and heading straight for the Ardsley Woods, the same way we had done on both previous enduros I entered with my big 74 Harley.

Less than a half-mile after leaving the hard pavement in Ardsley, I came upon a huge tree that had fallen across the trail. It was more than a foot thick, and the trunk was resting yet another foot off the ground. It lay horizontally across my path like a huge barrier. There was a course-marker arrow nailed to

A few popular New York Metropolitan Area riders of the '50s included (L to R) Jim Fennell, Tom Svack, Gene Baron (with tongue out), Don Brown, and Don & Leslie Pink, taken at the Pink's home in Yonkers.   Courtesy of Bob Roper

the trunk at exactly the center-point of the trail. I figured that since the club usually nails the arrows in a way that indicates which way we're supposed to go, I assumed that the arrow meant I was supposed to go OVER the fallen tree; and if I didn't, I'd be in violation of their rules, and maybe get disqualified. I was glad I didn't have the 74 Overhead.

I slid off the back of the seat as I turned up the throttle, which made the tiny machine stand almost straight up on its back wheel, and it allowed the bottom of the frame to come to rest against the fallen trunk. I reached back and picked up the rear end to get the bike up onto and over the tree.

I didn't think at the time that it was a big deal, since I was quite strong and the Hummer wasn't that heavy. As I held it there momentarily, teetering about two feet above the ground, I noticed that Tommy Svack, a club member and one of the top experts of the day, had stopped while on his way AROUND the tree to watch my efforts. In obvious sarcastic amazement he said, "Why are you doing that?"

I answered, "Because that's the way the arrow is pointing." He shook his head in disbelief and continued around the fallen tree, apparently laughing to himself. I learned something new about enduros every day! You don't really have to follow the arrows, literally. I assumed that the story of my act would certainly get back to Tracey's and become more fodder for their "tales of the trail," since he was also a regular there.

I managed to get the little Hummer moving quite fast along most of the trails and over the hills that day, and I got all the way up and over the rock-strewn Tompkins Corners Hill with minimal physical effort. Of course the Hummer lacked the awesome power of my 74, and I had to keep the rpm quite high most of the way up the hill. Only occasionally would I have to push it a little. I did have to push it through a few of the sloppier mud holes that I came upon, because the tires didn't have the knobby tread pattern that most of the other bikes had. But it was light and I was strong, so the mud holes didn't pose too much of a problem – not even the Yorktown swamp.

I learned quite early from riding the Hummer that one of the secrets of riding successfully was that it had to be a joint effort between the bike's power and handling and my own strength and agility. Whatever the Hummer lacked in power and traction, I made up for with strength from my arms and legs. I could throw the Hummer around with ease.

I got to the final checkpoint in Yonkers and felt pretty good about myself – it being the first enduro I had ever finished. Ralph and I lifted the Hummer and his Terrier back into my Hudson and we took them home. They had served us well. When I got the results in the mail several days later I saw that Don Pink had won the High Score, and that I had won first place in "Class B Under 200 cc." Ralph finished second in that class.

I also saw that out of 47 riders starting the event, I was eleventh overall in the final tally, which I thought wasn't bad. Only 13 riders finished the strenuous 150-mile course, and most of those were experts, or "A riders." I was considered a novice and a "B rider." I was the only B Lightweight rider to finish the entire course. I learned later that to become an expert I would have to receive a letter from the American Motorcyclist Association saying that I had accumulated the required number of points while competing as a novice.

Points were awarded in accordance with an "Endurance Rider Points System," which was written and controlled by Jules Horky, Chief Referee of the AMA. For regular endurance runs, a 1st place finish in each class was awarded 20 points, 2nd place 15 points, 3rd place 10 points, and 4th place 5 points; for endurance runs 225 miles and over, an additional 5 points was awarded for each of those places. For two-day endurance runs, including national championships, 25 points were awarded for completing the first day, 50 points for finishing both days, and 50 points for 1st, 2nd, and 3rd places, even if no one finished the run.

An accumulated total of 100 points would warrant advancement from Class B to Class A. The system was changed in later years when additional classes were introduced. All of the clubs that belonged to the AMA were required to send a copy of the run results to the AMA Headquarters in Ohio, using a specific format. I received 20 points for that first place finish, which set me on my way.

I felt that I was finally vindicated. I was proud of that first place trophy and I've always kept it in a prominent place and cherished it. The appendix of this book shows how the top riders of each class finished in this and several other enduros that I mention in this book. I usually kept the full result sheets with the names of all the contestants as keepsakes from the events in which I competed; although not every club mailed out result sheets. The appendix includes several runs that I mention in the book, and a selection of other runs.

Ralph and I rode one other enduro in 1956, for which I don't have the result sheet, although I earned a trophy there too. It was the Crotona Motorcycle Club's Halloween Classic, in which I finished second in the novice lightweight class. That second place earned another 15 points towards my becoming an expert. After having ridden only two events with the Hummer, I was already well on my way and more than a third of the way to earning expert status.

Most Crotona enduros of that era started from Art Chamber's Drive-in Restaurant in Yorktown Heights, which was less than 10 miles from my home. I could easily ride the Hummer to and from that event. The course would usually take us up into the thick woods of Putnam County, where there was an abundance of rocks, steep hills and fallen trees.

Another thing I learned from riding those first few enduros was that whatever time I would lose on the higher-speed trails and long, steep hills, where the larger displacement machines had a definite advantage, I could usually make up for in the more technical sections, where there were lots of rocks, fallen trees and mud holes, and where I could maneuver the little bike easily around and through the obstacles.

Jim Fennell with route markers, staple gun, brush saw and other necessities as he and Don Pink are "front-running" an enduro to staple markers to the trees.

Tony Granone receiving a little extra help from the Crotona M.C. layout crew to get his 650 cc Triumph over Tompkins Corners Hill. Don Whyte is pulling in the front, while Don Pink (bare-headed) and Jim Fennell are pushing.

I also did fairly well in the rain. Some of the sloppiest endurance runs would favor the lightweight bikes, while other dry, smooth trails seemed to favor the heavier weight machines with much more horsepower. Continuous soggy going would also require the extra horsepower of the bigger motor, while the Hummer would always labor in it.

I had to run in the lower gears at a much higher rpm level to get through many of the sections. The result sheets tend to indicate not only what riders, but also what motorcycles were putting in their best performances in various types of terrain and under various weather conditions.

Chapter Four

Learning the Game

1957 was the first year that Ralph and I rode enduros farther from home. Ralph bought a new Studebaker pickup for our transportation to carry the bikes to and from the events. The truck had a high-geared rear end and a very weak engine, where he had to shift down for every little grade, much like the Hummer. It would take us quite a while to get to a run and even longer to get home, because it was long before the interstate highways were built, and we would have to drive through heavy traffic in all of the cities and small towns along the way. Although tedious, those return trips would become a time for reflection and discussion about our experiences of the day before heading back to another workweek.

Lillian and I had already been blessed with our third child and she was pregnant with our fourth. If I were ever to justify continuing to spend a lot of the family's money on this enduro folly of mine, I would certainly be expected, at least by my own conscience, to cut corners; not that I wasn't already programmed by my Frisian heritage to do so.

I can't speak for Ralph's heritage, but he was just as tight with the buck as I was. He and I would always try to find the least expensive accommodations, and whenever possible we would leave for the enduros very early on the morning of the event to avoid having to stay over the night before. If it were possible to get home before midnight after the run, we'd leave as soon as we were both loaded up and even before all of the other riders were in, which would be long before the scores were figured and posted.

It affected the way I rode, because I wouldn't want to take a chance on breaking the equipment or blowing the engine, by riding on the edge, not to mention getting hurt. I couldn't afford the potential cost of either, and I'd still be able to take the machine out the following weekend without ever having to work on it. I believe I was usually a little more cautious than most of my competition, although there are many who would laugh at that statement. But I felt I couldn't afford to get hurt, because like most others, I had to be at work in the morning to make a living for my family.

I would generally wear my tires and drive chain much longer than most because I'd figure that I couldn't afford to change them until long after they were obviously worn out. Several of my breakdowns, and I had many, were due to chain problems, tire problems, or other maintenance problems from being inadequately prepared. I can't with good conscience, though, blame it all on my frugality, because much of the blame rests with my "good enough" attitude toward maintenance and preparation.

I didn't have a place of my own to work on the bike between the runs, so I used Ralph's garage. Usually the first time I'd get there to do anything to it, even to adjust the chain, would be the following Saturday, which was often the day before the next event; and then I'd often have chores to do at home. If I did manage to get there, I'd try to do whatever I could in the time I had to work on it, and I'd say, "Good enough!" Ralph would usually cringe and say, "If it's only good enough, then it's NOT good enough." But it would be as much as I would do, which would often backfire on me in the next run.

In the fall of 1957 we traveled to the famed Covered Wagon Enduro, sponsored by the Pioneer Valley Motorcycle Club, which started from their clubhouse in Southwick, MA and ran up into the Berkshires. A few weeks later, we traveled to Hoosick Falls, NY for the Maple Leaf Enduro, which became known as the Ray Goodrich Memorial. Then in quick succession we rode the Sandy Lane Enduro in Atsion, NJ, sponsored by the Meteor Motorcycle Club, where we rode in deep sand; and to the Great Eastern Championship Enduro at Meriden, sponsored by the Meriden Motorcycle Club of Connecticut, which was a great run in one of the rockiest and hilliest parts of New England, and a run that quickly became one of my favorites. In addition to those, we again rode the Crotona Halloween Classic and the Yonkers Turkey Run – all with the Hummer.

We couldn't possibly make the trip to Southwick for the Covered Wagon on Sunday morning, before the 7 a.m. starting time, so it became the first run where we had to rent a room for the night. It started early because it was more than 150 miles long. The Covered Wagon attracted many riders to the Berkshires from all over the Northeast.

The room was quite a memorable experience in itself. As Ralph drove around the neighboring city of Westfield, I kept my eye out for what I thought might be the most economical place for us to stay. I spotted a small, unlighted sign on the front lawn of a huge house that read, "George Washington Hotel." The place didn't look much like a hotel. It looked more like a huge old Victorian mansion situated on one of the side streets in a residential part of Westfield. Ralph pulled into the driveway and we entered the building by way of the porch stairs.

The entrance lobby was poorly lighted and dingy. There was a small manual bell on the counter with a handwritten sign saying, "Ring for Service," so I rang it. An old gent came out from what appeared to be a small room behind the desk and he asked what we wanted. He probably thought we were looking for someone, or needed directions. When I told him we were there for a room, he acted a little surprised, and began to search under the counter for a "guest book." He eventually came up with it and placed it in front of me. I scanned the page quickly to look for names of enduro riders that I might recognize, but there were no recent entries in the book at all. If I recall correctly, it cost only six dollars for each of us for the room.

The guy gave us directions to a large, stark room on the second floor, with a bathroom just down a dimly lit hall. I unlocked the door to the room with an old-fashioned key, and looked for the light switch, before noticing an old piece of string hanging from a bare single-light socket in the center of the room. I pulled the string and it broke. It was apparently rotted from age. So I took one of the old rickety, straight-back chairs from against the wall, over to the center of the room to stand on, and I turned the light on with the small chain that hung next to the bulb.

The light worked, but it was very dim. Whenever we talked, our voices echoed from the bare walls and bare floor. There was no radio or TV in the room to check the weather. The bathroom down the hall didn't appear to have been used recently either, but it worked. Being situated in a residential area, the place was quiet at night, with no street noises or noises from anyone in the building. So at least we got a good rest.

The Covered Wagon Enduro was one of the largest and most prestigious enduros in the Northeast at the time. Coleman Mitchell and Charles Chapman did most of the layout. Coleman also rode the course as pathfinder on the day of the run to ensure that all of the course markers were still up, and that the beavers hadn't built fresh dams during the night to flood some of the trails, which could make them totally un-ride-able.

Enduro markers were usually 4" by 6" (or larger) white cards with big black or red arrows printed on them. The cards were stapled to trees and telephone poles along the route in clear view of the riders, indicating the route that we were supposed to follow. Cards with right-angle corner arrows would be stapled before the corners, to show where to turn right or left. Wherever there was a dangerous situation anywhere on the trail, like a ditch along a high-speed trail, or anything that might pose a threat to the riders' safety, the pathfinder would staple several "straight arrows" pointing down, just ahead of whatever it was. Many arrows pointing down in a cluster were an ominous signal to slow down.

Where a rider might accidentally have missed a turn marker and gone straight, a marker with a big "W" was used, meaning "Wrong." In the heat of the competition it was easy to miss one of the turn arrows and also miss the W. Failure to see both markers could cost riders several minutes searching for the way back to the course, and it could cost them a trophy or even finishing the run. I've often been accused of having "tunnel vision," as it's happened to me a number of times.

It also happened occasionally that someone, like one of the local landowners or local kids, might come along and tear down a turn arrow – or tear down a lot of them. Of course the turns would also be noted on the route sheet, but many riders didn't take the time to read their route sheet in the woods, where they would be focusing more on the trail and would be relying on the arrows to be there.

The Covered Wagon attracted more than a hundred riders that year, which might have been a record entry for a New England enduro up to that time. It was a pleasure for me to see people in person that I had only heard or read about.

I recall that the enduro headquarters was in a beautiful clubhouse amongst the pine trees. The enduro sign-up was done there, and breakfast was served there for a small charge. The area around the clubhouse served as the starting area, as well as the final checkpoint. Scores were tallied and posted inside the clubhouse after the run, and the trophies were awarded there.

I missed a course marker during that first Covered Wagon and got lost. When I reached a blacktop road after having missed it, that turn came very close to matching one of the turns on my route sheet, which made me think I was still on the course. I eventually got miles out of the way, and by the time I got back to the course and went through a few more woods sections, I was more than an hour late, which disqualified me.

I rode only 52 miles of the course, according to the result sheet. Almost the entire run took place in the Berkshire Hills, which is beautiful country for riding. One of the most famous spectator points was a wide, although shallow, river crossing, not far from the foot of the Knightsville Dam. The river-bottom was strewn with very slippery round rocks, and the banks were usually lined with spectators. Riding across with the feet on the foot pegs was almost impossible due to the large number of round slippery rocks. Watching the riders as they struggled across, and seeing a few of them take a dive into the water, made the spectator's trip worthwhile.

Don Pink won that event on his big Harley KHK, with only 8 points lost. There were a few tight sections in the run, although most of it was laid out on logging trails and abandoned county roads, with plenty of open going, all of which favored the larger displacement machines. Don Pink, who would often alternate between his KHK and a Harley 165, depending on the type of terrain he expected, used his KHK for this run.

The run was laid out so that it was possible for the experts to maintain very close to the 24 mph schedule over most of the course, except for a few tight sections with rugged going. There were some places where they could fall behind, and other places where they could run ahead of schedule, which forced them to pay attention to their time. It was an ideal run for good time keepers, a factor that gave Don Pink an edge.

The trick was to maintain the 24 mph schedule, figuring time for all of the turns while dodging obstacles in the trail at the same time. That was the true nature and the object of endurance runs, aside from having the riding skills. It was the part of the game that would be lost forever with the advent of tiny on-board computers that were introduced several years later. I think Ron Webster described it well, "Time keeping in the woods was sort of like rubbing your stomach and patting your head at the same time. I found it to be quite difficult and even hazardous, especially when I was beat down from exertion."

Don Pink was a true expert at this part of the game; and being a local hero, he became one of my lifelong icons who I would try to emulate. My biggest handicap in emulating Don, not only then, but later, was making up time on high-speed trails, which was yet another aspect of the game and totally different from the ability to go fast through the tight woods. I had already begun to master the skill of going fast on narrow hiking trails, through the rough brambles, and over rocks and windfalls; but riding at speeds considerably higher than 24 mph on the old abandoned stagecoach roads to make up time, was an entirely different story, and next to impossible with a Hummer.

Of nine entries in the expert lightweight class, eight different brands were represented, including Joe Kastner on a Harley 165, Bob Maus on a Triumph Cub, Manfred Schmid on a DOT, John Miller on a small Indian, Drew Smith on a DMW, Les Beach on an Adler, Henry Zientek on a Maico, and Greg Lipsky on an Allstate. Leslie Pink, Don's wife, and the only girl in the event, also competed in Class A Lightweight with a Harley 165. They all finished in the order mentioned above. Ralph finished 12th in Class B Lightweight with his new DMW. As soon as he came into the final check, we loaded our bikes onto his pickup and left, hoping to be home before midnight.

A few weeks later we left home around 6 AM to make a 9 o'clock starting time at the Maple Leaf Enduro in upstate New York. We got there just in time to sign up, unload the bikes, tape the route sheets we were given onto our gas tanks, set our watches, and get the bikes running and up to the starting line. Usually whenever I had a little extra time, I would figure out the times that I would be due at some of the turns on the route sheet, so that I wouldn't have to do it in my head while riding, which was much more difficult.

Forty-three riders showed up, including Les Beach with the same strange-looking little Adler he rode a few weeks earlier at the Covered Wagon. He said it was made in Frankfurt, Germany and that its little 125 cc engine had a very high rpm rating, much higher than most bikes of that era. He started it and rode it up and down the road near the starting area so everyone could hear the high-pitched screaming sound it made when he turned up the throttle.

The Adler attained peak horsepower above 6000 rpm, which was high for those days, especially for an enduro bike. It attracted a lot of attention; but so did the Hummer, along with a few friendly chuckles. The Maple Leaf started near Hoosick Falls, NY and ran up into the western foothills of the Berkshires, not far from Mount Greylock. There were many steep climbs in the run that would prove to be quite a challenge for any 125 cc engine of that vintage.

At one point we crossed a wide stream where the only way out was over a steep muddy embankment. The first bikes through made a deep groove in the mud that most of the others were using. I managed to get the front wheel through it, and up onto the bank, but the rear wheel didn't quite make it all the way. I was out of the stream far enough, and still astride the bike, so I put my feet onto some firm ground, reached down and grabbed the little machine by the handlebars, and pulled it up between my knees, lifting it clear out of the deep mud rut and placing it onto the firm ground in front of me, like a bicycle.

It was a neat trick that I certainly couldn't have done with a heavier machine. Many spectators had gathered to watch the bikes cross the stream. Loud cheers and applause went up for my unique method of getting it out. Many years later I saw it on film, when Al Sedusky came to one of our RAMS club meetings to show some of his favorite enduro footage.

I finished fifth in my class that day. It was quite noticeable that I lacked the horsepower, as well as the ability, to make up any lost time. I learned that being competitive in the Berkshires certainly required a much stronger engine than the Hummer. Ralph did much better with his new DMW, sporting the 250 cc engine and knobby tires, as he finished second in the novice lightweight class. The run had many long, steep hills and high-speed trails that favored bikes with the greater horsepower, especially for making up time.

It was where we first saw the Milford Riders, probably the undisputed best enduro team in New England in the late 1950s. One of its members, Charlie Schumitz, won high score that day. Charlie was one of the top enduro riders in New England, riding a 500 cc Matchless. His teammates, Dick Chandler and Paul Walton, who both rode AJS 500s, were also active in scrambles racing, and were very good at it. All three were very consistent competitors. Charlie became the New England Enduro Grand Champion in 1959, which was the first year of the annual enduro championship series in New England.

The Sandy Lane Enduro was our next big challenge. A few days before the weekend of the enduro, Ralph and I were in

Charlie Schumitz – 1959 New England Grand Champion

Dick Chandler and Charlie Schumitz of the Milford Riders M.C. team

Both photos above by Grant Whidden

Al Knapp's shop, which had recently moved from Poughkeepsie to Highland, NY, a ride of about forty miles up and across the Hudson River for us. Ralph mentioned to Al Knapp while we were there, that we planned to ride Sandy Lane that weekend. Being a veteran of riding Sandy Lane many years earlier, and having been an expert enduro rider himself, Al asked what kind of bike I was riding. When I told him the Hummer, he laughed and said, "You don't expect to finish then, do you?" He predicted that I would never get "that puny little Hummer" through 150 miles of sand at Sandy Lane. I assured him that I would, but he was still laughing and ribbing me when we left his shop. I gathered he had quite a caustic personality!

The starting point for Sandy Lane was in Atsion, New Jersey, in the Pine Barrens along Route 206, which was in the sandy, southern part of the state. Since it was another long run, which started at 8 a.m. Sunday morning, we had to drive down on Saturday. When we arrived, we asked at the enduro headquarters where we might find accommodations. We were told that they had cabins right there behind the Pick-a-Lilly Restaurant. The price was right – only about $10 for the night for the two of us, so we rented one of the cabins, sight unseen.

Our cabin turned out to be a tiny, ramshackle building with only a single ¾-size bed in it. Everyone at the event used the same outhouse, which was close-by – too close! The toilet was already clogged by Saturday evening, and one couldn't sit without sitting in the waste. The stench for several feet around was sickening. As a result, most people used the woods.

When Ralph and I tried to sleep together in the tiny bed, the springs were so weak in the center that we couldn't stay on the edges without rolling toward each other. I spent practically the whole night holding onto the side of the bed so I wouldn't roll into Ralph. I was afraid of what might happen if either of us, in our sleep, would unconsciously (and accidentally of course) reach for the other, as one often does for his wife in the middle of the night! Consequently, I was afraid to fall asleep.

I remembered a possible solution I had heard, where a comedian once said you should lean over and kiss the other person on the cheek, and then HE would be the one to stay awake all night, allowing you to turn over without a care and get some sleep. Often in retelling this story to friends, I would say that I did, but I lied!

Don Pink at Sandy Lane on his Harley Davidson KHK

Photo by Boyd Reynolds

Sandy Lane was probably the most important enduro held in the East in 1957, drawing more than 150 entries. Several riders came in from Ohio, including John Penton who rode a BSA in Class A Open, the expert heavyweight class. I think it was a 500 cc single. I assumed that most of the Ohio riders all came to the run together. John Penton won first place in his class that day.

The run ended in a tie for high score between Jim Fennell of the Bronx and Ed Elliot of Amherst, Ohio, Penton's hometown. The tie couldn't be broken by the Emergency Check due to a problem with the check, which caused all of the scores from that checkpoint to be "thrown out;" so duplicate high score trophies had to be awarded to both riders.

I finished 10th out of 61 entries in Class B Lightweight, losing 100 points. Most riders in my class rode the larger 250 cc machines, or at least the 165. I thought I did well with my 10th place finish, especially after having been laughed at and told by a supposed "expert" that I would never finish the run.

I certainly wasn't enthused about riding in the sand, and the Hummer lacked the power to get through it with any real speed. It also lacked the power for making up time on the wide-open sand trails. I used my legs a lot that day, mostly for stability, to keep from dropping the bike. I think I had my feet on the ground paddling for most of the 150 miles. At least it seemed that way, from the way I felt. Combined with a lack of sleep, I was exhausted when I got back to the Pick-a-Lilly, and I knew I had finished a real test of endurance.

The stronger machines had a huge advantage at Sandy Lane. I noticed that Don Pink rode his KHK. I never did well in deep sand, even in the later years after switching to a stronger machine. Aside from the equipment, another excuse for my not doing well was my reluctance to go that fast, even when I had the opportunity. It was like an all-day cross-country race, where keeping time didn't mean that much. Ralph finished 17th in our class with his 250 DMW, having lost 280 points. In addition to the sand, there was also plenty of mud and water at Sandy Lane.

A few words about scoring: a score of 1000 points in an enduro is considered a perfect score. It means that the rider was neither early nor late at any of the checkpoints in the entire event. It's rare that a rider finishes a run with a perfect score of 1000 points, especially a technical endurance run of more than a hundred miles. The rules state that a point is deducted from that original 1000 points for every minute the rider arrives late at a checkpoint. For example, at Sandy Lane I lost 100 points, giving me a score of 900. Probably all of those lost points were for being late, and not early, at the checkpoints.

Checkpoints were usually spaced from as close as 5.2 miles apart, up to about 20 miles apart, so there could have been a total of 15 or more checks at Sandy Lane. I was probably late at almost all of those checkpoints, possibly only a few minutes at some, but up to 30 to 40 minutes at others. The total accumulation of late points deducted from my original score of 1000 was 100, which is how I got a final score of 900.

Two points were deducted from a rider's score for every minute he arrived early at a checkpoint. Later the rules were changed so that only the first minute early would cost the rider two points, but every additional minute early would cost the rider five points per minute; so where three minutes early at a checkpoint would cost 6 points in 1957, it would cost 12 points in the 1960s and beyond.

The rule change was made to impose an additional penalty on riders who would either deliberately run early as a strategy for building up a safety buffer for tough sections ahead, or for making a "race" out of it, as it was intended to be more of an exciting game that challenged not only riding ability, but also the rider's concentration, and his ability to stay on time.

I was really beat on the way home from Sandy Lane from a lack of sleep and from struggling with the Hummer in the sand all day. Wherever there wasn't sand on the trail, I was in deep water or mud. I was usually supposed to keep Ralph from falling asleep on the way home by talking with him. We would talk about the event and about the other riders, which was always an interesting subject; but on this trip I had problems staying awake to talk about anything, so Ralph was on his own to stay awake well enough to get us home safely.

The next enduro we rode was at Meriden, Conn. It was billed as the Great Eastern Championship. We were able to travel to and from Meriden on the same day because it was only 85 miles each way for us and it started at 9 a.m. Getting there was much easier than getting home. Our return trips from most places in New England would always take longer, because of having to go through so much traffic on Sunday nights in Meriden, Waterbury and Danbury – not to mention between those cities. We would sometimes get caught in stop-and-go traffic for miles, which is excruciating at any time, but more-so when you're tired and just want to get home.

The Meriden Motorcycle Club, one of the oldest in the country, had a really nice clubhouse in the woods, about five miles northeast of the city. I took an immediate liking to the Meriden group, their clubhouse, and their event. They were always friendly and congenial, and they always put on an excellent run, followed by a great turkey dinner in the clubhouse. There was no waiting around for the scores, as they were posted by the time we finished dinner.

I really enjoyed the enduro course there too, which was laid out by Sal Scirpo and other veterans like Frank Kokoszka. The course offered an abundance of excellent woods sections. One of the most challenging, known as the "blue trail," followed a rocky razorback ridge along the top of a mountain, where one could see for miles on both sides – that is, if you could take your eyes off the trail long enough to look. The run offered the kind of narrow, rocky trails that I was able to get through quite well, and making up time was rarely possible for anyone, since most of the trails didn't offer the opportunity to go even 24 mph, let alone much faster. A few sections were even designed to catch some of the top experts running early if they weren't careful.

No sooner I got into the woods at Meriden, not far from the clubhouse, and the Hummer's engine quit. I was getting off to investigate when Leslie Pink came along on her Harley 165. Without even slowing down, she glanced over and pointed to the Hummer's engine, and said, "Your spark plug wire is loose." That really impressed me! How could she possibly have seen that? I quickly reattached the wire and was on my way. The course was exceptionally challenging all day and I found myself passing other riders when the going got really tough in the rocks, and along the tightest and most technical trails. I don't think a single rider passed me for the entire distance.

I got to one very steep downhill where the course took us down through some trees along the narrow hiking trail. The brakes on the Hummer were practically useless, because of the road tires. It didn't have much of a front brake anyway, and there were no knobs on the tires to hold it back, even if I were able to stop the wheel from turning. I shut off the motor and started rolling slowly downhill, in-gear, with my foot on the brake, but as I inched forward, I started to skid faster and faster, until I thought for sure I was a goner.

The trees were very close on both sides of the trail, which zigzagged down between them. Just before the bike got completely out of control, I reached out and wrapped both my arms around a big tree, hanging onto the bike with my knees and legs. After catching my breath, I gradually let go and continued to skid and roll the rest of the way down the hill.

The course was only 112 miles long and I had gone farther than that on a tank of gas before, so I thought I could make it all the way to the finish without refueling; but I got almost to the clubhouse when the engine sputtered and quit. I looked into the tank and it was dead empty! Since I was on hard pavement at the time, and I knew I wasn't too far from the finish, I got off and started to push as fast as I could. I ran beside it almost all the way to the clubhouse, which was about a mile. I was huffing and puffing when I finally got there. I thought that I had still finished in pretty good shape, though.

After the scores were posted, I felt much better about things. For starters, I learned that I had finished 3rd in my class, Class B Lightweight, which qualified me for a trophy in what was billed as the Great Eastern Championship Endurance Run, attracting some of the top riders from the Northeast. Upon studying the final scores of everyone else, including the experts, I saw that I had finished 9th overall, out of 47 total entries. For the first time in a prestigious enduro, I had finished in the top ten! And I was still riding the Hummer in the novice class. Coleman Mitchell, the overall winner of the high score trophy, was riding a 500 cc Triumph.

The following article appeared later in the Metropolitan Motorcycling newsletter, dated December 1957:

Coleman Mitchell Tops In Meriden Enduro

November 10 saw the running of the Great Eastern Championship Endurance Run sponsored by the Meriden M.C., one of the oldest clubs in the country.

While old in charter it is young in blood! Chief layout men for the run were: Sal Scirpo, past Jack Pine Champ, and Frank Kokoszka, recent winner of Crotona's Halloween Enduro. They saw to it that this run had everything a championship enduro needs – hills to challenge a goat and streams to make a spawning salmon sit up and take notice.

Coleman Mitchell became one of my early icons for his ability to ride big bore machines through the tight woods. I didn't actually meet him until years later. Then I found him to be not only an exceptionally accomplished woods rider, but also a fine gentleman. He and his wife Lew were always a pleasure to be with. I believe this photo was taken in the late 1950s.

Photo by Grant Whidden

Portions of the course went not across streams, but upstream a half-mile or so. Leslie Pink, one of the few girl contestants in this man's run, thought this was a great spot and made it with little effort.

Coleman Mitchell, the eventual winner, racked up an impressive score on the hills and power line that followed. Don Pink, with an early number, was having trouble finding the course when a blinding snowstorm hit for a half hour or so. Jim Fennell was riding well, but a broken rear axle in the last five miles slowed him down. He still finished third in Open A. Piet Boonstra ran out of gas in this same last five miles but undaunted, he pushed the rest of the way to a well-earned third spot in B Lightweight.

Whitey Loud was making knots along some back trail when he connected with a rock sticking a little too high out of the ground. He says flying is great, but best for birds. Cost of this caper was one front end to his motorcycle. Joe Kastner, another local boy, always a threat when the machinery keeps up with his hard riding, had to spend some time for repairs. Sure does ride 'em hard, he does!

The last few miles of the run were the straw that broke the camel's back. After a long climb up a mountain, the trail became very narrow and wound along a razor-back ridge where you could look straight down and see into a valley on either side as you rode the two-foot-wide ridge. A slip left or right and you really went down! Shortly after the run the Meriden Club held a banquet for all entrants, where everyone gathered for dinner and a general get-together, after which the winners were announced and the "gold" was handed out.

This article appeared in the same newsletter:

Frank Kokoszka Wins Crotona Halloween Enduro

WESTCHESTER COUNTY, OCT. 27, 10 A.M. Strange-looking objects moving down the road and disappearing into the woods at one-minute intervals! First suspicion: a posse looking for fallen Sputnik. But no, this is the Crotona Halloween Enduro with 77 eager contestants in search of gold and glory. Not all of them will find it.

The course, starting at Art Chambers Drive-In, threads through some of Westchester and Putnam's most scenic back trails. But the poor contestants don't get to see much of it, since their eyes are kept straight ahead to decide which of the rocks ahead will be the easiest to bounce over. There are a few small hills, naturally, which this time they go down. Then back to Art Chambers – streams to cross, Tompkins Corners Hill, the finish – a straight-through ride, about 85 bouncing miles long.

Top man was Frank Kokoszka from Meriden, Conn. Frank is a wonderfully consistent rider, who has won many events up New England way. Chasing Frank all the way was Joe Kastner from the Bronx, N. Y. Frank would make a little faster time through the rough stretches, but Joe jumped up even with him once when Frank goofed one check a minute early. The Emergency check had to be used to break the tie.

Chuck Schumitz, the eventual winner in Class A Open, got a big kick out of the humorous signs the Crotona club posted along the way. On one stream crossing they had an old pair of handlebars just sticking out of the water with a sign that said, "Don't give up the ship." Chuck likes best the one that pictured a rider biting his fingernails and saying, "Have you missed any checks?" Seems that Chuck did just that a few weeks ago, so he picked up the sign to take home.

Dick Chandler, teammate of Chuck from the Milford Riders, threw a chain on the hill at Tompkins Corners. It took 20 minutes with the help of spectators to find the chain. Sky Ball, popular New Jersey rider from the den-of-woods riders called Cycle Alley M.C., showed the gang they raise winning material in New Jersey too, with his easy win in Class B Open.

The Crotona Club spared no effort in promoting this run. Jim Fennell and Don Pink, who sparkplug this run, have a unique system of putting markers up. All marking is done the morning of the run. Don and Jim start out at 5 AM with boxes on the front of their handlebars to hold markers and staple hammers. They figure on managing 10 mph while marking, and finish the job about an hour before the first man is due to finish. In this way, markers are fresh and seldom touched by local citizens. Even a spare machine is kept handy in case one breaks down.

Joe Kastner in a water crossing. He often wore those coveralls.

Photo by Grant Whidden

I had the pleasure of riding on a number just ahead of the winner of the Crotona Halloween Classic, Frank Kokoszka, and I got to see him ride his relatively heavy 650 cc Triumph in several different situations. After the run, I asked him, "How do you manage to drag that thing through the deep mud holes, Frank?" thinking of my own problems with the Harley 74 in the Yorktown Swamp several years earlier.

He answered, "You're not supposed to DRAG 'em, you're supposed to RIDE 'em." That was a good lesson. I saw him go through a few mud holes without even slowing down. Frank was a real "charger."

I saw Joe Kastner do the same thing that day with his Harley 165. Joe Kastner and Bob Maus were two of the top lightweight riders from the NY Metropolitan area. Joe was also somewhat of a charger, but he wasn't nearly the physical size of Frank Kokoszka. Joe would sometimes hit the mud holes at full speed, with muddy water splashing everywhere.

Chapter Five

Getting Better at It

Ralph and I returned in 1958 to ride many more enduros, including some of the spring runs. I learned that spring enduros were much wetter and sloppier than most of those held in the fall, and I usually did well in that type of run. I also made out better at the Great Eastern Championship in Meriden that second year, improving my place in the results from 3rd to 2nd in my class and finishing 8th overall, as compared with 9th the previous year; and I was still riding the Hummer as a novice.

When we arrived at Westfield, Mass. for our second Covered Wagon in September of 1958, the question came up with Ralph as to where we might stay for the night. We agreed that we got a good night's rest at the George Washington Hotel and that the price was right, so Ralph drove straight to the side street where we found it the first time. The same old guy waited on us and handed us the same guest book to sign. When I opened it to the current page, I noticed that our names from the previous year were on that same page, which meant that only a few guests had signed in all year!

We were given directions to the same room at the top of the stairs and when we entered (laughing), we saw that the string was still missing from the ceiling light. So I pulled the same old chair over to the center of the room to reach the short chain, and I turned on the light, feeling like déjà vu. I think the place was torn down shortly after that.

Déjà vu also struck me on the trail, only 14 miles from the start. I remember the incident well: I was coming down a long steep hill on a high-tension power line, moving as fast as I dared on the steep downhill slope with the Hummer. I struck one of the many huge water-bars across the trail, which threw me far out into the air. I landed on both wheels at the very bottom of the hill, like coming off of a huge jump. The hard landing and my weight broke the poor little Hummer in half.

The single-tube frame broke just forward of the front motor mount and the frame spread apart at the break. The underside of the bike hit the ground and dragged the machine to an abrupt stop. I couldn't ride it back to the start, so we had to come back later to pick it up with the truck. Ralph had a small welder at home with which we were able to fix it in time for the next event. That welder got a lot of use over the years from broken parts on our enduro machines – mostly mine!

Once during a different run, the right handlebar broke off the Hummer. I had to secure it temporarily with rubber bands, made from 4.00 X 18 inner tubes, which I always carried for all sorts of emergency uses. I managed to finish the run, holding the bike steady with only the left handlebar, while operating the throttle on the broken piece. Luckily I wasn't far from the finish.

We rode a very tough enduro in the spring of that year in Torrington, Conn. in the pouring rain. It was one of the wettest and muddiest runs I had seen thus far. There were only 32 entries, which was also one of the smallest showings I had seen for an enduro. Of those 32, only 10 made it to the final check. Christy Scholar won high score riding a huge 500 cc Matchless. I finished third in Class B Lightweight. Jim Forbes, who joined Ralph and me for the trip to Connecticut, finished second on a 250 cc DOT.

The winner, Christy Scholar, was a phenomenal woods rider, for whom I gained a great deal of respect, and he became one of my lifelong icons. The sloppier the run, the higher Christy would place in the results. He wasn't always the fastest rider in the enduro, or the world's greatest time keeper; and like me, he didn't go super fast on the high-speed trails. But there were few who could stay with Christy in the tight woods, especially if it was wet and slippery. He rode a motorcycle in the woods in a way that epitomized the image I would have liked someday to emulate, and he always seemed to be having fun doing it.

As the old saying goes, "when the goin' gets tough, the tough get goin'." The sloppier the run became, the better Christy seemed to ride. He reveled in the tough, sloppy runs. If it was raining hard, and the mud in the woods was the deepest and the slimiest, the bare roots were the slipperiest, and there was no trail at all for most of the run, you could rest assured that Christy Scholar would probably win the high score – and he'd be singing and talking to himself all the way.

Jim Forbes and I are securing the bikes onto Ralph's pickup, prior to the Torrington Run.

Some called him a "hippie;" maybe because he wore a beard, and before it was mandatory to wear helmets, he rode with a beret, and sometimes with small dark glasses. He was a wonderful, congenial, kind-hearted person with a great sense of humor, and he had good taste in blackberry brandy.

I remember one enduro in particular that we rode. It was a very sloppy District #5 Championship Enduro in northern New Jersey in November of 1960. I hadn't owned my DMW for long, and I was having problems getting used to it, especially stalling it in the woods a lot. I thought that I was doing well by even finishing the run. The miles of muddy trails and slippery roots had been giving me a lot of problems trying to get used to the handling. I was exhausted from struggling with it in the slop for hours. I was running about 20 minutes late when I finally pulled into the final check in the pouring rain. I asked the checker how the others were doing, and he answered that everyone was checking in very late.

I was about to leave the check and put my bike away on the trailer, when I looked back up the road and noticed that Christy was just coming in, so I sat and waited as he signed in. Riding a heavy 500 cc BSA single, Christy checked in 10 minutes early! It seemed hard to believe. Though early, he was technically on time because when the mileage and arrival time for a check is

Christy Scholar, on the cover of *Cycle Sport* Magazine, on his way to a High Score in a Snow Run in the mid-sixties. He's sporting a helmet decorated with the symbol of the RAMS M.C., and riding a big single-cylinder motorcycle.

printed on the route sheet as the final check usually is, it's considered to be a "known check," and contestants are allowed to arrive up to 15 minutes early without penalty. I asked, "How was it Christy?" He answered with a big smile, "Loved it!"

Later, when the scores were posted, they revealed that Christy had won high score, losing only 29 points for the entire day. His normal "home turf" was central Connecticut, and this was in New Jersey. I lost 262 points that day, almost ten times more than he did. The next highest score to Christy's was Bob Maus, another lifelong friend, on a lightweight 200 cc Triumph Cub, with 60 points lost, more than double Christy's 29. Only 37 hearty souls finished that championship event, of the 122 riders that started.

The Crotona Halloween Enduro that year started in a mixture of rain and snow. By the time we got to the top of East Mountain in Fishkill it was all snow, and it was coming down quite heavy. It became difficult to see, and it began to pack to the gravel road surface. I was running several minutes late with the Hummer when I was passed about 20 mph faster than I was going by Sal Scirpo, on a 500 cc Triumph.

We were in a long sweeping turn on a gravel road, and he was already sideways when he went by. His machine went into a full broad-slide, with gravel and snow flying for more than 50 feet, as he skillfully negotiated the turn, and then just as skillfully straightened the bike out again. I doubted that I could ever ride like that. I had heard that Sal was a flat-tracker in his earlier days, but by then he had already won Jack Pine twice.

A few miles up the road we got into a woods section where there were no trails at all. Don Pink and Jim Fennell had stapled the route markers to the trees that very same morning, but the snow was packing against the markers and totally obscuring them as fast as they were put up. Most clubs would tack up their markers at least a week before the event, while laying out the run, but Pink and Fennell would leave Yonkers before first light on the day of the event to start tacking them up, having laid it out earlier. It was quite a challenge to stay ahead of the riders, especially when it was snowing.

I was able to follow Sal's tire tracks to where the run was stopped at the end of that section, which was only 48 miles from the start. That was much shorter than planned, but it had to be stopped because Sal caught up with the pathfinders. I was one of only 10 riders to go those 48 miles, of more than 60 that started. Most riders probably got lost in the woods when they couldn't follow the trail in the snow. Sal won the event.

We had four children by the fall of 1958, and I began to wonder how much longer I might be able to keep up my enduro competition, especially since Lillian wasn't able to come to any of the events with the small children. Also, by early 1959 I was

Sal Scirpo enjoyed the pinnacle of his fame riding a 500 Triumph in the early 1950s, when he twice won the Jack Pine 500-Mile National Championship in Lansing, Michigan. Sal was good at every aspect of the game. I considered him to be among the very best in at least one of those aspects, making up time, especially when he rode the Triumph. He later rode a 250 Harley Sprint for years. There was probably no one who could stay with Sal on the back roads and sand trails of northern Michigan after he'd come out of a mud hole or river crossing, from which everyone would emerge late. Sal could get back on time in short order, which was often a key factor to winning at Jack Pine.

Photo by Grant Whidden

working at IBM for up to 80 hours per week, in the throes of getting out a whole new line of supercomputers, so I had much less time to devote to the enduros.

At the 1959 Yonkers Spring Run, not long before its retirement, the Hummer put in its best performance ever – or at least I finished higher. The run was extremely tough with lots of rocks, hills, and very tight going. Much of it was run in the Ramapo Fault area of Putnam County, where physical agility, as well as riding skills, played a major role in the way the run turned out. There was one very steep uphill that consisted almost entirely of huge, sharp-edged black rocks, where the tires rarely touched dirt. I think it was necessary for almost everyone to push his machine at least partway up that hill.

Everything came together for me as the run not only favored the lightweight machines, but it also favored those with the skill of coordinating physical agility with the bike's inherent maneuverability. I finished second overall behind Don Pink. Don scored 912 on his Harley 165, while I scored a 905 with the Hummer. Gene Esposito, another phenomenal enduro rider, scored 901 on a 500 cc Triumph. Who ever heard of an enduro rider from Brooklyn? And he was one of the best!

Gene Esposito, a member of the esteemed Cycle Alley Riders, was an expert in just about every aspect of the game, and he became my foremost competition and nemesis throughout the sixties in almost every type of endurance run. In particular, he was much better than I was at riding in sugary sand, and at making up time in 3rd gear after a tough section in almost any type of terrain. He was good at keeping time, he had good concentration, and he usually kept his equipment in much better condition than I did. The poor condition of mine was partly due to my having less and less time to work on it, and partly because I would end up riding it in the little time that I did have. Consequently, Gene would often outscore not only me, but also almost every other rider in the area.

I rode fewer events in 1959 than I did the previous year, due to my job, which also gave me much less time to devote to my equipment; but in October I received a letter from Jules Horky of the AMA, informing me that I had earned the necessary points as a novice to be advanced to Class A. They now considered me to be an expert. That letter gave me a new burst of enthusiasm as we headed into the sixties.

My 6' 4" frame was still far too big for this 165 Harley/Puckett. I didn't own it for long, but it treated me very well during the 1959 season.

I realized that the Hummer was getting tired, and I knew I needed a stronger machine to withstand the abuse I was putting it through. In spite of my fears that I wouldn't be riding enduros much longer, I bought a used Harley 165 from Gene Baron, on which he had installed a swinging-arm suspension on both front and rear. The engine had also been hopped-up with a full-Puckett rebuild kit, which gave it much more power – enough to attain and even exceed 70 mph.

Puckett Motors Harley Davidson of Orlando, Florida, well known in racing circles, supplied the kit. The bike handled exceptionally well in the tight woods. I could throw it around almost as easily as the Hummer and it had much more speed and power. Maybe it had too much power for the rest of the running gear, which was already well worn by the time I got it. I sold the Hummer to help pay for it, and it was an excellent machine while it lasted.

I went out the very next month with my newly acquired Harley/Puckett and won 1st place in the Expert Lightweight Class at the District 5 Championship in northern New Jersey, ahead of 16 others in the expert lightweight class, many of whom I had looked up to for so long, including Don Pink, Bob Maus, Sal Scirpo, Joe Kastner and others.

Of the 115 total entries, I had the 3rd highest score overall. The only riders with higher scores were on heavyweight machines. They were Dave Barnes, the overall winner, on a BSA single, and Jim Fennell on a 500 Triumph. I was the lightweight champion; and as such, I felt I had finally arrived, since that run was one of the toughest and most prestigious enduros in the area, known for being continuously technical, with rocks, roots, steep hills and tight trails. Good throttle control, particularly on the hills, and good physical agility combined with riding ability in the tight woods played a major role in winning the event. There were very few places along the course for making up time, so my handicap in that area didn't affect the outcome much.

I don't recall how many events I rode with that 165, but it didn't last a full season before I began to have problems with it. It also didn't fit my 6'4" frame that well. Yet another factor was that I was subjecting my machines to much more rigorous use, or abuse, as the case may be; and they simply weren't up to the task. I needed a machine that would last without requiring much maintenance.

At the beginning of the 1960 season I bought another well-used piece of iron – an old 250 cc Maico scrambler, which had been ridden hard for several scrambles seasons. It turned out to be another mistake, because I could never handle that Maico half as well as I could handle either of the two Harleys, and it was already played-out from too much scrambles competition; consequently it needed far more work between the runs than either of the Harleys. The "quick throttle" was also very sensitive, which was yet another handicap for me; and handling in the tight woods left much to be desired.

I rode the Maico in four or five events in 1960, the last of which was the 1960 Covered Wagon in the Berkshires, where it literally began to come apart. I lost the front fender, one of the foot pegs and part of the rear fender, as I pushed it extra hard through the Berkshires with the intent of winning, which I didn't.

But the good news was that I finished my first Covered Wagon, although when I got to the finish line there was nothing much left firmly attached to it but the seat, the handlebars and me. Even the seat was beginning to come loose. The engine was still in good working order, but the rest of the bike was shot, and it was simply not an enduro machine that fit my riding style.

If I were to continue to ride the enduros, it was time for me to buy a decent motorcycle – a new one that would fit me, and one that I could afford. It had to withstand the abuse and it had to be capable of an occasional overall win. Of all the motorcycles on the market at the time, the one that seemed the closest to what I was looking for was the British DMW.

Ralph had ridden one for a few years with no problems, and after I test rode his I figured I could probably do well with it. The DMW was designed especially for enduro competition, with good swinging-arm suspension, front and rear, and a 250 cc two-stroke engine. Since I made out well with a 125, and even better with a hopped-up 165, I reasoned that a good 250 with knobby tires would be even better; that is, if I could throw it around easily and if it would withstand the abuse.

The DMW had a longer wheelbase than either of the Harleys, making it fit my physical size better, but the longer wheelbase also meant a longer turning radius in the tight woods. The extra weight might also be a handicap, but I reasoned that I was strong enough that it probably wouldn't be.

Don Whyte, the distributor, lived only 20 miles from my home and he stocked parts for it, as well as maintaining one of the largest Villiers parts inventories in the country. His business was known as Crown Distributing. We later became fellow club members of the Crotona M.C. and lifelong friends. Don had already been a Crotona club member for many years.

It took practically the entire 1961 spring season to get accustomed to the different handling. I didn't just naturally fall into it like I did with the Harley/Puckett. The Villiers engine was also very temperamental, in that it would often stall in the woods and then it would take several minutes to get it restarted, which I'm sure cost me trophies and maybe even a high score.

The restarting procedure was also different every time, depending on the heat of the engine. Handling in the woods was different from both Harleys, probably because of the wheelbase; but I felt that I would eventually adapt to it. After having been promoted to department manager at IBM, I had very little time to practice between the enduros or to work on it. The only practice I got was riding the runs; and like with my other machines, I never did work on it much between runs.

In October 1960, I rode a short Westchester Closed Course enduro and didn't even reach the first check. The following month at the District #5 Championship, the same event in which I had done so well the previous year, I rode the DMW to a disappointing 10th place in Class A Lightweight. Both events were the kind in which I had previously excelled, with tight trails and many technical sections.

I didn't fare much better with it throughout the spring of 1961, but I managed to devote a little more time to riding it during the summer and I eventually got more used to the handling, to restarting the engine in the woods, and to keeping it from stalling in the first place. I came back in September to a particularly tough Great Eastern Championship at Meriden and finished 1st in the expert lightweight class, and 2nd overall. The only rider with a better score than mine was the master of the tight, slippery woods himself, my icon, Christy Scholar.

Two weeks later Ralph and I traveled to Cayuta, NY to try our hand at a 150-Mile National Championship that was laid out by Dave Barnes and put on by the Schuyler County M.C. It was my first attempt at a national, and I was excited about it. The bike performed well there too, as I won first place in the expert lightweight class at the second run in a row, and I managed to finish 8th overall. John Penton won the event on a 250 cc BMW R27. He was riding with conventional forks rather than the Earl's-type swinging-arm that came with that BMW. I thought at the time that the forks were from a 500 BSA, but I learned later that they were actually Ariel forks.

I thought I had finally acquired good control of the new machine and I had a good idea of what it took to win an enduro, but I had never won a High Score. I was able to go reasonably fast in the woods, through mud holes and over the steep hills, but I had seen others do the same thing and still not win overall. I felt that I had mastered much of the art of keeping time, in that I rarely hit a check early and I knew whenever I messed up that it was from a lack of concentration, or because someone's watch was off – either the checkers or mine.

I also realized that it was a factor of how fast I made up my lost time, which was becoming one of my major handicaps. It was often necessary to ride considerably faster than the 24 mph on woods roads, and even on the trails, to make up time that was lost in tight woods. I was never a cross-country racer and I was always hesitant about riding through the trails at the higher speeds, while dodging rocks, ruts, slippery logs and roots.

First of all, losing control at the higher speeds could spell disaster for the machine and for me. If I ignored the risks and the possible consequences, and pushed myself to ride that much faster anyway, I reasoned that I'd be putting too much emphasis on winning, thereby sacrificing much of the aspect of fun, for which I was out there in the first place.

I knew also that if I got seriously injured in an enduro I would probably give up the sport altogether for family considerations. I'm sure Lillian would never feel right about my competing again. I always had a fairly high tolerance for pain and discomfort, so fear of pain was never a consideration, then or now. My decision not to ride that fast was based solely on logic, although it sometimes left me with a sizeable handicap to winning, particularly at the nationals, where most of my competition opted for the greater risks. It's one of the differences between competing in a sporting event and racing, and I never considered riding enduros to be racing.

I decided to concentrate more on keeping closer track of my time in the technical sections, which was another area in which I could use some improvement, rather than forcing myself to go faster. It's necessary in an enduro to know how one is doing against his clock at all times, even in the tight technical sections, which often involved doing calculations in the head while the brain is almost totally dedicated to the steady stream of visual data pouring in through the optic nerves, processing it and reacting to it. Splitting one's concentration between keeping time and seeing where he's going was not only a neat trick, but it was also a factor to winning.

Whenever I lost track of my time in a tight woods section, it would become necessary to refigure my time quickly upon reaching a smoother section of the course, where making up the time might be possible. It was necessary to reestablish the relationship between time and mileage as quickly as possible when emerging from woods sections.

I'll cover time keeping more thoroughly in a later chapter, but keeping time had always been an integral part of our game, whereas in later years a mere glance at a computer would tell the rider whether he had to go faster or slow down, and how much time he had to make up or lose when he emerged from a woods section. With the on-board computer he could essentially forget about a watch, or the need to calculate time at all, for that matter, and he could concentrate virtually all of his mental faculties to his riding.

Two weeks after finishing well at Cayuta, we returned to the Berkshires, where I hadn't done well for the first three times I rode the Covered Wagon, although it was certainly my type of run and my type of terrain. The 1961 event was sanctioned as a 200-Mile National Championship and a few Midwestern riders came to ride, including John Penton with the same 250 cc BMW, and Norm Smith with a 500cc Triumph. I knew that both were excellent competitors. John and his unique machine attracted considerable attention in the clubhouse area that morning as many riders gathered around to hear him expound on some of his ideas, and to hear some the interesting stories he could tell.

I got an excellent lesson in concentration from John Penton during that 1961 Covered Wagon. As soon as we lined up for the start of the event, I realized that my starting number was only two minutes ahead of his. I had mixed emotions about that arrangement because on one hand I might learn something from seeing a famous guy ride, but on the other hand we might be getting into each other's way, since I was on my home turf in the beloved rocks and hills of New England, and I had just begun to do well with my DMW.

There were not many tight sections in the first hundred miles before our stop for lunch in Middlefield, so I didn't get to see him at all in the woods that morning. There was also no occasion during that first half where I was running more than a few minutes behind schedule, and I assumed that John Penton certainly wouldn't be running early. But soon after the lunch stop we began to encounter much tougher terrain, with tighter trails and some of the traditional, abandoned county roads and rocky up-hill climbs that I learned to love, as we worked our way deeper into the Northern Berkshires.

We got into one long, 10-mile section where much of the trail was narrow and sometimes marked from tree to tree, with no trail at all except for whatever trail the bikes were making. We got several miles into that section, to where everyone naturally began to run behind schedule. I kept expecting John to come up behind me at any moment. We were in a particularly tight section when I finally heard the "beep-beep" of a horn. I had never heard a horn in the woods before, and I assumed it was he, so I immediately pulled over and stopped, to make room for him to go by. He went by, but he went only about 10 yards, where he struck a slippery root at the wrong angle and dropped his motorcycle.

John Penton leaving the starting point of the 200-Mile National Championship Endurance Run at Southwick, Mass. in 1961.

Photo by Grant Whidden

During the time he was picking it up and restarting it, I began to build up another small lead, but it wasn't long before I heard the horn again. I pulled over for the second time so he could pass, but halfway by he hit another slippery root at the wrong angle and dropped the bike again. Dropping it twice in that short distance made me think that he might be riding over his head, because I almost never fell down in that type of woods, unless it was from total exhaustion or a lack of concentration on the trail. I passed him for the second time with renewed vigor.

Just as he was about to go by for a third time we broke out onto a wider trail where he could pass without my having to pull all the way off the trail and stop. It was quite rocky at that point, requiring considerable skill to maintain any kind of speed over the rocks. Our wheels rarely touched the ground as we rode side-by-side, only hitting the high spots. We were traveling very fast, and I took my abilities to their maximum as we rode handlebar-to-handlebar for the next 50 yards or so, going much faster than I would normally ride on that type of rocky trail; although riding the rocks on any type of trail, and at almost any speed, had become one of my strengths. We continued to ride that way until the trail smoothed out.

As soon as we hit solid ground, John pulled away and accelerated very fast – much faster than I cared to go, or probably could go, for that matter. Less than a quarter-mile from there, the trail made a left turn onto a power line. He was already a hundred yards ahead of me when he made that turn. As soon as I got there and rounded the corner, I looked up the power line, but didn't see him anywhere. I couldn't figure how he could have disappeared so fast. I thought that possibly the trail had cut back into the woods somewhere, or that he had fallen off and I couldn't see him; but in any case he was gone!

Within about a half-mile, the trail took a sharp right-hand turn off the power line and onto another trail, and then almost immediately out onto a blacktop road. The turn and the tarmac were both noted on the route sheet, so I quickly rechecked my time and mileage as I approached it. I realized that I was running between 10 and 15 seconds early, which confused me, because Penton should have been more than two minutes behind at that point.

I stopped and waited for about thirty seconds before making the turn, to make sure I wasn't early. As soon as I made it, there was a secret check, which I half-expected to find, since it was just before the tarmac, and the mileage came out to the "even minute" where there could be a check. I was on time, and the first thing I asked the checkers was, "Did John Penton come through here?" One of them said, "Yes, he was four minutes early and he wasn't too happy about it."

Even though Penton was a much more experienced and notably much better rider than I was, he totally lost his concentration for keeping time, and consequently he lost the high score trophy right there. Those four minutes cost him eight points, while he lost high score by only two. In later years those four minutes would have cost him 17 points. If ever I got a good lesson in concentration, and splitting one's concentration between riding and keeping time, it was then. I finished 4th overall at the Covered Wagon that day, behind Sky Ball, John Penton and Jim Fennell, in that order.

Not far from the end of the run I took my first tumble with the DMW, when I hit a wide gully on a high-speed trail. It was marked well enough, but I was looking at my watch at the time, and my odometer, and didn't see it coming. Nor did I see the many "down arrows" tacked to the trees, which I spotted at the very last moment as I went for the brakes – but it was too late. It was one of those wide dips in the trail for which I should have slowed down to ride into and out of on sloping surfaces. That end-o was yet another lesson on splitting concentration between riding and keeping time.

I hit the far bank hard with the front wheel and it threw me clear over the handlebars. I was lucky that I was able to slow down a little, or I would have bent the front end, and would have almost definitely gotten hurt in the process. As it was, I didn't damage anything on the bike, or on me, and I didn't lose any points. I was able to get back on and recover the lost time before the next check, which was the last.

A month or so later I recognized one of the unnamed photos in the October 1961 issue of Cycle Sport as being John dropping his BMW yet again, when he tangled with the slippery rocks in the Knightsville River crossing. Another lesson I learned that day was that it doesn't always pay to ride at or beyond the peak of one's ability. For one thing it takes concentration away from keeping time, and another is that one tends to fall much more often. My average tumble was only about once in four or five enduros. I had heard that some of the top riders, who apparently had a much greater desire to win than I did, fell at least a couple of times in practically every event. I would rather conserve my bones and conserve the bike by riding at 90 to 95% of my ability, rather than 101% and more.

That 1961 Covered Wagon was one of the first national championships where the Greeves made its appearance. Sky Ball was riding a Greeves when he won that day, as were Frank DeGray, Harold Dean and several other experts. There were nine

Greeves entered. Randy Wilson of West Boylston, Mass. was importing the Greeves from England, which was soon to become a major factor in enduro competition in this country.

The first Japanese motorcycle I remember seeing in an enduro also made its debut at that event. It was a Yamaha, ridden by Bob Hogan of Springfield who became a Yamaha dealer. The first Japanese bikes imported into this country for enduros left a lot to be desired in handling, strength, and reliability, but great strides were made in the next few years.

Following is an article that appeared in Cycle Sport about that 1961 Covered Wagon, written by a member of the Pioneer Valley M.C.:

Sky Ball tops Covered Wagon

October 8th was a lovely morning, but at the Pioneer Valley M.C. campgrounds the air was not quiet – not even at 6:30 AM. The participants were busily checking their bikes while Ralph Spencer (#1) and Jim Fennell (#101) were edging theirs to the starting line, where Ross Aborn would give them the "go" signal at 7:01 AM sharp. Within the next three-quarters of an hour they were all on their way, as were most of the spectators, after checking their maps for the points of interest and the locations of the "Gas Stops."

At 17 miles on their route sheets, the riders turned into the woods, and just two-tenths farther, there was a check, which was "zeroed" by many. The course consisted of easy-going old stage roads to get to the next check, but it was not easy for some to stay on time; then some dirt roads and a short stretch of rough stuff, where the riders found one of our humorous signs, "Ooops, sharp turn," and into the brook they went.

A "Gas Available" followed by a breather for the next 20 miles, with checks before and after the rough sections to keep the riders on their toes. Between check #4 and #5, the State Police were looking for 5 Boy Scouts lost since the day before. When the trailblazers talked with the police, their only request was that they be notified if any rider saw the boys.

During midmorning, the riders found themselves in some new territory, which eventually led them onto another old stage road, and then to the Knightsville River crossing, which had some of its usual surprises. Right where the trail entered the river there was a deep spot, which some hit and drowned out their engines, but many looked closely and avoided the deep water. The stones in the river were very slippery, which helped some riders to get their machines washed. We understand that "Tibby" Thibodeau, of Springfield made a beautiful crossing without "footing." It was also reported that the girls made it look easy! Not too much farther and there was a sign, "Billy says, 'Bet your feet are wet'". The next interesting spot is known as, "Beaver Dam Country." We didn't make them ride the dam – we made a road around it – fit for endurance run riders only.

Then came a check that caught many late. John Penton, Lorain, Ohio, was one of the few who zeroed this check, in spite of having dunked his machine in the Knightsville River and having trouble restarting it. The rest of the morning was rather easy, passing through some very pretty and very hilly country. (We threw in lovely fall foliage for an extra measure.)

Noon control was at Middlefield, Mass., in the midst of the beautiful Berkshires, where all welcomed something to eat and drink. A few repairs, gas and oil, and away they went, only to find that the afternoon was getting a little tougher, and it was harder to make checks on time. At the next check there was a sign at a bridge that was missing the planking, and had only bare rails to ride, "Did you cheat and go around? – Chappie wants to know." Note: Most of them did!

At 126 miles the riders came around a corner and found a red and white flag, and checkers who informed them that they would pass that way again in a few minutes. This was the first of the old trolley line that they saw a good deal of later. It was almost impossible to stay on time, and by the time they got back to the checkers, many remarked, "That was a cute trick. Who thought that one up?" Guess they could blame both Phil and Mitch (Phil Bourdon and Coleman Mitchell) for that one. The section after School House Rd. and before the West Granville Gas Stop found everyone losing points. This was where the girl riders finally ran out of time. Five miles of "free territory" followed, but not easy to make up any time. A brook, a little pipe line, onto the big pipe line, and then a combination secret and emergency check kept the boys doing their best to stay on time.

Sky Ball on his Greeves, winner of the 200-Mile National Championship at Southwick, Mass. in 1961.

Photo by Boyd Reynolds

R.G. "Randy" Wilson and Bob Hicks were two very prominent figures in the New England motorcycle scene. Randy was the importer and distributor of many brands of European motorcycles, including the Greeves, which became a major factor in enduro competition in the U.S. in the 1960s.

Bob Hicks was editor and publisher of Cycle Sport Magazine, which later joined with Trail Rider Magazine to report on all motorcycling off-road activities in the Northeast. At the time this photo was taken, Bob was recovering from a fractured wrist, which he sustained in scrambles competition. He rode in many forms of off-road competition, including the International Six Days Trial twice; first in Germany in 1969, and then in Spain in 1970. He rode an Ossa both times. He went on to serve as the Ossa team manager in the 1971 and 1973 ISDT, and as the Yankee team manager in the 1972 ISDT.

Photo by Grant Whidden

Frank Degray – Certainly the top New England woods rider of 1960, Frank DeGray was not only the Enduro Grand Champion that year, but he also topped the Trials Lightweight Class, missing out on the overall Trials Grand Championship by a small margin. He again won the overall Enduro Grand Championship in 1962, and he continued to finish high in the standings throughout the sixties. Frank is credited with having invented the first route sheet holder, described later in this book.

Photo by Grant Whidden

Oops! Those rocks are slippery. John Penton gets wet in the Knightsville River crossing. I learned that even the experts fall down sometimes.

Six well-placed checks later and everyone relaxed, for the run was over. We are sure that Frank Dean, Souderton, Pa. was thanking a fellow Pennsylvanian, Bob Wagner, who had fixed his broken shifting lever, making it possible for him to start and complete the run – and even to finish First in the Senior Class. We are sure there were many other examples of good sportsmanship as there always is at enduros.

We certainly hit the Jackpot for compliments on the run. With riders from the New England states, N.Y., N.J., Penn., Md., and Ohio, we felt well pleased when many said it was one of the top runs they had ever participated in. The lovely trophies and special souvenir pins and a covered wagon with oxen, engraved with "1961 200-Mile National" also rated many compliments. We want to take this opportunity to thank the companies who donated trophies, the AMA, which gave the beautiful Grand Championship trophy, and the many who assisted us in the checking. The Pioneer Valley M.C. members feel that it was a very successful day.

I also learned that passing efficiency in the woods is a very important factor to winning. I remember once while "waiting time" out on the trail with Christy Scholar, he said, "Are you having as much trouble getting by some of those fellows as I am?" I think we were in New Jersey at the time, and several slower riders on numbers directly in front of us weren't giving up any trail at all for passing. When I answered yes, he said with a little smile, "I hate to knock someone down, but sometimes it just can't be helped."

My own procedure for passing on narrow trails was to first call out, "Trail," as loud as I could, which was a non-intimidating way of letting the person know that I was there, and that I wanted to pass. As soon as an opportunity would arise where I felt it was possible for the guy to have pulled over, whether he did or not, I would start the pass, and either yell a little louder, "On your left," to let him know I was coming by, ready-or-not, and on which side I was coming; or I might just move in alongside, and say practically in his ear, "Coming through!" Then as I passed, I would usually yell out, "Thank you," even though he might never have yielded any trail at all. I found it to be much easier once we all got to know each other, and the other riders learned that I would eventually be coming by, one way or another.

The DMW became an excellent partner for me, except that sometimes it lacked the power to maintain a constant speed on the longer and steeper hills, or for recovering the speed quickly after having slowed down on a hill. I found it to be excellent for the tight woods, which usually favored the lighter weight machines. I think I could have lived with it, if only it had been more reliable restarting in the woods after having stalled for one reason or another. But I still thought I could do better with more power; and I felt that I had the ability to control more power. I was certainly strong enough to handle it, although I wasn't particularly anxious about riding a heavier machine.

I rode the DMW throughout 1961 and the spring of '62, and it served me well for more than a year, but in spite of my good showings, even at the nationals, I still hadn't won a high score, and by the middle of 1962 I began to look around for a machine that would do it for me.

I analyzed the result sheets and I could see that most riders that were turning in better scores than mine, when I was putting in my best effort, were riders with a better power-to-weight ratio. I could see there were events where a little more power could have made the difference between a win in the lightweight class, and winning high score overall.

I had looked often at the 500 Triumph, but I still had a soft spot for the singles, like a BSA or Matchless. I would have preferred finding a 350 four-stroke machine for the ideal power-to-weight ratio; but Gene Esposito and Jim Fennell were both doing very well on their 500 Triumphs in the Metropolitan area,

Proudly holding the 1st Place Class A Lightweight Trophy that I won at the 1961 200-Mile National Championship Covered Wagon Enduro, run in the Berkshires. I won it riding the 250 cc Villiers-powered DMW shown above.

as were several good riders in New England. I felt that I could also do well with one.

During the spring of 1962, around the time that I began having mechanical problems with the DMW, I started looking more seriously at the options. The Villiers two-stroke engine still wouldn't always restart when it was hot, and I stalled it far too often in the woods, which I rarely ever did with either of the two small Harleys, so I was anxious to get something else.

The tank on the DMW developed a serious gas leak while I was competing in one of the spring runs in New Jersey. Every time I stopped at a check, the gas would drip down and sizzle on the hot engine. I finished the run, winning first place in Class A Lightweight again, but by the time I got to the last check, the tank was leaking badly. I rode it to where my car and trailer were parked, and dropped it on its side to avoid the possibility of fire. I left it there until the engine cooled down while I changed my clothes.

A young guy came over to look at the bike lying there like a dead horse. He said he had never seen a DMW go through the woods as fast as that one. I didn't ask whether he was a spectator or if I might have passed him on the trail; but I did ask if he might be interested in buying it, and he answered with an enthusiastic yes.

I quoted him a good price, and he went to talk it over with his mentor, John Fenimore, who was a longtime fan of DMWs and somewhat of a collector. He returned a few minutes later with John, who asked if I was serious about selling it, and would I take his personal check. We talked about the problems I had been having with it, which didn't seem to bother them, and I went home without the DMW.

I probably would have been able to do much better with it, if it had a slightly stronger and more reliable engine. I imagined at the time that putting a good 350 cc four-stroke engine into that motorcycle, along with a better gas tank and a few other improvements, would have made it an ideal enduro machine, which would have been capable of beating just about anything out there. I still believe I could have won a high score with it just the way it was if the run was laid out totally in tight woods.

The DMW preceded the Greeves out of England by a few years, and when the Greeves arrived, it seemed to fare much better in New England enduros. Ralph quickly bought one, which I test rode, but by that time I was anxious to move away from two-stroke engines, and consequently I never got serious about owning one. There were many other models of the Greeves through the years, which were equipped with much better engines than what was in the DMW, and which would have fit my needs quite well, but I never did own one.

Ralph and I talked a lot about what changes the manufacturers ought to make to produce a better enduro bike, like folding foot-pegs, better bottom protection from the rocks, stronger chrome molly frames, engines that would start easily, cold or hot, better power-to-weight ratio, and many other characteristics that we would have liked to have.

While waiting for the results to be posted that day in New Jersey, I studied Dick Heins' 500 Triumph, and I asked him if I could take a ride on it. By the time I got back, I was convinced that it would be my next motorcycle. The four-stroke power seemed so much smoother and more controllable than the two-strokes, and the power was really impressive. I bought my first 500 Triumph the following week, a new 1962 model, from Jim Fennell and Whitey Loud, who had a shop in the Bronx at the time called *House of Triumph*.

Chapter Six

Triumph at Last

The 1960s were certainly the golden age of enduros for me, as I think they were for almost everyone who rode enduros in that decade, especially in the Northeast. The sixties were before factory-sponsored enduro riders existed in this country; it was before European and Japanese manufacturers began to mass-produce special enduro bikes for US consumption; it was before most clubs started more than a single rider on a minute; it was before the colorful, plastic "body-armor" existed; but most of all, it was before on-board computers took over the brain-work and the concentration involved in keeping time, which was one of the greatest challenges facing a serious enduro contestant. Staying on a precise time schedule, using a simple old-fashioned wind-up watch, and a brain, was what enduros were all about. Computers basically changed the nature of enduro competition forever from a brain-challenging sporting event, or a game, to a race.

The sixties was also a time when having fun doing it, as well as the sportsmanship involved, was more important than winning. I certainly don't mean to imply that winning wasn't also fun. Winning an enduro then was just as much a boost to the ego as I'm sure it is today, but I for one was always aware that it wasn't a race, and that there were other more important things involved, like the personal satisfaction derived from playing the game vigorously and fairly.

If someone chose to ride faster on a given trail section than I did, and he let me know he wanted to pass, no matter how heated the competition, even if we were both vying for the same trophy, or the same place on the result sheet, the trail was his for the asking, and vice versa; even if I were running late, and about to drop out of my minute, where every second counted. It was truly a matter of sportsmanship, and when everyone played the game that way it became somewhat of an unwritten rule, although I learned later that in other parts of the country they didn't always play with the same set of rules.

If I were to see someone take a tumble out there on the trail, no matter how much every second on the watch meant at the time, I would always stop to see that the rider was OK before proceeding, even if it was a championship event, and even if the other rider was a novice and not a well-known champion. Camaraderie and consideration for the other guy would always come before the competition. It was fun, and we often went out of our way to keep it that way.

The first run in which I rode my new Triumph was the Ray Goodrich Memorial in the fall of 1962, in the western foothills of the Berkshires, near Hoosick Falls, NY. I had ridden the Hummer there five years earlier, and it was an enduro where I noticeably lacked power. I was anxious to see how I'd make out with the stronger machine, especially in the Berkshires. The Triumph was barely broken in at the time, but it fit me perfectly, and it was an awesome piece of machinery as compared with other motorcycles I had owned.

I got only about two-thirds of the way through the run, doing exceptionally well, when I got a flat tire on the rear. So rather than coming home with the big trophy, which I was shooting for, my first enduro with the Triumph turned out to be a big disappointment instead.

I had been running about 10 pounds of air in the rear tire with the DMW. I soon learned that 10 pounds wasn't enough for the heavier weight of the Triumph and the way I was charging over the rocks with it. I weighed around 225 pounds, and the combined weight of the machine and me was far too much in the rocks for only 10 pounds of air. So I brought it up to 12 in both tires, and that's the way I rode it for years. I would still get flats occasionally, but I was willing to accept the trade-off.

I also began using heavy-duty tubes, which wouldn't pinch quite as easily. I would still have to be careful how hard I hit the largest and sharpest rocks, or I might still pinch the tube, especially in the rear, which had more weight on it and less suspension. If I ran with too much air in the rear tire, the Triumph would tend to bounce over the rocks, and if I ran with too little pressure I would pinch the tube and get flats. Not long after that, I began to use a larger 4.00 X 19 "Trials Universal" on the front to soak up the impact from hitting the larger rocks. The stock Triumph T100C came through with a 3.50 X 19. The front suspension on bikes then was less than half of what it became a few decades later – even a few years later for some bikes.

The next run I rode was the Great Eastern Championship at Meriden, CT, which was one of my favorites, and it was one in which I would have liked to do well with my new machine. I was not only determined, but also convinced that I could win my first high score at Meriden. The Triumph fit my riding style perfectly and I had adapted easily to its extra weight. I would probably have done just as well, or even better, with a lighter weight machine, but the power-to-weight ratio of the bikes at that time was such that I couldn't get enough power from the 250 cc engine; or the reliability either, and I was strong enough to handle the heavier machine.

Meriden was a particularly tough run that day with lots of rocks, fallen trees and tight trails, as there usually were plenty of at Meriden, which was in my favor. I arrived early for sign-up to get an early number, which I usually did well with.

After passing everyone who had started in front of me, I saw no one all day. I was hitting every checkpoint in good shape, "zeroing" most, with no early arrivals. The very last section of the run consisted of more than 10 miles of woods where there was no trail at all in some places; just markers stapled to the trees, where even the pathfinder's tire tracks were often not visible. I was making excellent time through it, and eventually I caught up with Bob Butterfield, the pathfinder.

"Keep going, Piet," he said, "the markers are all up." So I did, in spite of the fact that I knew the AMA rules stated that if an early rider overtakes the pathfinder, the run should be called right there. I proceeded until I got to a huge group of spectators at a brook crossing a mile or so after passing Butterfield.

The trail led to the edge of the water where I could see what appeared to be the continuation of it on the other side. I hesitated for a moment because the water looked very deep, but the spectators were all pointing and yelling, "Go straight through." I glanced up and down the stream and didn't see another place to cross; so trusting the spectators, which isn't always a good practice, I charged right into the deep water.

It was in fact the way Butterfield had intended for riders to go, but unfortunately someone had dammed up the stream that morning, probably for an additional spectator thrill, making it much deeper than it normally would have been. I'm sure if the pathfinder had gotten there before I did, he would have cleared the blockage, or at least directed me to a different spot to cross. The water must have been 3 feet deep where I plunged in, which was above the air cleaner. The bike not only drowned out, but the cylinders filled with water and hydro-locked the engine.

I got help dragging it out and up the embankment on the far side, but I worked on it there taking out the plugs, pumping out water and trying to get it restarted for at least twenty minutes. The ignition points were wet, and the stock air cleaner, which looked like it had been made from some kind of cloth fabric was clogged with water. I worked on it for almost a half-hour before the second rider, Dick Turmel, came through. When I finally got it running, I figured I could still win the event since only one bike had gone by. I charged out of the area as fast as I could ride. It was only three-tenths of a mile to a paved road.

I expected to see a turn marker as I approached the road, but there was none. When I reached it, the thought occurred to me that I should have come through a check. But I spotted a course marker on a pole not far away, so I turned onto the road and started following arrows and trying to make up some of the time I had lost – hopefully before I hit what I assumed would be the last check.

The farther I rode, the more worried I became about not having seen a check after completing the long, 10-mile technical section. I knew from quickly refiguring my time and mileage, and from figuring where a check would most logically have been placed, that I should have seen one either a tenth of a mile before, or three-tenths after reaching the blacktop.

The clubhouse was almost five miles from there, which was a sure sign that something was wrong with this picture, but I kept going, driven by the need to make up time. As soon as I pulled into the clubhouse grounds I looked for the check there too, but I didn't really expect to find one anymore; even though by that time I hadn't seen one since I originally entered the tight woods about 15 miles back. I kept yelling, "Where's the check?" and the only answer I got was, "What check?"

Someone from the club eventually told me that the final check was in the woods a tenth of a mile before the tarmac. It turned out that it was between the brook crossing and the road; and I had been too much in a hurry, causing me to miss a left-turn marker at an obscure fork in the trail where either way would have led me to the same paved road, but only one way went past the checkpoint. I was actually on the wrong trail when I reached the tarmac.

I was of course disappointed with failing to finish two runs in a row, and I wondered how much longer it would be before I could prove, at least to myself, that I had the potential to win a high score, especially now that I had the equipment.

My next enduro was the Bushwacker, held in the rocks and tight woods around Somers, in north central Connecticut. It was another area in which I normally did well. In later years the Bushwacker was an enduro that I could win handily by a comfortable margin. I only vaguely remember riding this one. The following report appeared in *Cycle Sport*:

Bushwacker Enduro

On November 4th the Conn. Ramblers held their 3rd annual Bushwacker Enduro. Thirty-seven riders left the starting line for an enjoyable ride through some of the finest woods trails to be found anywhere.

Much to the surprise of Conn. Ramblers' member Ron Alleman, Harold Stone, a hardy enduro rider from Lebanon, N.H. was already waiting to ride, long before anyone had arrived at the start. Early arrival must be his secret, by the way, because he won his class that day.

Soon however, after the rest of the club members arrived, things were humming. Frank DeGray pitched his tent so anyone so desiring, could get out of the brisk fall weather. Fred Marsh and Roger Walker soon got a charcoal fire going, and coffee and the works were soon hot. Meanwhile, Ed Emory had signed in the riders, the checks had all been set out, and the riders began leaving the starting line. Due to a slight shortage of help, the always willing Jean Scholar and Ed McIntyre volunteered to help out at the checks and everything was set.

Before very long, two riders came limping back to the start. Seems they were rushing just a little too much in a slippery turn when a few rocks lining the trail decided to get in their way. At the first check Vern Warren, a new rider, came walking in and asked how far he had gone. When told 5.2 miles, his incredulous exclamation was that he had figured it was much closer to 45 miles. The miles do seem to stretch out for those new riders, don't they! Rusty Brittain, the lone girl entry, rode 13.3 miles though. She only quit when her machine started to act up. Gives you something to aim for, wouldn't you say, Vern?

Meanwhile, a couple of our Senior riders, Mabel and Bill Robinson had arrived as spectators, but were soon working along with the club members. Mrs. Robinson was a lifesaver at the close of the run helping Fred Marsh dish out the much needed coffee, hot dogs and donuts to the famished competitors.

At last everyone was in or accounted for and the results were being checked. When the smoke cleared, who should emerge as High Point winner but Greg Lipsky. Some guys will do anything to sell a few machines, and it appears that Jawa couldn't have anyone any better at pushing their product than Greg.

All of us at the Conn. Ramblers would like to thank the riders who participated, and those generous people who chipped in and helped with the work, especially Veto Bonan and Frank DeGray who laid out the run. Here's hoping we see all of you back again for our annual Snow Run which is held in February. Until then, happy riding!

The magazine reported that Greg Lipski's score was 981, and that I had finished second overall and first in the expert heavyweight class with a 979. Third overall and second in the heavyweight class went to Christy Scholar with a score of 977. I could rationalize that it was in Greg's "backyard," giving him a slight edge from knowing the trails and knowing the most likely spots for checks to be placed. Christy had always been one of my idols, especially in the kind of tight, rocky trails they had at the Bushwacker, so coming away with a higher score than Christy and the rest of the field was satisfying enough for that day, but I was still looking for my first high score.

The District #5 Championship was scheduled to take place in New Jersey the following Sunday. It was being sanctioned as a 100-Mile National Championship and would be run over the same course where I had already done well with the 165 Harley, when it actually favored the stronger machines. Gene Esposito had won it the year before, and Christy Scholar the year before that. I was convinced I could do well there with the Triumph, and I was looking forward to the opportunity to prove it at a national. I had gotten all the practice I needed by that time, and I had ridden the Triumph through the tightest woods sections and over the steepest hills. In spite of having had problems in a few of my earlier outings, I felt that if I could pull everything together I could do it that day.

I presumed that everyone out there had good days and bad days, and that many factors had to come together in order to take home the big trophy, especially at a major event like a national championship; but I also felt that I was overdue. I accepted my handicap of not being able to make up time as quickly as others on high-speed trails, but if the entire run was tight, like District 5 usually was, I had just as much chance to win as anyone. One didn't always have to be the fastest rider, or the best time keeper, or have the best motorcycle.

Even with all three, which were certainly essential at a national, there were still many factors that could prevent a top rider from winning. I had experienced just about every one of those, including mechanical problems, flat tires, missing course markers, inability to pass others on the narrow trails, hitting the checks early and a myriad of others. About the only thing I hadn't done was crash. By riding just short of my full capability and by keeping in mind the object of the game, which to me was having fun doing it, I was usually able to minimize my falls and prevent serious injures.

When Ralph and I arrived, we noticed that several of the top national riders were there, including Bill Baird, the national champion of the previous year, John Penton, Norm Smith and others. I also saw several top riders from the East, including Gene Esposito, Bill Decker, Sky Ball, Bob Maus, Jim Fennell and Dave Barnes. Any one of those riders was fully capable of winning high score, and they didn't have to have a particularly bad day to lose; but I would certainly have to have a good one to win.

One of the primary obstacles that could cause problems on the trail at District 5 was "Impossible Hill," which was a long, steep hill on a gas-line right-of-way, with rocks and loose gravel all over the face of it. It was tricky to get over without getting stuck somewhere on the hill, as the tires could easily break traction on the loose ground, or the bike could rear up and come over backwards.

It didn't usually cause much of a problem to the experts if they could choose a good path and if the hill wasn't already cluttered with stalled bikes, causing a traffic-jam. The hill called for a running start, good throttle control, and an unobstructed path most of the way up. Once the rear tire lost traction, the chances of moving forward again were slim, especially for a heavyweight. If there were many other riders stuck on the hill it was often difficult to pick a good line. Having an early starting number had its advantages. Starting numbers were drawn at random by the club, and luckily I got an early number that day. I also never had much of a problem with steep hills.

One of the other obstacles at District 5 was "Snake's Den." It was probably a huge swamp at one time, which became overrun with trees and eventually became a morass of slippery roots. Motorcycles made what was probably the only twisty path through it, after years of having used it in the endurance runs. The entire trail through Snake's Den was usually very slick.

Here too, early riders had an advantage, as it was possible to lose time getting around slower riders between the trees, where it was often difficult to pass. Even getting an early number didn't guarantee not losing time, but it helped. I remember one day when someone tore down the markers in Snake's Den, and tacked them up going in the wrong direction. Practically everyone got lost that day.

I left the starting line with high hopes for a good ride. I zeroed the first few checks and was about thirty miles out when the course turned onto a grassy power line. I was running late in my minute at the time. The trail was smooth with very few rocks showing, but the beaten path meandered in an erratic line, and I wasn't quite maintaining my 24 mph average.

I realized that I would "go out of my minute" if I didn't increase the speed a little. The easiest way to do that was to take a straighter line. So I ignored the path and chose a straight line through the grass. Bad decision! Suddenly a huge rock appeared, which was hidden in the tall grass. I veered away to avoid hitting it head-on with the front wheel, but I couldn't quite miss it altogether, as I was traveling much too fast. The bottom on one side of the bike struck the rock very hard, and the impact threw the machine into the air and twisted it to an almost 45-degree angle, as it ricocheted off the rock. I held on, but with little hope of regaining control.

After being airborne for at least 15 to 20 feet, the bike landed on its side with me still on the seat and holding the handlebars. I landed hard on my arm and shoulder. The worst of it was that my foot had slipped off the bare metal foot peg, which had lost its thick rubber cover earlier that morning. The stock Triumph foot peg was famous for losing that rubber cover.

The 5-inch-long solid steel peg, with a spear-shaped knob on the end, which was supposed to hold the rubber on, then became a weapon that pierced my boot and went clear through the fleshy part of my heel pad, hitting the inside of the boot on the other side. I didn't feel it go through because of the shock of landing so hard on my side, but when I tried to pull my leg out from under the bike, I couldn't because my foot was pinned there by the foot peg.

The next rider to come along was Norm Smith on a 500 Triumph. When he stopped to see if I was OK, I told him that I couldn't get my leg out from under the machine. He got off and tried to lift it from my leg. I realized that the peg was actually holding it, so as he lifted the weight of the bike, I forced my other foot between the bike and the pinned foot and pried it off with the other foot. I felt the pain then as the knob withdrew through my heel pad.

As soon as my foot was free, and after Norm put my bike on its side-stand, he said he would tell someone I was there, and he took off. I was sure it cost him at least a few points at the next check, which could have cost him high score, but that's the way we played the game, and I was glad Norm played it that way. Several minutes later a four-wheel-drive carryall arrived with two guys, who carted me off to a hospital. They said they'd come back later for my bike.

Being Sunday, the emergency room people had to call in a surgeon from home to work on the hole in my foot. I laid there on the emergency room gurney for hours before the doctor finally showed up. The initial shock had worn off by then and the foot really hurt.

The nurses tried to clean and sterilize the wound as well as they could without getting deep inside. When the doctor arrived, he cleaned it out thoroughly and put a plastic tube deep into the hole for draining; and then he stitched it up. To say I was feeling the pain would be a gross understatement. Even with the injections I was given to anesthetize the foot, it was just about all I could take. The attending nurse said my face turned several colors every time the doctor drove the needle into my heel, while sewing it up. It took several stitches.

When Ralph arrived later, he had my Triumph on the trailer with his Greeves, ready to take us home. I had asked the guys that picked me up to tell Ralph about my problem and to tell him where I was. I was instructed to keep the foot elevated on the way home, but there was no way of doing that in the Studebaker. The pain was excruciating, especially from the foot being that low. I managed to make it to work the next day. I never missed a single day of work from injuries or recuperation related to an endurance run in all the years that I rode.

When the results arrived in the mail two months later, I learned that there had been an official protest lodged. The following notation was made on the result sheet:

"As you know, the 100-Mile National Championship Endurance Run has been protested. The American Motorcycle Association has notified Referee Charles Watson that while he acted according to the AMA Rules, they feel that the results of this run should be scored to the end of the run at 109 miles.

The awards therefore were based on the scores up to that point. The American Motorcycle Association has also decided that under these conditions this run <u>WILL NOT</u> be classified as a 100-Mile National Championship Endurance Run, just as a 100-Mile Endurance Run. Trophies will be mailed out in early January 1963."

Sky Ball was named the eventual winner of the high score trophy, and since a separate trophy was awarded to the District #5 Champion for the highest scoring rider from District 5, he also took that one. First place in Class A Medium went to Gene Esposito on his 500 Triumph. My friend Ralph Spencer won the Senior Class for riders over 45.

Bill Baird, John Penton, Norm Smith, Jim Fennell and several other top riders were given credit for completing 48.0 miles, having caught the pathfinder somewhere between 34.4 and 48 miles, which I think was the problem that caused the protest. For me it meant a winter to recover and think about what I had done. It was the first and one of the only injuries I ever sustained in all the years I rode enduros.

My time eventually came in March 1963 at the very next run I rode. It was at Camp Smith, north of Peekskill, which is a National Guard training area just five miles from my home. Laid out as a closed-course enduro, it was made up of five 4-mile laps within the rocky, hilly, closed-in restricted area belonging to New York State. The run was very short as endurance runs go,

Astride my new 1962 Triumph, holding the Reggie Pink Memorial Perpetual High Score Trophy that I had just won at Camp Smith in Peekskill, NY.

but continuously tough, as the spring thaw and recent rains had created a muddy, slippery morass for all of those 20 miles.

Ironically, it turned out to be more of a race than a time keeping enduro, but it served to prove that one of my strongest suits was riding in the highly technical terrain with lots of mud, rocks, slippery roots, and other obstacles.

A check was set up approximately halfway around each lap, with another check at the end of the lap, totaling ten checks. It was possible for only a few of the top riders to be early at the checkpoints; but because of the deep mud and the technical nature of the course, it was very difficult for anyone to maintain the prescribed average speed and still be able to look at the watch and figure out the seldom-used time schedule of 18 mph, rather than the usual 24 mph.

Being unfamiliar with figuring the 18 mph schedule in my head, I figured out much of it beforehand, like most of the others did, and I wrote the times onto the route sheet. It was still necessary to check my watch occasionally to keep from being early at the checks, which made it more like an endurance run rather than an all-out cross-country race. About half of the sixty-five riders who started the event completed the five laps.

I not only won high score, but I turned in a perfect score of 1000 points. I suspect that a few of the top riders lost points for being early, since it was difficult to concentrate on the time while negotiating the trails. There was no smooth terrain or roads in the entire run, on which to make up any time lost, as it was simply a continuous, tough obstacle course.

Four weeks later the Crotona M.C. put on their annual Split Rock Enduro, a closed-course event at Monterosa Lodge in the rockiest and hilliest part of Putnam County, about 25 miles north of my home. The terrain and conditions were perfect for me, but I arrived at one of the checks a minute early. It was a check that was positioned partway around the first lap. The infraction cost me two points, as well as the high score trophy.

I lost those two points because I had been running too close to the "head-end" of my minute, where my watch said I was on time, but there was a difference of a few seconds between my watch and the checkers watch. My watch was running a few seconds slow at the time, which compounded the problem. I'll discuss this subject in greater detail in a later chapter; but I missed winning the high score by a few seconds.

Chapter Seven

A Few Early Nationals

Having put together a few encouraging finishes with the Triumph, one a high score and two others very close to the top score, I gained the confidence I needed to try my hand at a few Midwest national championships, particularly the longer ones like the 250-mile Little Burr and the 500-mile Jack Pine. I was anxious to see how I might fare under different riding conditions on foreign turf, as well as pitting the skills I had learned in the Northeast against a whole new set of riders. At least two of our popular local riders had already won the Jack Pine – Don Pink and Sal Scirpo; and I was doing well against both, although mainly in the shorter and much more technical runs.

Ralph and I used his pickup for most of our multi-day and overnight jaunts so that I could leave the car home for Lillian, because like most families of that era we owned only one car. Leaving on a long trip where we would be away from home for three days and two nights, and sometimes longer, also meant leaving Lilli home alone to cope with our four children, three of whom were eight years of age or younger.

It was a tough decision to make, since I played a major role in the children's discipline. It would have been even tougher if she hadn't encouraged me to go. I'm sure she had hardships during those times, but she never complained. In hindsight, I suspect that my leaving for a while offered her a break from the daily routine of caring for many of my needs, in addition to those of the kids.

Enduros were not the only thing that kept me away from home during that period, because as a manager at IBM at a time when they were struggling to get out an entirely new line of supercomputers, I was being asked to work a great deal of overtime, as well as spending almost two hours a day getting to and from work; not to mention the occasional field trips, since I was one of the only troubleshooting specialists who would be asked to go out and solve the unsolvable technical problems in the field, after the field engineers would become totally stumped and even the development engineers were unable to get their own newly designed machines up and running in the customer's office.

As a last resort they would call in the "manufacturing ace" with the excuse that it was probably a manufacturing defect, which it usually wasn't; but I'd fix it anyway. I often ran into conflicts between my work and the enduros, but work always came first. Unfortunately they both appeared to be taking precedence over my family. In spite of that, I was once told by one of my IBM managers that, "If you didn't stop riding that motorcycle, one of these days you're going to be on the outside looking in!" I think I outlasted him with the company.

I was working 30 miles from my home at IBM's plant in Poughkeepsie, when I decided to travel to the national enduros. I was managing a department of manufacturing engineers at a time when it was necessary for the entire department to be working a great deal of overtime designing test equipment.

The only time I could find to ride my motorcycle was on the day of the event, which left no time for practicing; and practice was an important factor for finishing in the top five or ten, especially at a national championship. It also left insufficient time to service the bike between enduros, which resulted in all kinds of problems that kept me from even finishing many of the local runs, and now I was headed for the big ones.

Our first effort was at Little Burr, held in central Ohio on Memorial Day Weekend, and which of course was not the greatest time for a family man to be away from home, especially since we usually had a backyard family picnic on that day.

Little Burr was sanctioned as a 250-mile national championship. We learned after arriving in Columbus that there were more than 250 entries signed up to ride, and that they would be starting four riders on a minute. I had never seen more than two riders on a minute and I wondered what kind of traffic problems I was in for, especially since passing slower riders was not one of my stronger suits by far. I had gotten used to riding with practically no one in front of me, sometimes for the entire run. I certainly didn't welcome having four riders on every minute getting in my way.

The starting numbers were determined by a random drawing at least a week before the day of the event. Luckily I got #305, which meant that I was one of four riders on the fifth minute. It also meant, however, that there would be 16 riders within those four minutes, and it would be a while before they would thin out. More than a few of those people caused problems for me between every check for the first hundred miles or so.

I noticed from studying the list of entries posted on the clubhouse wall that John Penton would again be riding close behind me, even closer than at Covered Wagon, where he finally went by in the afternoon. He was #206, in the minute directly behind mine. I would certainly see him more often than I did at Covered Wagon, being that it was his home turf; although as it turned out I didn't see him at all until we ran into a few miles of very slick trail early in the afternoon, where we were both late and he was willing to risk riding a lot faster than I would.

He went by me like I was an amateur. I've always been leery about riding on smooth, slick surfaces at high speeds anyway, which gave me yet another handicap for that part of the country, since there was a lot more of it there. I can usually handle 24 mph on just about any uneven surface, but when it comes to riding faster than that on wet clay, forget it.

I learned in the very first woods section that most of the slower riders wouldn't give up an inch for passing, and the trails were narrow and fast, which made my passing problem even worse. When someone is traveling on a relatively narrow footpath at a speed close to 24 mph, he isn't about to slow down to let someone go by, especially in a national championship where he's got high hopes of finishing with a trophy. Passing required much more risk and daring there than I was accustomed to in New England, where I "broke trail" in most of the runs; or worst case, there would be only one rider on a minute.

As long as I was safely within my minute, I'd be content to follow the slower rider and wait for a better opportunity to get by; but as he would continue to lose time, it would bring me to a point where I would certainly drop out of my minute if I didn't go by the guy, which is when I'd be forced into taking on the greater risk.

The first time it happened, which was in the very first woods section, I tried my New England method of calling out, "Trail," followed by moving in closer and yelling "On your left." It went totally without response, even though the guy had plenty of room and ample opportunity to yield a little of the trail.

I judged his speed to be too fast, and the trail too narrow for me to squeeze up next to him and yell, "Coming through." I was concerned that I might knock him down, which seemed like too much of a bully tactic, especially so early in the game; but eventually I'd either have to wrestle with the guy for the trail or do something else to keep from dropping out of my minute.

I rarely ever had to wrestle with anyone for a trail at home; partly because there were fewer riders, partly because they were more willing to give up room on the trail when asked, and partly because in New England they'd usually know who was there; whereas in Ohio, as Rodney Dangerfield would say, "I get no respect!" It would also seem to me to change the attitude of the sport. Enduros at home were never quite like that, nor was it like that to most of the people I rode with. There seemed to be more sportsmanship in New England.

An alternative on that first encounter was to simply take to the brambles to go by; although to pass, I would have to go much faster in the bushes than he was traveling on the smooth trail, which was quite a trick. I would do that occasionally in New England in the later years when I was more capable, and when I'd be reluctant out of courtesy to ask the guy to move over or to wrestle with him for the trail because he was probably out there with an even greater desire to win than I was in the later years. I liked to think that I was there mainly for the enjoyment of riding the runs.

I remember passing a past New England Grand Champion along a very tight trail in the Berkshires. Being reluctant to pull up alongside and wrestle with him for the trail, I waited for an opportunity to chop a corner and reenter the trail in front of him. I accidentally hit an obscure rock while doing it, and I came crashing through a clump of bushes airborne, landing only a few feet in front of him. He hadn't expected it, so it probably startled him, and "shook him up." He came over later and said, "Boonstra, I don't think you're wired right!"

The first time I left the trail to pass in Little Burr, only a few miles from the start, I hit something obscure there too, which threw me clear over the handlebars. It's a good thing there were very few rocks around, and plenty of bushes, because I could have broken my collarbone or worse. I landed hard and got shook up a bit.

After picking myself up and getting back on, I quickly caught the same guy again, and started to go around him a second time the same way. This time I hit a hidden branch or something at the wrong angle and took another nasty spill. It took three tries and two falls to get by the first rider in the first woods section – not a great start for my Midwest national debut!

It reminded me of John Penton in the 1961 Covered Wagon when he also fell twice going by me, except that I pulled over and gave him plenty of room each time he beeped for the trail. I soon learned that riders from his home state weren't quite as cooperative. Of course I could have taken on the attitude that Christy mentioned, "I hate having to knock someone down, but sometimes it just can't be helped." Unfortunately, that's when our game stops being fun.

In hindsight I would have been much better off wrestling for the trail, which is what I figured was the accepted practice out there, and apparently a regular part of the game as they played it. I thought at the time if I had to pass very many riders between every check, and I fell down every time, I'd get punchy after a while.

Soon after coming out of a woods section, the same slow riders would go by me on the road as they made up their time. I'd then have to pass the same guys again a few minutes later in the very next woods section. It became quite frustrating! In a section where the average amateur rider might drop two minutes, I'd have to pass as many as eight riders to stay on time. It never got quite that bad, but I hoped at the time that I wouldn't have a problem for the entire 250 miles. I fell a total of five times that day, which was more than I usually fell in an entire season in New England, and every fall was while passing, or trying to pass a slower rider on a narrow trail.

The good news about the passing problem was that more than three-quarters of the less-experienced riders "went over their hour" early in the day, after having dropped more than an hour behind schedule, and after having been disqualified. Of the total entry of 255 riders, only about a hundred finished, so it wasn't nearly as crowded in the afternoon. I certainly didn't have as many passing problems. I don't think any of the sidecars made it past lunch, as they were disqualified earlier for being more than an hour late. A 250-mile run is a true endurance run though, which is the thing I liked most about Little Burr.

Another thing I learned from that first Little Burr and didn't care much for, was that the Ohio soil has a much greater consistency of clay, making it a lot slipperier than most trails in New England, especially after a rain, and especially at the higher speeds. The trails would become extremely slick in some places with a small amount of moisture. It was on this type of wet clay that John Penton went by me. It was shortly after a technical section from which we both emerged late, and were making up time. I saw only a few rocks in Ohio, and very few long hills, which would have been where I might have put in a much better performance. I gave the run my best effort though, and I enjoyed much of the riding in spite of the negatives.

About fifteen miles from the end I was on a narrow, high-speed trail with bushes growing close on both sides, when suddenly I spotted what appeared to be a huge 3-inch-diameter jousting pole sticking out of the bushes and pointed straight at me, and I was traveling around 25 mph. If I hadn't let my right hand fly off the handlebar and twisted my entire body sideways in a very quick evasive move, it would have caught me in the shoulder, or maybe even in the chest. As it was it grazed my coat sleeve. I tried not to think about what it might have done, and I wondered how everyone behind me would deal with it. A few minutes later I came out onto a road where there was a check. I told them about it, but there wasn't much they could do.

A short while later as I was "waiting time," John Penton pulled up alongside to also wait his time. The rules say that checks must be positioned at least five miles apart, making the first five miles after every checkpoint "free territory," where riders can safely run early. We had gone five miles from the last check on roads, and I was running a few minutes early. I stopped there to wait for my watch to catch up, as did John. This can occur many times in an easy enduro.

He didn't look good, so I asked, "Are you all right, John?" He answered, "Did you see that thing sticking out back there?" I said, "Yes, I saw it. It almost caught me." He pointed near his shoulder and said, "It hit me right there and threw me clear off the back of the motorcycle."

He reached inside his jacket and said, "Does this feel right to you?" I felt it and could tell immediately that his collarbone was in two pieces, one of which was poking against the outer flesh. I said, "It broke your collarbone, John."

He answered, "Do you think so?" I said, "I'm sure of it. I can feel the broken piece. Do you want me to tell someone you're here?"

"No," he said, "I'll be all right."

We exchanged a few more words before it was time for me to leave. There was a check a mile or so up the road, where I told them about the stick and about John's collarbone, in case he didn't show up at their check, because it looked to me like he was hurting. From that point on, the course went into some of the tightest woods we had all day. It was like a tough 5-mile finale for the run, which was otherwise quite easy. I was making good time through it, but I couldn't help but think about how John was dealing with it. I thought he would have a great deal of difficulty getting through, especially with his broken collarbone being on the throttle-hand side. There were water splashes and a few fallen trees, and some of it was quite technical.

I came out onto a gravel road at the end of the five-mile section. The final check was about a quarter-mile up the road. I checked in and said, "John Penton is back there somewhere riding with a broken collarbone. I doubt that he could ever make it through that last section." At that very moment someone said, "Here comes Penton now."

After I had thought he couldn't possibly make it through at all, there he was, all slouched over the machine, coming down the road. And he signed into the final check on time! At first I thought he must have aborted and taken a different route, and that he was no longer in the event, but it appeared that he was not only still in, but he checked in on-time.

Later, as the scores were being tallied for more than a few hours, John hung around the clubhouse area, socializing. Once when he pushed his undershirt back to show his injury to someone, I could see that it was bleeding quite a bit internally. Most of the flesh in a wide area was deep purple. I asked why he doesn't go to the emergency room to get it taken care of. He brushed it off and said, "I'm all right. I'll go later." He stuck around until well after the scores were posted.

When the scores were posted, they revealed that John had won first place in his class with a score of 980, a single point behind the overall winner Sox Brookhart, riding a 650 Triumph. Sox is a big fellow, with hands like a side of beef. He could ride a 650 through tight woods as fast as most with lighter machines. I rode a minute away from him a few years later at the "Little Bone" in western New York, where I got to see him ride. I said to him after emerging from the "Seneca Highlands" section, that I was amazed at the way he was able to throw that big 650 around. He turned to me and said with a smile and a southern-Ohio drawl, "You ride 'em just like you do the road, boy."

Bert Wieland of Michigan tied with Sox for high score with a 981. The Emergency Check broke that tie. I finished third in Class A Medium Weight with a score of 956. Norm Smith took 1st in that class with a 963. Bill Baird won the Medium Weight Class Championship with 970.

Looking over the results, I realized that I had finished 11th overall out of the 255 entries, which I rationalized wasn't too bad for competing against the country's best for the first time, where the riding conditions were foreign to me; especially the high-speed passing on narrow trails and the fact that one of the only ways to make up time after a technical section was to go even faster on the narrow, sometimes very slippery trails, which I normally wouldn't do.

I concluded that if I rode in that area often enough, I would probably develop the necessary skills needed for passing, and maybe even for riding much faster than 24 mph on slick trails to make up time lost in the technical sections, although I didn't care much for either. The thing I liked most about Little Burr was its 250-mile length.

At a checkpoint in a later Little Burr, waiting for the checkers to find my name on the score sheet. Patience was not one of my stronger virtues.

Photo by Boyd Reynolds

I thought it was unfortunate that a 250-mile national championship couldn't be held in the rocks and hills of New England, which would place more emphasis on the skill of riding continuously tough terrain, which also requires conserving one's physical strength as well as the machine. In Ohio we rode all day at relatively high speeds on over-crowded narrow trails, mostly to make up time lost in relatively short technical sections. The continuous toughness of a long event like that in New England would make it a true endurance run.

Ralph's and my next effort was the Jack Pine 500-Mile National Championship, which started at Lansing, Michigan, right in the middle of town. It was a 2-day event held on Labor Day weekend, which was yet another family holiday that required being away from home for four days and three nights. A few years later, wanting to make it a vacation for Lillian, and for the children as well, we all went to Michigan together. Ralph and my family served as my pit crew that year.

Their vacation didn't turn out quite as well as we had hoped, because taking care of the children at the spectator points, walking the long and sometimes muddy trails to get to and from the spectator points, and controlling the children in the car, turned out to be quite a chore for Lillian and Ralph. It was the time Ralph coined the phrase, "Oh my jangling nerves!"

My first Jack Pine in 1963 was quite a production as compared with any other enduro I had ever ridden. Oscar Lenz, "The Old Jack Piner" himself, hosted a huge banquet on the eve of the start of the run, the Saturday night before Labor Day. There were guest speakers and Oscar himself got up to the microphone to tell some of his favorite stories about how it "used to be, way back when." Oscar won the Jack Pine seven times between 1923 and 1936, before taking over the layout and promotion of the run. He was 69 when I first saw him there, and he still took part in the layout with a sidecar rig.

I recall Oscar talking about sticky gumbo mud that he claimed to have found after having searched for it for years. He said the mud was the consistency that it would build up quickly under our fenders until it would eventually bind and lock the wheels. He talked about how one run had to be stopped right there because no one could go any farther.

I had heard that at one time during the mid 1950s Don Pink performed at that banquet. One of Don's tricks was to get up onto the long banquet table and ride a unicycle from one end to the other and back. He also had a stand-up comedy routine that he delivered there. I heard the routine once at one of our Crotona Club meetings. We got out of the dinner quite late, and I didn't get any sleep at all that night, from the excitement of the evening and from having drunk too much coffee.

The enduro started from the center of Lansing at 7 a.m. Sunday morning. The course took us north out of the city over US Highway 27, where we had more than 25 miles of relatively straight, hard pavement before entering the first woods section. By starting five riders on a minute, it put hundreds of riders out on the long, straight highway at the crack of dawn, in a seemingly endless string of enduro bikes.

More than 450 riders left Lansing that morning, including sidecars, buddy-seat riders, women, and several hundred solo riders on small bikes, big bikes, and a lot in between. Every place where US 27 would take a slight bend, I could see a string of enduro bikes for miles ahead and miles behind, all moving at the same 24 mph speed through the dim morning haze; some making the blat-blat-blat sound of two-stroke engines, while others made the throaty rumble of the four-strokes. Being so early on Sunday morning of a Labor Day weekend, there were practically no other vehicles on the road.

The first trails were wide, sandy, and relatively easy to ride. They led us to an early crossing of the Grand River, which was at least 200 feet wide at the place we crossed, and quite shallow with a hard and relatively smooth bottom. Hundreds of spectators lined the riverbanks. The Grand was the first of three rivers we crossed in two days at Jack Pine.

We crossed the Tobacco River that same day, after dropping off a muddy embankment into the water and making our way across a deep, moderately strong current to the far side. We then climbed out over another muddy bank. The Tobacco had a smooth bottom with no holes or rocks.

The Rifle River on the other hand, which we crossed on the morning of the second day, was a lot trickier, with deep holes on the bottom, which caused some bikes to almost disappear below the surface; and there were many huge rocks around. Even more people lined the banks there, as the Rifle River was the top spectator point at Jack Pine. Some stood up to their knees in the river, waiting to pull bikes out that weren't making it across.

It was easy to drown the engine as the fast-moving current obscured most of the rocks and holes. I saw one guy drop his bike in a deep spot, and it almost totally submerged, leaving only one end of the handlebar sticking out of the water. The current in the Rifle was much swifter than either the Grand or the Tobacco, although when I rode the run a few years later, after a drought, they were all shallow. A check was usually positioned on the far bank of the Rifle River.

Crossing the Tobacco River

Crossing the Rifle.
Both photos above by Boyd Reynolds

Our scheduled overnight stop was in the town of West Branch, which appeared at the time like an old western town with dirt streets. I saw hitching posts in front of many of the quaint shops. West Branch is about 150 miles north of Lansing by roads, although the route we took to get there was over more than 250 miles of mostly sand trails. Many townspeople in and around West Branch offered their homes for the contestants' overnight stay, at a small charge, and a local church put on a dinner (see inset for ticket). The entry price for the event included the banquet on the eve of the run at Lansing, and also the church dinner at West Branch.

NATIONAL JACK PINE RUN
DINNER
AT ST. JOHNS LUTHERAN CHURCH
HOUGHTON AND FAIRVIEW ST.
WEST BRACH, MICHIGAN
START SERVING AT 5 P.M.

Ralph and I signed up for accommodations in one of the private homes. I slept that night on what must have been a child's bed, which was far too short. My feet extended out onto a chest at the foot of the bed, where I put one of the pillows to support them. I figured the people must have thought enduro riders were built like jockeys. Not having gotten any sleep the night before because of the banquet, and after having ridden almost 275 miles over rough sand trails to get there, not to mention struggling through a few major obstacles, I slept well in spite of not fitting into the bed.

The thing I remember most about the next morning was the pain I felt in practically every part of my body for the first hour or so. My arms, my shoulders, my legs, and my back were all sore. I had all I could do to get my leg over the machine that morning. I felt much better after everything loosened up, which took about 20 to 30 minutes of pounding along the sand trails. I figured that if I were going to like the longer runs, I'd have to tolerate the pain that comes along with them, although I didn't always relish that part of it very much.

Most of northern Michigan is flat and sandy, similar to South Jersey, with many monotonous miles of two-track sand trails and roads; and some of the sand was deep and sugary. We used the sand roads for making up time, after sporadic technical sections, like at Sandy Lane, except that Sandy Lane had a larger percentage of tougher trails. Most of the technical sections in both places consisted of huge mud holes that would stop hundreds of riders. The trick would be to get by everyone stuck in the mud as quickly as possible, and then to make up the lost time on the roads or faster sand trails.

The sand at Jack Pine came in various depths.

Waiting to sign into a secret checkpoint at my second Jack Pine in 1965. The rider signing in is Paul Kiger on a 650 Triumph from Lancaster, Ohio. His number was 213, putting him in the minute directly ahead of mine.

Both photos by Boyd Reynolds

I rode on #455 at my first Jack Pine, which put me half way back in the pack with almost 230 riders in front of me, riding five on a minute. Whenever I got to a mud hole or other obstacle, it would look like half of the field was right there. It was always a problem getting through, as they would block most of the choice paths.

I would stop for a moment before diving in, to plot out the best way through. Then after quickly developing a plan and choosing a route, I'd go for it. The trick would be to weave through and around everyone, often breaking new trail, with the mind focused on only one thing – the other side. I could often leave most of the field still struggling in the mud holes. The next trick, upon clearing the morass, would be to make up whatever time was lost, as quickly as possible, after I'd figure out how much time I had to make up.

I entered one mud hole in 1965 that I actually got through much too fast for my own good. I had been riding on a number very close to Bill Decker and Gene Esposito, the same year that Bill won high score at Jack Pine. By the middle of the second day I was also running with an exceptionally good score. I don't mean to imply that the score was high enough to be in contention for the high score, but I certainly would have made out much better than I did that day. I was doing very well up until that point.

I came over the crest of a hill to see hundreds of bikes stuck in this huge mud hole, and they appeared to be totally blocking the way. The narrow uphill trail on the far side was also blocked with riders that weren't making it up the slippery slope. It was quite an awesome sight! I quickly plotted my best course through the mess and went for it. Luckily I chose an excellent path, zigzagging my way around everyone in the mud without losing more than about 40 seconds.

The next challenge was the hill, where I chose to go straight up through the woods. It was very steep, but there were no other riders trying it that way. Had I been on anything less than the Triumph, I would never have even attempted it, because I was breaking new trail through soft soil and over windfalls, on an exceptionally steep climb.

With help from paddling my big feet, I quickly cleared the hill too, and reached a gravel road. I rechecked my time and realized I was only a little over a minute late. I turned onto the road and sped up to around 50 or 60 mph, anticipating a check nearby. I got back into my minute in less than a mile, so I cut back my speed to 24 mph and was rechecking my time when suddenly my tires began to pick up soft mud from the wet road surface, slinging it up under the fenders. Before I knew what was happening, the fenders were totally clogged with the soft, sticky, clay-type mud.

It got so thick that it actually stopped both wheels from turning, in spite of the power of the engine straining to overcome it. It was the same gumbo mud Oscar Lenz had talked about at the first Jack Pine banquet I attended, – and I thought he was kidding. By the time I came to a stop, my 350-pound machine must have weighed over 500 pounds with the mud stuck to it. The light-gray soft mush totally enveloped both wheels, and it bulged out from under the fenders. I dropped the bike to its side and began trying to pull it out with my hands. I looked for a strong stick to dig it out with, but couldn't find anything.

I looked up and down the road to see if anyone else was having the problem. There was no one because every rider who passed was doing at least 50 mph, making up time, and the mud wasn't sticking to their tires at that speed. It took at least 20 to 30 minutes to clean enough of it out to be able to drag the bike over to a grassy shoulder where I was finally able to get it moving again on the grass. As soon as I got up enough speed where the mud wouldn't stick, I swung back out onto the road. Needless to say, I didn't do well at that Jack Pine. I finished 10th in my class with a score of only 902. Bill Decker, who won the high score, finished with 976.

Another somewhat infamous obstacle and a favorite spot for spectators at Jack Pine, was "Skyline Drive." It was a section of trail along a ridge, covered with deep, sugary sand. There was a long, steep hill coming all the way from the top, with the same deep sand, where spectators would usually line both sides of the downhill. It was the spot where Bill Baird made a spectacular departure from his bike, over the handlebars, in the late sixties. Bill got up from his spill, got back on, and probably zeroed the check at the bottom as he continued on his way; but he was dazed from the fall, and remembered nothing about the rest of the run, having apparently sustained a mild concussion.

Although there were five riders on a minute at Jack Pine, there was much more room for passing on most of the trails than there was at Little Burr, even early on the first day, when practically everyone was still in the run. Four-wheeled vehicles often used the same trails, but on different weekends. The only time that passing became a problem for me was in passing sidecars. On the first year I rode there, one of the only four sidecars entered had a number four minutes in front of me. I would often have to pass him in the tight technical sections, where he would totally block the trail. He finally lost enough time to go over his hour and I was clear of him for good.

I came upon another sidecar that was still running on the second day. The guy was holding up a whole string of riders on a two-track, sandy trail with bushes growing close on both sides. He was doing well, and running close to his 24 mph schedule, but after a while he had this big string of bikes behind him, all waiting for an opportunity to get by. There would sometimes be enough room where he could have given up a few feet, and slowed down a little at the same time, but he wouldn't give up an inch, and he wouldn't slow down either.

I gradually passed the string of solo bikes behind him and I yelled out several times to let him know I wanted to pass, but got no response at all; probably the same problem the others were having. Finally I started to pass on his left with a loud, "Coming through." He still wouldn't give an inch. He was doing close to 30 mph at the time, and it even seemed as though he sped up when he heard my yell.

I managed to get shoulder-to-shoulder with him, but he wouldn't be intimidated and he still wouldn't give any ground. I leaned my shoulder hard against his and yelled loud in his ear, "Thank you!" He still wouldn't move over nor back off. He actually tried to push me off the trail, while holding his speed constant. I finally managed to get by with a sudden burst of speed. I don't know how the other riders made out. Eventually I learned to do that quite well with solo riders too, although most riders – back home anyway – would usually yield a little trail when asked. It's called sportsmanship.

I didn't have a pit crew to meet me at the gas stops the first year I rode Jack Pine, so I'd have to keep an eye out for gas stations. I don't recall that a "gas truck" was ever used in those days. There were always concerns about the safety of carrying a lot of gas cans on a single truck; so individual pit crews carried gas for their riders. I think much of the mass gas-carrying business started when some of the newer two-strokes began to use much more gas. I don't remember anyone ever carrying gas in the Northeast when I started riding enduros.

Most official "Gas Stops" were located close to a gas station, although I remember once at Jack Pine that I had to go a few miles out of the way to find gas. "Gas Available" locations would also be noted on the route sheet. The difference between an official gas stop and "Gas Available" was that the organizers allowed extra time in the schedule for the official stops, whereas you'd be on your own time everywhere else. Another difference was that I usually knew I could get gas at gas-available locations, whereas it was not always the case at the official Gas Stops.

Some of the extra time at the gas stops would be used to make minor adjustments to the chain, get a quick drink of water or soda from the pit crews, clean the goggles or glasses, and other small preventative maintenance chores. The gas stops were anywhere from 5 to 15 minutes in length.

I remember once in New Jersey where I went out from an official gas stop to look for a gas station. I eventually found one about a half-mile off the course, except that a big sign on the pump read, "Gas, $3.00 per gallon." It was selling at the time for less than half that. I could hardly believe my eyes. I suspected that the owner got tired of being bothered by selling only a few gallons at a time to the enduro bikes and he used that sign to scare them off. It scared me off. I didn't even stop to ask if it was a joke. I didn't need gas that much and I wasn't about to pay three dollars a gallon for it.

I felt like the Lone Ranger at the gas stops in Michigan, especially my first time there. It seemed as though just about every other rider had at least one other person to meet and greet him at the gas stops with gas, water, refreshments, a quick snack, and a little friendly chatter. Some riders used a friend's pit crew for their gas and refreshments. Even with no pit crew at all, I made out fine; that is, if I could find a gas station.

If I spotted someone I knew from New England or the NY Metropolitan area, I would usually stop to ask if they knew the location of the gas station. They or someone else from the East would often offer some of their gas; but I'd be concerned that it might leave them short, so I would usually decline the offer and continue looking for the gas station. Some crews only carried the two-stroke mixture, which I would only use in an emergency.

At one of the Jack Pine runs, while riding on the Crotona club team with Bob Maus and Ralph Spencer, Bob's wife Frieda graciously offered to pit for Ralph and me. It was a year that I got a bee up my jacket sleeve on the first day that stung halfway up my forearm. I managed to kill it, but I didn't get the stinger out until late that night at West Branch. My arm swelled up during the night and it ached all the next day.

When I got up Monday morning my forearm was badly swollen and I had to force it into my jacket, and I had a slight fever from an allergic reaction. When we left West Branch that morning, Frieda offered to pack an extra sandwich for me for the noon layover, along with snacks for the gas stops.

In the early days, Bob Maus (above) could keep a Triumph Cub running better than most in the sport. He won first place in Class A Bantam at this 1965 Jack Pine. In the background Ralph Spencer is helping me by checking the oil in my Triumph at the Noon Layover, while I'm about to light up and relax.

Photo by Frieda Maus

     She asked if there was anything else and what kind of drink would I like at the gas stops. I handed her the remainder of a pint of blackberry brandy that I had bought the night before, and I asked if she would mind carrying my "medicine" for the bee sting. Before handing it over I took my first dose!

     My forearm gave me problems that day, especially on washboard surfaces where the handlebars would shake violently. The bee sting was on the throttle-hand side, so I was never able to rest it. At every gas stop, as well as at the "Noon Control," I would take my medicine. The sting didn't bother me much after I'd take it, but I sweat a lot that day from the fever, and probably from the booze. In spite of my discomfort, I did have a lot of fun that day!

When I finally rolled into Lansing at the end of the second day of just about every Jack Pine experience, I knew that I had ridden two days on more than 500 miles of trails. My body felt every mile of it, and I felt totally beat. But knowing I had finished what was probably the granddaddy of all US endurance runs, I did get a fair degree of personal satisfaction from it.

I wasn't sure after finishing that first Jack Pine that I ever wanted to come back, for several reasons. One because the riding was far from the kind I got the most enjoyment from. I thought I might come back at least one more time. After all, it was the biggest and probably the most prestigious off-road event east of the Mississippi, and maybe in the entire country. On our way home, Ralph and I would talk about how we might improve our next showing and how we might make it a more enjoyable experience the next time around.

One of the more disappointing things I heard about Jack Pine was that since the trail markers had to be tacked up long before the run, some of the local riders would go out weeks before the event to practice the course. That fact alone was disturbing enough, but when I heard that the locations of the secret checkpoints were also known to some, making it possible for them to safely ride early until just before a check, I lost a lot of respect for the run, as well as for some of the riders.

It was not uncommon to see someone "waiting time" alongside the trail less than a mile before a secret checkpoint, instead of 5 miles after the check, which was the normal place to wait time. From what I had heard, the reason for marking the locations of the checkpoints ahead of time was so that the checkers could find the exact spots where they were supposed to set up their checks on the day of the event, without the need for one of the lay-out crew to go out with every group. The marks that were left by the layout crew were not easily discernable to others riding the course, except to those who might have worked with the layout crew in past years and knew exactly how they were marked, and where to look.

One year I noticed the same guy waiting time within a mile of a check more than once, and I saw that he had a number that should have put him behind me. When I checked the results later for that number, I recognized the name as someone who consistently got better scores than I did at Jack Pine, and he was a relative unknown at other national events. Of course that doesn't make him guilty of cheating, but it was unnerving to see and hear that some might have been doing it.

The author is checking into the finish line at Jack Pine in Lansing. Sometimes spectators would line both sides of the street for blocks to see the finishers.

Photo by Frieda Maus

Even if a local rider and/or former club member didn't know the exact location of a check, he could still gain a huge advantage from practicing the course, as it would make him familiar with the general layout; and since most checks are placed after tough technical sections, the rider would become familiar with all of the obstacles and could figure out where the checks would probably be placed.

Jack Pine had a limited number of technical sections with hundreds of miles of interconnecting secondary roads, sand roads, and high-speed trails. Unprincipled contestants might decide to avoid the technical sections or obstacles altogether by plotting ways around them beforehand. It was also possible for riders to come from other areas and do the same thing, which cast a somewhat unfavorable light on the event for me.

In one of the later years that I traveled to Michigan for the Jack Pine, I reserved a room at a motel in West Branch for our night layover. When I pulled into the motel area Sunday evening, the host walked over and handed me what he called a yard-of-beer. It was a long, tapered glass that held a full 12-ounce can, with a long, thin pedestal at the bottom like a huge wine glass. He was quite friendly and I got talking with him, as I hosed some of the mud off my Triumph.

I had noticed that West Branch had become somewhat of a tourist town, so I asked why he rented his units to bikers who would be there for only a single night, when he could have booked the rooms to other tourists for the entire Labor Day Weekend. He replied, "Oh, I enjoy having the motorcycle guys here; and besides, some of them, like Joe over there, (not his real name), have become like regular customers. This is the third time he's been here in the past three weeks. You know, twice for practicing and today." I recognized the guy and answered, "No, I didn't know that." – but I never forgot it.

A local Michigan rider won the high score the first two years I was there. Many of the highest-place finishes in several of the classes also went to local riders. Three of the top four riders in the expert medium-weight class, in which I rode, were from Michigan; as well as the rider who won first place in the novice medium-weight class. I knew that a few of them were excellent riders. I finished 11th in my class that first year at Jack Pine, as compared with 11th overall at Little Burr. My score wasn't one that I was particularly proud of, but I rationalized that I had fun, and I generally enjoyed the weekend, which I thought was possibly the best I could hope for at Jack Pine.

It should add an extra degree of satisfaction to the wins of riders from the east like Sal Scirpo, Don Pink, Bill Decker, Jack Wright and others, as well as riders from other areas of the country that have won Jack Pine and traveled there only for that weekend, without practicing the course ahead of time.

I remember one time when I was competing in a different national championship. I was riding about a hundred yards or so behind one of the top Midwestern riders at a point where the route sheet and the arrows clearly indicated a turn into the woods. This guy kept going straight without turning. I wondered if he simply hadn't seen the clearly marked turn or if he had gone by for some other reason. It was a tough technical section in which I lost several points at the next check. The rider I had seen didn't pass me in that section, but the scoreboard that night indicated that he zeroed the check at the end of the section.

In hindsight I drew both positive and negative conclusions from Midwest enduros. On the positive side I would meet and get to know a whole different group of riders, and enjoy the riding experience. It was also satisfying to pit my own riding skills against those of some of the best in the country in the technical sections, even though the skills were of a different nature than those I had learned in New England.

On the negative side, aside from the somewhat obvious cheating, it wasn't my type of terrain or my type of riding. I enjoyed the challenge of riding the rocks and struggling through long technical sections that were tough, but totally ride-able; sometimes with no trail at all – just well-marked virgin woods; and with a time schedule designed so that the fastest riders had to continually watch their speed, and continually keep track of their time. I also loved long, steep, rocky up-hills, where skillful throttle control was essential to making it over the top. Finally, I enjoyed competing where the only trails available to make up time were old, abandoned wagon trails, where the fastest speeds attainable were less than 30 mph.

Most Midwest enduros seemed to put a lot of emphasis on a few major obstacles that could seriously delay or even stop many riders, followed by miles of relatively smooth trails on which to make up time; consequently a greater percentage of the total distance would be devoted to making up time, and most of that time keeping would be done on the roads. This doesn't test the rider's ability to ride longer, moderately technical sections while being forced to keep time within those sections, which is where the real endurance run skills come into play.

I had already become one of New England's top enduro riders, where I was becoming known as the master of New England rockery. I was developing a reputation, not for speed, but for my riding ability in the toughest and most technical, yet still ride-able, sections; and for keeping time in all types of woods sections, as well as on the roads. I was unable to put together anything that even resembled that kind of performance in the Midwest enduros – not at Little Burr, and especially not at Jack Pine.

Another negative about riding that far from home was that in spite of Lillian's tolerance with my being away for days at a time, I was always aware that it wasn't fair to her. I remember one case where a rider from the East won Jack Pine, but came home later to find that his wife had moved out. He claimed he didn't even know she objected that strongly to his being away. Granted, it could have been for entirely different reasons.

I knew another rider who had trouble convincing his wife that what he was doing was something that she "probably wouldn't understand, but it was something a man has to do." He came home from one of the weekend runs to find her gone. The note she left behind read, "You're probably not going to understand this, but it's something a woman has to do."

Chapter Eight

It's About Time

The 1965 RAMS Spring Run started from a small field off Kibbe Road in Ellington, CT. I arrived for the run around 8:40 for a 9 a.m. starting time. I thought as I was driving in that I had plenty of time, but the club had reserved the #1 riding position for me again, figuring that by now I had laid a permanent claim to it. It was one of the tougher enduros, where no one wanted to "break trail." To get ready, I had to sign in, unload the bike, cut and tape my route sheet together, install it into its holder, get dressed, set my watch to agree with the "master clock," and finally get myself and my Triumph up to the starting line – all in less than 20 minutes. I just made it.

I pulled up to the start at the very last moment, passing all of the bikes lined up and waiting. I got there with about ten seconds to spare, as I looked at my watch and began to follow the second hand. When the hand reached the 12, at exactly 9:01:00, it was the exact moment for me to get some kind of signal from the starter to go. Ed McIntyre was the official starter, as he was at many of the RAMS events, especially around Somers where he lived. He, Greg Lipsky and Perley Parker had organized and laid out the run.

I looked up at Ed, anticipating his giving me the go-ahead signal, but he just stood there chewing on a dead cigar and staring at his watch, which I figured couldn't be more than a few seconds different from mine, since we both would have set them from the same master clock only minutes earlier. I thought possibly in my haste I had set my watch wrong, so after about 10 seconds of not getting a signal to go, I asked Ed to show me his watch. He did; and as soon as I saw it, I could tell that it wasn't running!

I said. "Ed, your watch stopped." (Expletive deleted.) He looked at it, slowly moved it up to his ear (Ed wasn't known for his fast moves), and he gave it a few slow turns, like twisting his ear. After looking back at the watch, he bit down a little extra hard on his inch-long cigar, grunted, and said, "Go ahead." I didn't know what he did about starting the rest of the riders, but he probably walked over and got the master clock.

That example was typical of the watches being used by some of the clubs in the late 1950s and early sixties. Most of the checkers in those days would set their watches to the master clock just before going out to their check, which of course was the thing to do; but many of the watches being used were their personal watches; and some of those didn't even have a second hand; just two tiny hands, and sometimes no marks for the minutes. As I got more capable of vying for high score, it became more and more crucial for my watch, as well the checkers' watches, to be accurate.

In November 1964 I came very close to winning high score at one of my favorite runs, the District 5 Championship in northern New Jersey. I finished second overall the year before to Sky Ball. This time I finished in a tie for high score with Bob Maus, as we both got 992. The winner was determined by seconds taken at the Emergency Check. I lost out by just a few seconds, which could have been due to the inaccuracy of my own watch. The Emergency Check watch was usually the most accurate watch in the event. It had to be set to the exact time, and it had to be capable of staying on time.

The second hand on my own watch was becoming a much greater factor to my winning or losing the enduros. Prior to that, my reason for not winning would usually be a breakdown, due to inadequate preparation, although once I started riding the Triumph, it hardly ever broke down, even when I didn't maintain it properly.

The accuracy of my watch was not only important for the Emergency Check, where one is expected to arrive at the exact center of his minute, but it was also important at every secret checkpoint, where it was merely necessary to ride within a one-minute window of time; but the earlier the better in that window, without being in the previous minute.

If I were always to ride near the center of my minute in anticipation of being exact for the Emergency Check, it would leave only 30 seconds of safety buffer to the end of the minute for all of the other secret checkpoints. That strategy is usually used for road rallies, where one hardly ever drops behind schedule more than a few seconds, but a much larger time buffer was needed for enduros, to anticipate losing time on rough trails.

For example, riding 5 seconds into one's correct minute gives a full 55-second buffer to work with, in anticipation of losing at least that much time on rocky trails. Since many secret checkpoints in an enduro are much more important than a single tie-breaking Emergency Check, the best place to ride would be as close to the start of one's minute as possible, without risking early arrival.

I would sometimes take on that extra risk, depending on the exact mileage that the course enters the woods section. Since checkpoints can only be set up on "even minutes," it leaves a limited number of spots on the course where they can be placed. All of the area between those even minutes is free territory, where a rider can be early without the risk of penalty. The even minutes will always fall at multiples of 0.4 miles from the start.

It means that if the route sheet has a turn at 29.0 miles, that turn is in free territory, since the multiples of 0.4 miles from the start fall at 28.8 miles and 29.2 miles. The entire 0.4-mile area between those two points, which includes the turn, is in free territory. Maintaining a constant awareness of all of the locations where checks can possibly be placed in the entire run is where one's concentration pays off.

The above example means that it is feasible for a rider to enter a woods section running a few seconds early, although he then has to keep very close track of his time until he is certain that he isn't still running early when he nears the 29.2-mile point, where there could be a check. This strategy allows for a few extra seconds of buffer when anticipating a very tight section of trail in the first 0.2 miles of woods; but again, the rider has to remain vigilant of the exact time, to the second, within those 0.2 miles, and his watch must be exceptionally accurate.

If he were then to find a check at 29.2 miles, he would still try to lose a few seconds before entering the check, to allow for a possible difference in the checker's watch and his. If he didn't lose any time at all on the trail, or actually gained time between the tarmac and the check, he would need to kill even more time. If he entered the check without the ability to kill any time at all, he would almost certainly be clocked a minute early.

Even being 5 seconds into his minute when he enters a check, doesn't guarantee that he'll be scored on time, or scored correctly. Both his and the checker's watches must be accurate, and both watches must be read correctly, which requires that both have precise sweep-second hands that can be seen at a glance by the rider, and of course read accurately by both.

If he were to enter the check at 3 seconds into his minute according to his watch, but his watch was 4 seconds faster than the checker's watch, he'd probably be scored early, and lose two points; that is, if the checker's watch was accurate, and if he (or she) read it right. Unfortunately, some of the checkers of that era wouldn't be as careful in setting their watches exactly to the master clock, or be as careful reading it, as some of the riders.

It happened quite often, especially at the local enduros, where the checker's watch would be a few seconds slow, which can make the rider early even when he isn't actually early. In net, the closer one chooses to ride to the head-end of his minute, the more risk he takes on for being clocked-in early, and the more he gambles on the accuracy of his watch and the checker's watch.

Arguing with a checker over the accuracy of his watch is usually futile; but if I knew that a checker gave me an incorrect time, I would take the extra time to ask to see his or her watch. They could have read the watch wrong, or their watch could have been considerably off. In the latter case, the check could be protested and possibly thrown out at the discretion of the club referee. The checker's first reaction, whenever I asked to see their watch, was usually that I was trying to put something over on them, or that I was trying to intimidate them into changing their time, when actually their watch would often be wrong, or they might have read it wrong.

Prior to the early sixties I used a very cheap dime-store watch because I seldom came close to winning the high score. But when I began to get closer to winning, I decided to invest in a better watch, which I could read easily and I could trust. I bought a Hamilton "Railway Special," the same watch used by many riders of that era. It had large bold numbers and a visible sweep-second hand.

When my watch was new, it kept perfect time; but later, after using it in many enduros, it began to gain time. I would fine-tune the speed of the watch at home, and get it to keep perfect time, but it would still gain time during the enduro. I assumed it was because the watch was being subjected to rough handling and vibration. No intricate mechanical mechanism with delicate movements and springs could be expected to keep accurate time under the conditions that I was subjecting it to.

I would hang the watch around my neck on a long piece of twine, and I'd usually stow it in my top jacket pocket while I was riding -- that is, when and if I had the chance to stow it. I would look at the watch hundreds of times during a run. I would usually pull it out at a time when I could make my left hand available for a few seconds. It would also have to be at a point where I could afford the time to read it. Sometimes on rocky trails, it was very tricky to take one hand off the handlebars to whip out the watch and read it. I also wouldn't always have the time to get it back into the pocket after reading it, so it would

My Hamilton Railway Special can be seen dangling from my neck in a tough section where I didn't have time to get it back into my top pocket or slip it inside the striped vest. It's impossible to look at a watch in a section like this, but as soon as I would reach a smoother trail, I would check the time to see how late I was running, to determine how fast I had to ride to make up whatever time I had lost. My scorecard can also be seen dangling from my neck near the watch. My route sheet holder is attached to the left handlebar. The two main attributes I became known for in New England were riding the rocks and time keeping. Boyd Reynolds took this photo in 1970 at the Back Mountain 100-mile National Championship near Dallas, PA.

just swing and dangle from my neck until I could put it back into my pocket, or at least flip it inside the vest.

Here is the text of a letter I wrote to the Hamilton Watch Company about my watch, and their answer:

Dear Sirs:

About 30 months ago, I bought a new Hamilton "Railway Special" watch. I use it solely for motorcycle sporting events, which are similar to sports car rallies. I carry the watch in a chest pocket attached to a safety string around my neck, and I pull it out often during the contest to read it. I have never dropped the watch or struck it against anything hard.

After the first few months of use I noticed that it would gain about four to five seconds an hour while being carried, although it would always run to within one second in 24 hours when not being carried. It got gradually worse until about six months ago when it ran about 30 seconds per hour fast while it was in use, although it would still keep perfect time while standing still.

I took it to a reputable jeweler three months ago and related the problem to him. He took the watch and worked on it for many hours, and he kept it for more than a month. He said that he completely overhauled it, having removed, inspected and reassembled every minute part. He charged only for the overhaul because he found absolutely no cause for the watch to gain time. He said that he took up some of the endplay in the balance wheel by adjusting the jewels, hoping that this might have contributed. He said, however, that he was not completely satisfied with its operation, although it ran perfectly in all positions while lying still. He returned the watch to me and apologized for not having corrected my problem.

The first time I used the watch after that, it gained about seven seconds in four hours, which was a definite improvement, but still not satisfactory. I have used it twice since then, with similar results. It continues to run perfect when not being carried. Last weekend I carried the watch while merely walking around, and it gained 35 seconds in eight hours, which indicates a further deterioration. I have borrowed a friend's "Railway Special" on several occasions and have spoken with other owners who use the same watch under identical conditions. They all run perfect, which infers that the problem is unique to my watch.

I am willing to mail the watch to you for your analysis and testing; however, when I mentioned this to my jeweler, he said that he doubted whether the factory could do anything more to the watch than what he has already done, although he added that there is definitely something wrong with it. I will send it to you if you are reasonably certain that it is a problem that can be corrected; but I must have prior assurance that I'm not wasting my time. My competition season reopens in about two months, and unless 1 can be assured of a permanent correction, I will be forced into purchasing a different watch, which 1 do not wish to do at this time.

Yours truly,

I received this reply:

Thank you, Mr. Boonstra, for your letter of January 19 relating your experiences with your grade 9928 railroad watch.

It is unusual that your watch performs differently than others of the same model under the same circumstances. All of these watches are manufactured as closely as possible to the same specification and are subjected to identical tests before being shipped from the factory.

It would be necessary to examine your watch and again submit it to our testing procedures to determine if all adjustments are still as they should be.

You report that you purchased your watch about 30 months ago and use it only for motorcycle sporting events. Actually the watch should be kept running to keep the oil fluent and the complete movement should be thoroughly cleaned and re-oiled at intervals of no more than 24 months.

Since we have no control over work that is performed outside our factory, we cannot guarantee the quality of such work. Nevertheless, we shall welcome an opportunity to examine your watch and give you a report.

To send us your watch, please package it carefully and ship by insured mail. A letter should be enclosed referring to this correspondence.

Shown above is a typical arrangement used by many riders. The speedometer, route sheet holder, and case to hold a pocket watch (shown empty) are mounted where the rider can see them. Soft sponge rubber would surround the watch in this case, as the watch contained delicate spring mechanisms and movements that could easily become damaged in this arrangement.

Photo by Boyd Reynolds

Incidentally, a pocket watch that is allowed to swing freely sometimes will not keep time as closely as one that is laying in a flat position or held more firmly in a watch pocket. At any rate, Mr. Boonstra, we are suggesting that you send the watch to us for an examination.

I didn't send the watch, and I continued to use it for years. I rode with a route sheet holder mounted to the left handlebar in reach of my left hand. During the 1940s and 1950s, we would tape the route sheet, with its turns and mileages, onto the tank or onto a makeshift holder made from a large fruit juice can that could be turned and read.

Frank DeGray of Ellington, CT was the first to design a route sheet holder like the single and dual roller models shown in the illustrations on the these pages. The route sheet could then be cut into vertical strips about two inches wide. The strips would

A later version of the route sheet holder originated by Frank DeGray. Walt Nye made this dual-roller model. The roller on the left held the route sheet, while the roller on the right held the time schedule. This example has an obvious error in the time schedule, having skipped 8:05, which would be at 2.0 miles. I competed without a printed time schedule, figuring all of the times in my head.

Photo complements of Jake Herzog

be taped together length-wise. A single strip of the route sheet could be anywhere from a few feet up to 18 feet long. When attached to the rollers, like film in a camera, it could be cranked past a magnifying window for viewing.

Upon arriving at an enduro, one of the rider's first chores was to prepare his route sheet. Many riders would figure out and jot down a time schedule for themselves beforehand on the route sheet for many of the turns, especially turns that fall on even minutes. This could be done before cutting the route sheet into strips for assembling in the holder. Even though it was possible for some, like myself, to figure their time while riding, it was still helpful to have it written next to the mileage on the route sheet, so that one's concentration could be devoted more to what's coming up on the trail.

An easy way to figure mileages at 24 mph, simply by looking at a conventional watch, is: rather than multiplying the number shown on the watch by 5, which one normally does to tell time, multiply that same number by 2. For example, looking at the face of a watch, when the big hand is on the 7, rather than the 7 meaning 35 minutes (7x5 = 35) past the hour, it could instead mean 14 miles (7x2 = 14); and if the big hand is three divisions past that seven, then those little divisions, rather than meaning minutes, could mean 0.4 miles each, hence three "minutes" past the 7, (38 minutes), would then become (7x2) + (0.4x3), or 15.2 miles. It's really quite simple.

If you think it's too complicated, it's actually less complicated than having your small children learn to tell time by looking at those same numbers on the face of the clock. Do you ever remember saying to one of your children, "When the big hand is on the 4, it's not 4 minutes past, it's 20 minutes past!" It's now your turn to learn that when the big hand is on the 4 it's not 20 minutes past, it's actually 8 miles (4x2).

Figuring in the opposite direction, going from miles to minutes, becomes slightly more complicated:

Let's start with a mileage less than 24, like for a turn that's shown on the route sheet at 19.6 miles: First ignore any miles, plus fractions, that are <u>above</u> the last <u>even number</u>. The last even number to 19.6 is 18, so we'll figure it for 18, with the difference, 1.6 miles, set aside for a moment.

Divide the 18 in half to get 9, which is the same 9 that's shown on the face of your watch. Since you've known from childhood that the 9 on your watch means 45, you're already halfway there. Now divide the 1.6, which was set aside, by 0.4 (each minute being 0.4 miles). Hence, 1.6 divided by 0.4 is 4. Add the 4 to the 45 previously figured, and you have the time that you should arrive at 19.6, which is 49 minutes past the hour.

For mileages over 24 miles, first subtract as many 24s (multiples of 24) from the mileage, as needed, to get the number down to 24 or smaller. For example, let's say the turn on the route sheet is 94.8 miles. First, as before, set aside any amount above the last even number, which in this case is 0.8 miles, leaving an even number of 94. Subtract 72 from that 94 (since 72 is the nearest even multiple of 24, less than the 94). The result becomes the base number (94 minus 72 is 22).

Now divide that number in half, as before, and get 11, which is the 11 on the face of the watch, or 55 minutes. Next divide the 0.8 that was set aside, by 0.4, and get 2. Add the 2 to the 55 minutes, and it says that the correct time to be at 94.8 is 57 minutes past the hour. You should know which hour it is.

Now try doing it in your head while negotiating a motorcycle through the rocks and mud ruts at maximum speed, while also concentrating on where the most likely spot for the next check might be. That was the real challenge of riding enduros in the sixties, and it's the part of the game that was lost when computers eliminated the need for that brainwork, and virtually changed our wonderful little brain game into a race.

A Connecticut rider, Ron Webster, designed and built the very first enduro computer almost a full decade before they were reinvented and became standard equipment for all top enduro riders. Ron was an outstanding design engineer at a local instrument company at the time. The idea was spawned at a Connecticut Ramblers club meeting when he and Frank DeGray were discussing time keeping as being one of the tougher aspects of winning the enduros. Frank said something like, "What we need is a gadget . . ."

Some number of months later, Ron presented Frank with that gadget, which was the very first enduro computer, and which Frank promptly named, "Gonculator." When I asked Ron to comment, he wrote:

"It was obvious to me and to others that, of all the competitors, you were by far the best time keeper. I always envied you for this ability. It was obvious also that 90% of the competitors out there couldn't keep time competitively, so they "leeched" on riders like you, with the time keeping abilities. I was as good at time keeping as almost anyone, except you, and perhaps a few others. Time keeping was sort of like rubbing your stomach and patting your head at the same time you were riding fast through the woods. I found it to be quite difficult and even hazardous, when I was already beat down from exertion. I knew that if I could automate the time keeping chore I could virtually eliminate the time keeping aspect of the game, thereby improving my chances of winning against those who were good time keepers, because even good time keepers made errors.

I also realized that enduros were a game and not a race, and that it required numerous attributes, including time keeping, knowing the rules, going fast in the tight stuff, bike reliability, concentration, consistency, cunning (note my comment above about leeching), preparation, physical fitness and others. Each attribute was something that could and should be worked on for improvement. It seemed like the one with the most perfected attributes had the best chance of winning the game.

At a Ramblers meeting one night Frank Degray said, "What we needed is a device, a black box, with a green light and a red light. If the green light comes on, speed up. If the red light comes on slow down."

Ron Webster's Gonculator – the very first enduro computer.
Photo courtesy of Ron Webster

I set about to make the gadget that Frank described. I started out by making three different devices, using three different methods; but none of them worked right. Either they failed from the pounding, or from temperature fluctuations. I just couldn't get them to maintain an accurate mileage indication. Remember, this was before digital logic chips, memory, etc. My fourth generation worked flawlessly, and it was so rugged that it still runs today, when I switch it on. I thought about marketing them, but I never did.

The device gave a numerical indication of mileage as a function of the event's average speed and the time of day. All that was necessary was to keep the motorcycle odometer matching the display on the device. At one point, after I began to use it, the New England Sports Committee tried to make it illegal, but they never did. It was a neat instrument and all done electro-mechanically with some smoke and mirrors, plus four AA mercury batteries. It would be nearly 10 years before there was anything else like it available.

The Gonculator removed the time keeping problem; but I never did totally trust it, because I made it, so I would also run the usual time keeping scroll in a Frank DeGray

Ron Webster riding a 500 cc Yankee in Oregon in 1972

holder, and I used my watch. However in the tight stuff I often relied on my Gonculator. It was simple to keep time by merely glancing down and comparing the Gonculator reading to the corrected odometer reading.

Although Ron began riding enduros in 1964, he first got my attention in 1967 when he won the prestigious Salmon River Ramble, one of my favorite runs, over an impressive list of entries, including that year's grand champion, Dave Latham. The run was held on a miserable rainy day in December, as it usually was, and there were at least a half-dozen major water crossings in the 100-mile event. Everyone got cold and wet, even if they didn't fall in. Ron lost only 46 points riding his Greeves, while I dropped 55 with my Triumph to get the second highest score.

Winning the Salmon River Ramble in 1967 gave Ron the points he needed to become the New England Enduro Lightweight Championship that year. He won the lightweight championship a total of four consecutive times and went on to win a gold medal in the 1971 ISDT at the Isle of Man. By that time Ron had switched from Greeves to the 250 cc Spanish Ossa, as did several other top lightweight riders.

John Taylor selected Ron to ride one of his 500 cc Yankee motorcycles in the 1972 ISDT in Spain. He subsequently rode several qualifiers with the machine, but it suffered mechanical problems on the 5th day in Spain. Ron was again slated to ride a Yankee in the 1973 ISDT in the Berkshires, but at the last moment John Taylor withdrew the Yankee and Ron rode an Ossa instead.

Chapter Nine

My Glory Days

By the end of 1963 I was able to take home a trophy from just about every enduro I entered in New England or New Jersey, unless the machine broke down. Most often I would win a first or second place in the heavyweight class, and occasionally I took the high score. Which trophy I took home would usually depend on how well I was able to concentrate on riding and how well the bike held up. In 1964 I managed to win high score in the rocks and hills of New England, and also in the sand trails and swamps of New Jersey.

The win in New Jersey still didn't make me enjoy riding in the sand. The Battle of Monmouth, in which I won high score, was held in the spring, making it tough all the way through, with deep mud in addition to the sand; and it happened to be on a rainy day, which was also in my favor. There was very little opportunity to make up time at the higher speeds like there usually was at Sandy Lane.

My ideal run was at least 100 miles long, the longer the better, with a schedule that was barely attainable by the top experts for the entire distance; yet totally ride-able, with a minimum of high-speed trails or roads connecting the tougher sections; and with no showstoppers. I liked it to be a test of time keeping, as well as one's riding skills in continuously technical off-road terrain. Even when dry, the run should be tough; but when dry it would favor those who could keep time. With heavy rains an event like that would become a test of survival, where even the experts would wind up with relatively low scores.

The time lost by the less-experienced riders in that type of run would become cumulative and much of it would be carried to the finish, if they were able to finish. More than one average speed is OK, but only when necessary to retain the time keeping aspect of the game. Whatever different average speeds are used should be set so that the top experts can barely maintain the schedule for the entire distance, and possibly run early. Most amateurs would naturally run late, and most novices would probably go over their hour before the final checkpoint.

My contention has always been that high speed on the trails without the time keeping, like with international rules, can be a lot of fun, but it's an entirely different game than endurance runs. Call it hare scrambles, cross-country racing, ISDT, or by any other name, but not endurance run. Speed does sometimes become the primary factor for closed-course and other short enduros, but they would still meet the classification of endurance run if they were continuously technical and if the time keeping aspect was retained. I enjoyed the shorter events that used all three: skill in the technical sections, endurance and keeping time.

I turned 40 in 1965, and although I was probably already past my peak in physical strength, endurance and reflexes, I was still gaining in experience, and hopefully in the skill of riding the enduros. I still had lots of enthusiasm and I was still having a lot of fun doing it, as I approached the pinnacle of my enduro career. I often felt that if I had started at a younger age I might have peaked with all of my competitive qualities in my early-to-mid thirties, and possibly achieved more in my competitive years, but as I've said before, I have no regrets.

In February 1965, at the Connecticut Ramblers Snow Run, held annually at Warehouse Point, I was invited to join the RAMS Motorcycle Club of New England. I felt honored by the offer and I accepted. Club competition in New England had become quite popular and the RAMS hoped that I would shore up their team effort. From a personal standpoint, I felt as though the group that I had been riding with and competing against for so long had finally accepted me.

I'm sure some members still had mixed emotions about my joining, since I would become eligible to compete for the annual enduro championship, possibly depriving someone of a place in the final standings; but there was a vote and I was voted in, which I considered to be a show of excellent sportsmanship.

Christy Scholar said at the time that the RAMS acronym stood for Rider's Actions Means Sportsmanship. Christy and Jim Stebbins, both riding 500 Matchless, and Phil Bourdon with a 500 Triumph, were among the RAMS club members who figured high in annual heavyweight championship competition, and would have the most to lose.

I was immediately assigned to the RAMS #1 Team, which was later to became not only the top club team in New England, but also one of the top club teams on the continent. The

New London M.C. team of Don Cutler, Bill Perry and Al Semmelrock was the team to beat in New England at the time.

Bill Perry had already been named the 1964 Enduro Grand Champion, riding a Greeves. Don Cutler won the heavyweight championship that year on a Triumph and was second overall for the grand championship. Al Semmelrock finished 2nd in the expert heavyweight class on a BSA. The three continued their winning ways in club competition during 1965, in spite of my contribution to the RAMS effort.

When I began to compete for the individual enduro championship, Don Cutler was my most formidable rival. He was not only a top enduro rider, but he had also, since 1962, finished high in both the scrambles and trials championships. In 1962 he won the Class B Heavyweight Championship in both enduro and scrambles competition.

Known as the Quiet Man, because he didn't say much, Don's silence was a sign of genuine modesty. That silence, as well as his physical size and slight build was deceiving, as he was an outstanding natural rider with a mastery of both the stand-up riding style and balance. Don Cutler was an excellent off-road motorcycle rider in every aspect of the sport.

During 1963 Don was selected to ride on the prestigious New England Scrambles team against the Canadians at Grafton, VT; although later, soon after having been involved in the same serious scrambles accident that took the life of a very popular rider of that era, Babe Aldo, Don began to concentrate more on riding the enduros – and he became exceptionally good at it.

In 1965, which was my first year of competing for the annual championship in New England, Don won the overall title, while I won the heavyweight championship. It was the first time that the overall grand championship went to a heavyweight rider since Charlie Schumitz won it back in 1959. After winning the championship, Don also eased off from his enduro riding to heal a painful pinched nerve in his shoulder.

He returned to full-time enduro competition four years later at the Salmon River Ramble in December 1969, riding an Ossa Pioneer, and he won that exceptionally tough event. He immediately went on to win two more consecutive high scores in the Snow Run and in the Lost Hour enduro.

Don won the enduro grand championship again in 1970, five years after first winning it in 1965, and he subsequently competed in six consecutive ISDT events in Europe between 1970 and 1975, first on a 400 Husqvarna in Spain, where he won a bronze medal, and the then five times on Ossa, winning three silver medals – two at the Isle of Man and one in the Berkshires.

Don Cutler astride his Ossa Pioneer in the 1970 Berkshire International Trials.
Photo by Marcia MacDonald

Don Cutler's return to competition may have resulted, at least in part, from the additional woods riding he was getting in teaching Marcia MacDonald how to ride enduros. Marcia certainly had an excellent tutor. After getting himself back into shape with this tutoring activity, Don realized that the shoulder wasn't bothering him that much anymore.

I first met Marcia MacDonald in the fall of 1969 at a RAMS fall enduro that started out of Northampton, MA. I had chosen to work the event as a "sweep," which called for leaving several minutes after the last rider. My job was to ride the entire course, making sure no one was left stranded in the woods. My primary function was to help riders who had broken down to get their machines out of the woods and back to the starting point, which sometimes meant arranging for them to be picked up. I got to ride the entire run, often alone, on well-worn trails.

Marcia had apparently never ridden an enduro before and picked a good one to start, where the trails are challenging and there's an abundance of rocks, mud, water and hills. The first rider I met out on the trail that day was Marcia, way out in the woods struggling with her bike in a mud hole. I parked mine and helped her to get through, after which I asked what her number was. When I learned she was well over her hour, I began to give her directions on how to get out of the woods and back to the start. She looked at me as if I had just insulted her, and said, "What are you trying to say?"

I tried tactfully to tell her that she was well over her hour, that the checkers would have already gone home, and that there was no point to her continuing. She glared at me and said, "I have just as much right on these trails as you do, you big gorilla" and she took off down the trail. I followed her all the way to the finish, making sure she didn't get stuck again, and helping whenever it appeared that she needed it.

Later, as I was lashing my bike onto the trailer, I turned to find her standing there with Don Cutler, neither of them saying a word, just smiling. She had apparently put her bike away and changed clothes. She looked and acted much more ladylike, as she stood there with her arm linked to Don's, and with a smile on her face. I think she had a flower in her hair, making her look somewhat like a hippie flower child. Don, who never said much, just stood with a big grin.

I said, "Hi Don." He said, "I understand you've met Marcia," and he went back to his big grin. We all chuckled about it, and Marcia and I became good friends. From that point on, she would always call me, "The Gorilla" or "Gorilla Piet."

Marcia soon became the top woman rider in New England, as well as one of the top women riders in the country. Most of all though, she became an enthusiastic member of our enduro community, where she was recognized for her riding ability, her good-natured personality, her sportsmanship, and her overall contributions to the sport; all of which tended to blur the gender difference; and I think that's the way she preferred it. I took a ration of good-natured bantering from Marcia through the years, but we have always remained friends.

About a year after we met, on a rare occasion that I took my family to a run, a 100-mile national championship in eastern

The incomparable Marcia MacDonald

Connecticut, I was walking through the pit area with Lillian and the children before the run started, when suddenly I heard a loud scream, like a war-whoop, from behind. A split-second later, Marcia landed on my back with both arms in a chokehold around my neck and her legs around my waist. As she landed, she screamed, "The Gorillaaaa!"

We stopped and Lillian gave me the strangest look. For the lack of anything better to say, I said, "Lilli, I'd like you to meet Marcia," while Marcia was still perched on my back, looking like a female gorilla hitching a ride. Later, after she slid off and disappeared, Lilli wanted to know what that was all about, and what was going on at these enduros. I had quite a time explaining the innocence of it, but I don't think she appreciated the humor in it either, as I did.

I spoke recently with Marcia and asked if she would like to tell her version of the events that led up to our meeting that day in the Berkshires, about the meeting itself, and a few words about Don Cutler. Here is her response:

> *After an extended hiatus from riding, Don Cutler appeared out of the blue at the final enduro event of 1968, the Salmon River Ramble, on a well-worn Bultaco that had seen a lot of custom framework. Don, in his usual quiet style, left the start unnoticed and slipped into the icy woods.*
>
> *Hours later he emerged, having outscored most of the entries, including Enduro Champion Dave Latham by almost 70 points. Dave turned to Bud Peck when the scores were posted, and asked." Who the hell is Don Cutler?" Peck replied." If he ever comes back, you'll know who he is!"*
>
> *Bud and Piet certainly remembered Don well, as they had ridden with him in 1965, the year he won the New England Enduro Grand Championship. But he then virtually disappeared after suffering a shoulder injury, and most of his competition never knew what happened to him.*
>
> *Don quietly slipped back into his garage in East Putnam, Connecticut after that Salmon River, to resume tuning Triumphs for a team of National riders he was supporting. He reappeared only briefly in 1969 to take a High Point on his ever-versatile Bultaco, in a trials event.*
>
> *Late in the summer of 1969 this woman appeared on Don Cutler's doorstep with a van full of road racing parts. The parts, in the end, were supposed to resemble a Rickman-Metisse Triumph. While pleading with Don to build the bike, she looked around his garage in utter fascination at the array of motorcycles, most of which bore National number plates. There were short trackers, half-milers, road racers, trials, and enduro machines – and even an engine from Champion Carl Wickstrand's Triumph hill-climber. She was instantly*

hooked. Sooo, – when an opportunity arose to ride an enduro in the Berkshires, it seemed to her like an opportunity not to be missed.

Borrowing a new 125 Penton from her then-employer Gordon Razee, who was also riding for Donald, she donned jeans, equestrian riding chaps, and a pair of L.L. Bean rubber boots; she had a 10-minute lesson on how to ride a dirt bike from Gordon, and then left for the RAMS fall event in Northampton. She had high hopes that some of Don's, or Gordon's, or George Cunha's, expertise might rub off on the way to the starting line.

The start was at one end of a large field, just wide enough to allow riders to spread out before the course funneled into a single track that foretold of a tight, nasty woods section before the 1st checkpoint. Marcia made it across the field and drove the Penton right up a birch tree, where it hung from the branches with the motor still running. That was the start of a very long day in the Berkshire woods!

Countless crashes and many miles later, after being engulfed in yet one more mud hole, she looked up to find this rather large creature wearing a blue-and-white striped vest, and very yellow-tinted glasses, sitting atop a thumping, snarling Triumph, hovering over her. Close to exhaustion, she gladly accepted the giant's offer to help push her mud-encompassed motorcycle to higher ground. Was he mumbling something about being "over her hour?" About Quitting? About going home on the road? – QUITTING?

Obliviously he didn't understand that she had come with Don Cutler, and Gordon, and George, and was not about to go back and tell them she had QUIT – given up? They would never take her to another one of their God-awful events again. Who was this big gorilla anyway? Frustration, and now anger, kicked over the Penton, and off she went down the trail, followed by the striped giant. Well, she thought, maybe he would come in handy at the next mud hole, or at that river crossing that loomed just ahead.

Finally, back at the finish, her humbling experience netted her last place out of 13 women; and two days in a bathtub soaking in a bottle of Absorbine Vet Liniment, with a battalion of black and blues, – and an incredible urge to do it again! But, she needed a bike, and a coach, to improve her pitiful results and aching body. She knew just where she could find one; but Don Cutler would somehow have to be talked out of his "retirement."

Don accepted the challenge; and after riding his aged Bultaco to a "DNF" in Meriden's Bone Yard closed-course enduro, he changed the steering configuration, and the bike became Marcia's new competition machine. Don dug out his old 500 Triumph, which he had used for everything from riding observed trials to motocross, with a few enduros thrown in. The Triumph's re-debut was a mud-strewn event in Bennington, Vermont, where Don took first place – as well as Marcia, who after Don's training, and getting advice from Gorilla Piet about how to ride through mud holes: "Think other side!" – began to actually enjoy the challenge of enduros, and all the wonderful people she was meeting – even the striped giants in mud holes!

The closed course at New London, Connecticut brought back visions of many a hard fought battle between the three Triumph riders, Bud Peck, Piet and Donald. Don remembers starting on the same minute as Bud and riding with him for the entire event, until just near the end, where the trail separated into two trail options – one longer and safer, and one shorter but far riskier. Don took a chance on the shorter route, and with his trials-riding skills, he edged Bud out for another win.

The trio met once again at the year's final event – Salmon River. Freezing temperatures, rock hard, frozen, rutted trails and icy river crossings, always made Salmon River an event for only the daring and the insane. Don again edged out the competition for the High Point, and Dave Latham finally came to know who Don Cutler was.

Don was seen after the finish taking a spin on a new enduro machine – the Ossa – and he decided, "That was the machine to have!" After winning most of the early events in 1970, Don was asked by Yankee Motor Company's President John Taylor to ride for him in the two-day Berkshire International Trials – an event that organizer, Al Eames was grooming for the ISDT. Don took one of the very few gold medals, other then the ones awarded to the trade-supported riders of the Penton dynasty, over a rain-soaked course that decided the U.S. team to ride in Spain in October. Don went on to represent the United States on six ISDT teams, and won several New England Championships.

Oh, -- and Marcia did all right too.

A few years before joining the RAMS, I joined the Crotona Motorcycle Club of White Plains, NY, where I was eligible to compete for the Metropolitan Sports Committee's Woodsman Class Championship. Joining the RAMS also made me eligible to compete for the enduro championship in New England, where I was doing most of my riding.

In 1965, Leslie Pink wrote the following article that appeared, along with the photo on the cover of this book, in Cycle Sport Magazine:

Ranking very high on the list of top enduro riders is Piet Boonstra of Buchanan, NY. You can hardly read a write-up on an endurance run without reading good things about Piet. He is a hard man to beat in the rough, and his fine sportsmanship is also very hard to beat.

Piet is no newcomer to our sport, having ridden a motorcycle for 19 years, 17 of which have been spent in competition. During World War II, Piet shared a tent in the South Pacific with an avid motorcyclist, and after Piet listened to this buddy for so long, he thought he'd find out what this guy was talking about. Soon after he was discharged from the Navy, he took his mustering out pay and bought a brand new H-D 74. Needless to say, he liked it. When the Korean War broke out, Piet was again in service, this time with the Air Force. After that mess was over he started to get down to business in the woods-riding department.

Piet is married, and his wife Lillian has presented him with 5 lovely children, ranging from a teenage daughter to a 5-month-old son. Our 40-year-old rider is the Manufacturing Administrator of IBM's latest and fastest giant computer. No wonder he is such a good time keeper. Piet's daughter, Kathy, has a motorcycle of her own, and maybe it won't be too long before she is keeping her Dad company along the trails.

Crotona M.C. is Piet's hometown club. This season the New England riders were generous enough to invite Piet to join one of their clubs so that he may also earn points in their activity contest. Needless to say, this was a great thrill for Piet, and it shows the fine sportsmanship of the New England Endurance Run riders. He became a member of the

RAMS M.C. of New England. Piet enjoys New England endurance runs best, and one of his favorites is the Salmon River Ramble in Conn. He likes a run to be at least 100 miles, and he enjoys mountain trails - and even no trails at all.

Piet's advice to a new rider is to choose the proper equipment for the job, keep yourself in good condition, and get a lot of practice. When riding in an event, to not ride over year head, as you run the risk of breaking your equipment and possibly yourself. He stresses the point of always being a good sportsman. Piet rides a Triumph 500 and regrets that it took him so many years before he found the proper machine for him. When Piet drapes his 6'4" frame on that 500, he makes it look like a Cub.

Piet has ridden many Jack Pines, Little Burrs, and almost all the enduros in the immediate area. His job keeps him so busy that he just about finds time to ride on Sunday. After trying a few scrambles, Piet said "Well. They're all right, but I like a good day's ride -- give me an enduro any day".

I rode more than 20 enduros in 1965, many of which were in New England, although some were also in northern and southern New Jersey, and I rode several national championships that year. When I competed in New Jersey, as well as in the nationals, I would often ride on the Crotona M.C. team with Ralph Spencer and Bob Maus, and sometimes with Don Pink and Bob Maus. In New England I always rode with the RAMS #1 team, usually with Dave Latham and Bud Peck, and at some runs with Phil Bourdon and others.

I rode far too many enduros in 1965 for the amount of time I had to devote to the sport, as opposed to devoting to my bread-winning activity, which of course took the higher priority. I was still unable to find time to work on the machine. I would often do nothing to it between the runs unless I knew that something was broken and needed welding, or if something was seriously out of adjustment.

I would often ride two or three enduros in a row with only a chain adjustment, and sometimes I didn't have time for that either until after I unloaded the bike from the trailer at the next event. Even then it was only if I had time to do it before starting, as I usually arrived late. I didn't bother washing it unless it was so heavily laden with mud that I thought it might become a deterrent to handling. I once rode Jack Pine with practically no knobs on the rear tire and a half-worn chain, and all because I didn't have time to change it before leaving home.

My favorite national enduro was Cayuta in western New York State. I liked Cayuta because it came the closest to what I thought an enduro ought to be. Dave Barnes did an excellent job of layout. It was tough all the way through, and time keeping was an important factor. The only part I wasn't too crazy about was the mud pit on Connecticut Hill, which was like bottomless quicksand. I struggled through that hole every year, while I often suspected there were ways to avoid it. I didn't even mind the steep hill that so many complained about – probably because I never had a problem with steep hills.

The Corduroy in the Haliburton Highlands of central Ontario was another of my favorite runs. Soon after I rode it the first time, they changed from AMA rules to a variation of international rules, which was the only negative from my point of view; otherwise it was a great two-day, 350-mile ride. The international rules eliminated time keeping and made it more like a race, although it was still great fun.

On the opposite end of the spectrum from those favorites were runs like Jack Pine, which I thought had several negatives; one being the bottlenecks, which were more of a game-of-chance than an obstacle. It was usually followed by high-speed sand trails and gravel roads, where the less-experienced woods riders could easily make up time they had lost in the sporadic technical sections. On the following pages I relate a few of my experiences in a few of the runs I rode in the late sixties:

Salmon River Ramble

The RAMS first organized the Salmon River Ramble in central Connecticut in 1963, more than a year before I joined the club. I rode it that year and it quickly became my overall favorite run. The exceptionally tough course usually crossed the Salmon River three times and ventured up into the blue-dot hiking trails of the Salmon River State Forest, where the going gets really tough and stays tough. There would be very little letup for the entire 100-plus miles; and coupled with the weather, it could be a nightmare for many novices, as it was traditionally held on the first Sunday in December, when the weather was usually bad. Christy Scholar did the original layout, although Phil Bourdon took over the chore the following year.

The temperature was in the mid-30s at the start of that first one, and it was raining, mixed with sleet and snow. Only about thirty hearty souls showed up to ride. Learning that Christy had laid it out, brought me there the first time. The RAMS stopped "allowing" Christy to lay out their runs after that one, as too many riders complained about its toughness. Being one of Christy's fans, and liking the same type of terrain he did, I thought it was great, although I admit he was a bit of a sadist.

The run started from a small state park along CT Rte. 16, a few miles east of East Hampton. When I arrived, I noticed that everyone was standing around the sign-up table under a picnic shelter, and no one wanted to volunteer to sign up first, which would give them the #1 riding position; and which might require them to "break trail" over some virgin terrain.

Entries at almost all New England enduros were "post entries," which meant that everyone signed up on the day of the event and starting positions were given out in the order they signed up. Most riders preferred tracks to follow; or if they weren't too good at time keeping, they preferred to follow a time keeper. No one wanted to ride up front because it was often difficult to see which way the course goes, especially where there were very few tire tracks, except for those left by the layout crew. Sometimes the only sign of a trail would be the arrows, although as long as the arrows are properly stapled to the trees, in the line-of-sight, seeing them was all part of the game.

I volunteered to be the first because I would rather break trail and take my chances on getting lost, than to have a bunch of slower riders getting in my way in the technical sections, where there's often very little room for passing. From that point on, the RAMS would often reserve the #1 riding position for me, even when I arrived late for sign-up and almost everyone else would have already signed in. By leaving the starting line before everyone else, I would often see no one all day except the checkers. I would have the trail all to myself, which is the way I preferred it. The only downside was that I never got the practice of passing other riders, which later became one of my weaker points, especially where there were many riders on each minute.

The run started out with an almost immediate crossing of the river, and if my memory serves me right, we crossed it two more times that day at different spots. The course took us up into the state forest, where much of it was run along tight, rocky hiking trails and through deep woods with no trails at all.

There was very little letup all day; and due to the rain, there was a lot of sogginess in the woods, with an abundance of mud, which makes it even trickier – especially where there are lots of bare roots and fallen trees to go over. When the tires are wet and coated with mud, it's important to approach every stick and bare root exactly perpendicular to it, or else a tire would slip out, and you end up dropping the bike and losing time. But it was the type of terrain I enjoyed the most.

While the scores were being tallied after the run, I heard someone mention that one of the experts, who had signed up near the back of the pack, couldn't get his bike started after signing up. When it came time for him to leave, he was still working on it. His time to leave came and went before he could get it running, which was well after the last man left the starting line. When he finally did get the bike going, he was reassigned a number several minutes after the last man had left.

That didn't sound quite fair to me, and I said so. The trail would look to him like a well-worn, well-defined path, and he would have no traffic problems at all, which would give him the best of both worlds – a well-defined path with no traffic. Of course I had no traffic riding in the #1 position either, but I had no tracks to follow, which made it even. I argued that getting the bike started was all part of the game, and that if I couldn't get mine started, I would have kept my original number, and simply left the starting line late. I suggested that they could have given him the next sequential number after the last man, or at least checked to see what the rulebook said.

I soon realized that my argument wasn't nearly as popular as the young rider in question. The club referee told me in no uncertain terms that enduros in New England are not necessarily run under the same strict rules and regulations that they might be run in New York; and that they would certainly extend the same courtesy to me if my bike hadn't started; and if I didn't like that ruling, I should go back to New York where I came from, because "here in New England we don't necessarily adhere that strictly to a printed rulebook."

The referee compared my argument and me to another well-known New York rider of that era, who had lodged a few official protests in the past. I accepted the ruling and never questioned the way they chose to run the enduros again. After all, I wanted to get along with everyone, and I was out there for the same fun and enjoyment that they were.

Later, when the results were posted, it revealed that the rider who had been given the special consideration won the high score; and that my score was only a few points behind his for second overall and first place in the heavyweight class. In spite of not winning high score that day, I enjoyed the run, which I felt capped off a very successful season for me, and I was totally satisfied with my first full year of riding the Triumph.

The next Salmon River, in 1964, started from Phil Bourdon's back yard in the big field behind his goat barn. He and Gus Cornelis laid out the run that year. It was literally pouring rain, and it was very cold. It was raining harder than at any run I had ever ridden, with the temperature in the low 40s. It was not a nice day at all for riding, let alone in the woods!

They saved the #1 starting position for me and I broke trail again, with 37 riders behind me. I didn't realize until later that Sal Scirpo, one of my foremost competitors of that era – when he wanted to be – had arrived several minutes after I left the start. He signed in and got the very last number, at the tail end of the pack.

I didn't see anyone all day except the checkers. I crossed the Salmon River three times and went up into the state forest again along the rocky, blue-dot hiking trails. The run was at least as tough as the one Christy had laid out the year before, if not tougher; mostly due to the heavy rain – but I loved it. It was very sloppy in the forest and it was hard for me to see where I was going much of the time. I wore no glasses or goggles all day. I had a ball out there, riding all by myself, breaking trail. I signed into the final check and proceeded to load the bike onto the trailer and change into some dry clothes, after which I broke out a bottle of blackberry brandy to warm up with; and I relaxed to wait for the others to finish.

More than a half hour passed with no one signing in. I began to wonder what happened to everyone. Finally I heard someone yell, "Here comes a rider now." It was Sal Scirpo. He had passed every other rider on the course, going from dead last to second to finish. Eventually, only about a dozen other frozen and totally drenched souls trickled in to finish within their hour.

I won high score that day with a loss of 21 points, while Sal was second overall, losing 39. He probably lost most of those points behind other riders, and I'm sure he had a tougher time passing everyone in the mud than I did breaking trail. It was without a doubt much muddier and sloppier for him; but knowing Sal, I'm sure he enjoyed it as much as I did.

The 1965 Salmon River was run under much better conditions, although it rained a little, and was cold as usual. Sal won that event with 995 points, losing only five. I tied with him, with an identical score, but the "old pro" beat me out at the emergency check. I assumed he might have been riding deeper into his minute, and closer to the center, whereas I usually rode very close to the head end of my minute. Don Cutler, who was rated the top enduro rider in New England that year, and won the overall championship, scored 994, as did George Ellis. Cutler won that tie. Don and George both rode 500 Triumphs.

View of an icy Salmon River crossing, on any 1st Sunday in December.
Photo courtesy of Bob Hicks

Probably my most memorable Salmon River was the one in 1966, which started in front of a little tavern in the hills behind Cobalt, CT. This particular Salmon River carries very fond memories for me because I was tied for the top spot in the final enduro standings for the annual overall grand championship with Al Gendreau. We were both aware before the run that the championship would be determined that day at Salmon River.

I came to the event with Ralph, and when we rolled our bikes off the trailer, it was only 15 degrees, windy, and with occasional snow showers. Ralph tried for a long time to get his BSA 441 started, as it refused to start in the extreme cold, until a few of us pushed it all over the place to "bump start" it. Several others had similar problems. Ralph made it to the second check that day, including a tough 18-mile section in the state forest, which was farther than many others were able to make it.

We didn't have heated grips in those days, so we had to depend on thin gloves or mittens to keep our hands from freezing. I used the same cheap pair of work gloves that I had bought at my local hardware store. There were many ice patches on the roads and trails that day, and there was ice in the streams and on the riverbanks.

Phil Bourdon, the pathfinder, would break through the ice less than an hour before I got there, riding in my usual #1 spot. The water would already have begun to refreeze in some spots. After splashing through a few brooks and crossing the river a few times, my Triumph was totally coated with ice. My pant legs were frozen stiff like stovepipes, and icicles hung from the brake cables and fork legs. It was cold, and everyone felt it.

Eleven riders managed to finish within their hour, out of more than 55 who started. Only George Ellis and I had scores above 900. Mine was 921, while his was 911. George lives right there in Cobalt, so for him it was like riding in his backyard. Only three others scored above 800. Sal didn't ride that day.

Al Gendreau, my primary competition for the overall championship, went over his hour in the very last section riding a 250 Greeves; so by virtue of my final score, I not only won Salmon River that day, but I also cinched the title for the 1966 New England Enduro Grand Championship.

Bud Peck wrote the following article about the run, which appeared later in Cycle Sport:

Salmon River Ramble

The RAMS M.C. held their fifth annual Salmon River Ramble at Cobalt, Conn. The 93-mile enduro was run at a speed of 18 mph for the first 18 miles, and 24 mph for the remainder. This schedule would have worked out very nicely on a warm, dry day; but the weather didn't cooperate! The temperature when I left home at 5:30 AM was 13 above zero, and it never got up to freezing all day. The temperature had also been below freezing all the previous day, causing the ground to be frozen solid, except in the deepest mud holes. This frozen condition, coupled with about an inch of fresh powder snow on the surface, made for very slippery riding on the trails, and even on the roads.

The run started on pavement, but went into the notorious "blue trails" of the Connecticut State Forests within a half-mile; and other than a few park roads and a stretch of power line, it didn't come out of the woods for about twenty miles. Then, on to the old railroad tracks, which were actually a joy to ride after having had the ties removed. It was great at 40-50 mph until where EVERY OTHER tie was still in place, with monstrous holes in between.

Then, on to a stretch where the ties were untouched, and the riding was great at 45 mph; but watch out for the next pothole! Oh my poor rims! So it went, with several good, very rough power lines, lots of trails, some road, and then the Salmon River crossings - THREE times, no less, and the river was wide and DEEP. While getting from one Salmon River crossing to the next, by way of various woods trails, we had to cross yet another stream twice. At the second crossing of that one, the frozen bank dropped off vertically about two feet into the water. I don't know what the others did, but I killed the engine, just in case I should drop the bike in the water. I dropped the front wheel over the bank, wrestled the rest of the bike over, and ended up with the machine standing in about six inches of water parallel with the bank. From there I cranked up and took off.

After the run, the ice that had formed on boots and clothes made it impossible to change until after you stood around in the heated tavern for about 20 minutes. Surprisingly, I was not cold at all during the run, as the coating of ice seemed to act as insulation.

It was a tough run, yes, but enjoyed by all 55 who started, and enjoyed even more by the 11 who finished. The biggest bugaboo for the riders – "B" riders especially, were those nasty little snow-covered logs and sticks, lying at an angle with the trail. The snow makes them about twice as nasty as they usually are.

Piet Boonstra, the master of New England rockery, took High Point with a score of 921, with George Ellis a close second with 911. Not one of the 22 riders in the "B" lightweight class finished; however, Jim Helliwell made it to the seventh check with 183 points lost to take first place in that class on his Greeves.

Dick Turmel topped the "A" lightweight class on his Triumph Cub. Here is a fellow who has done real well this season after several years' layoff. John Soltys, Jr. of the Meriden M.C. came through with a well-deserved win in the "B" heavyweight class with a score of 786 on his BSA.

Our thanks to layout crew Phil Bourdon and Gus Cornelis for the excellent job of laying out the run.

Bushwacker Enduro

The Connecticut Ramblers put on a great run called the Bushwacker. They often ran it twice a year, and it was tough, whether or not it rained. Even when it didn't rain, the Shenipsit State Forest offered some excellent tight enduro trails, which were right up my alley. It was one of the first runs I rode with the Triumph after switching from DMW in 1962, when I finished second to Christy Scholar. Here is a report on a later 1966 Bushwacker, after I had gotten more practice:

8th Annual Bushwacker Enduro

PIET BOONSTRA HIGH POINT MAN
AT RAMBLERS' ENDURO

The Connecticut Ramblers held their 8th Annual Bushwacker Enduro on October 23rd. It was a beautiful day and 78 riders showed up to compete in the event. The skies were clear and the temperature rose into the high 60's by mid afternoon.

The first rider to be dispatched from the starting point at the Bergstrom farm in Ellington, Connecticut was Al Gendreau, of Southbridge, Mass. The course headed east from the starting point and took the riders directly into the Shenipsit State Forest.

Most riders made it to the first check in good time, but the "blue trail" was encountered soon after that, where the going got quite rough for a while. This put the kibosh on having any good scores at the second check, which was only fourteen miles out. Between this point and the third check the ride featured a sticky mud hole that was located near the 16-mile mark. Later, an encounter was made with some railroad ties that caused the riders a few anxious moments, and then a ride through a dry riverbed that was full of boulders, logs and brush. A few miles after that, they arrived at the third check, which was in the Monson, Mass. area. This was near the midway point of the run, where the route began to double back toward Ellington.

After the third check, the tempo eased up a bit for several miles, which allowed many riders to make up some much-needed lost time; however, a long muddy section tended to dampen their spirits just before arriving at check #4. Between there and check #5, there were many stretches of easy trails and dirt roads that provided an opportunity to make up even more time. Piet Boonstra, the eventual high point winner, was the only rider who arrived at check #5 exactly on time.

Soon after this point the trails became much more difficult, and the riders found themselves back on the old rough & rocky blue trail. At about the 50-mile point, a steep downgrade had to be negotiated. This was one of the most popular spectator points. Many of the riders dismounted and

A few photos taken at different Connecticut runs in the late 1960s.

In one Connecticut enduro, the club got permission to ride through a nudist colony and convinced a few of the residents to "man" one of their checks. Shown here, Ron Webster's smile says it all, as he is checked in.

Photo complements of Ron

walked their machines down a zigzag path until they were able to remount and continue on. This contributed to losing much time, and many were clocked in very late, or did not arrive at all at check #6. The last ten miles proved to be just as hard as any other part of the course. The layout crew must have had hearts of stone! Back into the blue trail they went, one more time. At this point only about one-third of the original contestants were still in the running. The best scorer

at check #7 arrived fourteen minutes late.
    Even though it was a tough run, most of the riders had favorable comments to offer.

Greylock Enduro

The Greylock Riders of Pittsfield, Mass. put on an excellent endurance run in the northern Berkshires known as the Greylock Enduro, which was one of the forerunners of the Berkshire International Trials. It was the enduro in which Al Eames gained a good deal of experience organizing and laying out runs, as well as getting to know hundreds of miles of trails and many of the landowners in the area.

Although the Greylock was a relatively short enduro, it was one of my favorites, in that it was tough and it was run in the Berkshires. I managed to win it a few times in the late 1960s. In the early 60s, both the spring and fall versions of the run started from Dick March's plumbing shop on the outskirts of Pittsfield. Don Lohnes won at least a few of those on a 250 Greeves. The start was later moved out of town, to the Hinsdale Home Club, where there was a restaurant and more room for parking.

The enduro often scaled the top of Mt. Greylock, the highest point in Mass. I remember coming up the backside of the mountain at least a few times, over an exceptionally steep, rocky trail that was barely ride-able. Many riders needed help getting their machines up and over the last few hundred feet.

Al also used several great abandoned roads and other old woods roads that were becoming more and more familiar to me, like Old Florida Road, Tunnel Road, Petersburg Mountain, and Sucker Pond. Some of those roads had also been used in the Covered Wagon and the Maple Leaf Enduro. Following is a report on the 1966 run that appeared in Cycle Sport:

Greylock Enduro

108 enduro riders converged on the Hinsdale Home Club in Hinsdale, Mass. on October 2nd, for the opening event of the 1966 fall season in New England. It was a 100-mile enduro sponsored by the Greylock Riders. Layout man Al Eames, had used much of the trail also used this year in the Berkshire International. The speed was set at 24 mph over relatively easy going; but heavy rains the day before added a lot of surface water to the trails, so it was mud, mud, mud, all the way, with deep water crossings.

Piet Boonstra was the first rider away and ended up as the first rider on the scoring list, taking High Point with 988, over the large field of entries. Closest to him in the competition for High Point was Al Gendreau, who wound up with 983. Al took top spot in A Lightweight. The second place rider in A Lightweight, Dick Turmel, was impressive, as he rode a 125cc Moto Guzzi against the 250cc field.

Frank DeGray was the top Heavyweight, after Boonstra. He rode his Grumph, a 500 Triumph that he set up in a Greeves frame, finishing with 979 points. Phil Bourdon and Myron Hooker, placing behind Frank, were matched almost in scores by B Heavyweight top places, Herb Walker, Joe Veal, and Paul Winters.

The B Lightweight finishing order was highlighted by the closest point match, as Jim Moroney edged Arthur Solomen 956 to 954, and Arthur had but one point in hand over Jim Helliwell. Out of the huge entry in this class, these three nearly tied.

The big 100cc entry found the going too tough, only two went all the way, Dick Baj on his Honda edged out John Taylor on a Lobito. The large number of trail bike entries was encouraging, as from amongst these are sure to come future top enduro competitors.

A smorgasbord was laid on by the Hinsdale Home Club, and the club bar was busy as the scores were being tallied, the whole event was successful in many ways, a tough test for new riders, and challenging enough for the stars to be kept on alert all the way.

I experienced a mental turning point in my enduro career the very next year, 1967, at that same run. It happened soon after I had won several high score trophies in the spring, won the Best Opposite Class Championship at the Corduroy Enduro in Canada just three weeks earlier, and first place in Class A Medium Weight (4th overall) at Cayuta the week before, in an especially tough 150-mile national championship. At that point in time it looked as though I had cinched the overall New England Grand Championship for the second consecutive year.

Al Eames again laid out the event, which started and ended at the Hinsdale Home Club. It was an excellent ride, although not quite as tough as usual, with 190 entries, which was almost double the previous year. When it was over, I loaded my bike onto the trailer and took a sip of brandy while I waited for the others to finish and the scores to be posted.

I knew I had done well. I thought it had been my kind of run and I expected an easy win; but when the results were posted, they revealed that I had finished in a three-way tie with my two teammates, Bud Peck and Dave Latham – the three of us with identical scores! The tie with Bud was to the exact second. Here is how it was reported in Cycle Sport:

Huge Entry at Greylock Enduro

The Greylock Enduro on September 24th, run in the Berkshire Hills, was a 120-mile event that drew a record entry for any New England enduro, with 190 riders signing up for a try at the hill country. More than 30 riders entered on 100cc bikes, even – a very good showing. The turnout submerged the old regulars in a flood of new hopefuls, and the run did not disappoint the newer riders, though less than half the entry finished. Some experts were caught by checks placed in a way to catch them running early in slower sections, so they had to be on the ball, though the going was relatively easy. Rain arrived in the afternoon to toughen the going for many late-runners.

Piet Boonstra and Bud Peck finished with a dead-even tie for High Point, both to the exact second at the emergency check, as they lost 14 points apiece. Katey Holland rode 90 miles of the route to take the Powder Puff win. Her competition for the day was Grace Hanson, out in her first-ever enduro.

The 100 cc winner, Ken Wood, lost only 58 points, as 9 of the 36 starters in his class finished. The B Lightweight class fielded 96 starters, of which 47 finished. 10 of the 30 B Heavyweight entries went all the way. Riders in Class A fared better of course, 8 out of 11 in the Heavyweight class, and 14 of 17 in the Lightweight class, finished.

Dave Latham won the A Lightweight class with a score equal to the High Point men, but he was a mere 20 seconds off at the emergency check.

I had a freshly lighted cigarette in my hand at the time, which I threw away and swore off cigarettes for the rest of my life, thinking that it would bring back my edge. I haven't touched a cigarette since that day and I had been smoking for 25 years. But it would have taken more than just quitting smoking to hold off the inevitable. I realized that when one reaches the top, the only way to go from there is down, and this seemingly innocuous event gave me a very subtle hint that I probably wouldn't be at the top for very long.

Dave Latham, my teammate, who was getting very good very fast, went on to win the New England Enduro Grand Championship that year, in spite of the huge lead I enjoyed coming out of the summer; and Bud Peck, my other teammate, won the overall championship the following two years in a row. It couldn't have happened to a couple of better guys.

Dave Latham was a scholarly astronomer working at the Smithsonian Observatory in Cambridge, Mass., studying for his doctorate, which he earned a few years later. He was less than 30 years old at the time he wrested the title, not only from me, but also from a very impressive list of up-and-coming riders.

I first noticed Dave in the summer of 1966, at a rocky closed-course enduro hosted by the Springfield M.C. at Becket, Mass. He was attacking those rocks with a BSA 441 Victor like few people I have ever seen. I had seldom witnessed anyone so passionate about his sport as Dave Latham seemed to be that day. It was an extremely hot 90-degree day, and I think he might have been wearing only a T-shirt.

I thought at the time he looked a little like Bill Baird, and I thought, "Here comes another one." I later heard a number of reports about his fervor on the trails, and how he would sometimes crash almost immediately after passing someone. I actually didn't think he would last out the season. Dave's name only began to appear on Class B result sheets with that run, and he managed to win a 3rd place in the Class B Heavyweight Championship that same year. He went on to win the overall New England Enduro Grand Championship the very next year.

Dave had switched to Greeves by then, after breaking the BSA a number of times through his raw enthusiasm. It wasn't until he joined the RAMS, in 1967, that the RAMS #1 team really began to click. He, Bud Peck and I would consistently win club team awards in New England, as well as just about everywhere else we rode, including the Corduroy in Canada and several national championships. Dave won the high score at the 1969 115-mile National Championship in Dallas, PA, which was a tough event in the mountains of Pennsylvania.

Bud Peck was a self-employed stonemason. He had been riding motorcycles for quite a bit longer, and was several years older than Dave. While still a teenager, Bud was involved in a serious road accident with an Indian Chief. That accident, along with a few unsuccessful operations to repair his right leg and right knee, left his right knee so it wouldn't bend more than a fraction of its normal range. When he was an up-and-coming woods rider on a Greeves, many thought he had an artificial leg. A photo of Bud once appeared in Cycle Sport, with the caption, "he doesn't let an artificial leg stop him."

This disability left Bud with a significant handicap for being agile in the tight woods, a physical trait that was one of the most valuable assets an enduro rider could have. He made up for it in skill, determination and an optimistic approach to just about everything he undertook. He not only became a champion enduro rider and one of the top observed trials riders in New England, but he was also one of the most skilled road riders I have ever known. If it weren't for his inability to fit that leg behind a racing fairing, I think he probably would have been a champion road racer as well.

When Bud sat on a dirt bike, he usually sat on the tail end of the seat with his right leg almost straight out. He would modify his brake pedal so that he could operate it with the stiff leg in either the sit-down or stand-up position. Along higher-speed trails and woods roads he often stood up, as it was a much more comfortable position for him to use the brake. He was a master of the stand-up riding style as well, and often placed high in the annual observed trials championships.

While he cherished every one of his accomplishments, including twice winning the overall Enduro Grand Championship in his beloved New England, and winning the "Best Opposite Class" Championship in Canada at the 1968 Corduroy, Bud's "finest hour" came with his incredible performance in the 1970 Berkshire International.

There Bud emerged with the only heavyweight gold medal among a huge field of top international riders with much newer, high-tech, purpose-built motorcycles, while he rode his well-used, well-worn, 4-year-old, 1966 Triumph. One particular section on the Colrain power-line separated the men from the boys. It was almost thirty years later that we spread Bud's ashes on the downhill section at the end of that power-line trail, where in 1970, a thick layer of mud flowed off the mountain like a river, faster than most of the bikes descended from it.

Bud Peck had skill, determination and an optimistic approach to just about everything he undertook. He was the New England Enduro Grand Champion in 1968 and 1969. Bud was everyone's friend, and my best friend, and all who ever knew him looked up to him, and respected him for his integrity and his exemplary character. He was truly, as my wife Lillian once said, "the salt of the earth."

Photo by Dave Latham

Dave Latham on his 250 cc Greeves. Dave was the New England Grand Champion in 1967. In 1969 he won high score in a tough 115-mile National Championship at Dallas, PA.

Photo by Boyd Reynolds

Sandy Lane

The Meteor Motorcycle Club of central New Jersey had been putting on the Sandy Lane enduro for many years before I first rode their twentieth annual in 1957. Sandy Lane was held in the midst of what is known as the Atlantic Coastal Pine Barrens, much of it in the Wharton Tract, a huge piece of land now owned by the State of New Jersey. Atsion, where the run started, was once a thriving iron community; and prior to that, it was the "Atsion Farm" of Joseph Wharton. My first visit to Atsion was with the Hummer, when the sand almost brought me to my knees. I returned several times after that with the Triumph.

The Meteor M.C. ran their first endurance run from Atsion in 1935 using a 225-mile course. It was originally known as a "night run," because it started at 10 p.m. on Thanksgiving Eve and ran all night long. Only four riders finished the run that year. There were so many complaints about its toughness that they moved it to daytime the following year.

By 1947 they were granted a long-awaited sanction by the AMA for a 500-mile national championship. According to the club's history, it went off like clockwork. Only 14 riders finished. Julie Kroeger won that first AMA-sponsored event. The club cut the length back to 225 miles the following year when it was determined that a 500-mile run was a bit more than they could handle. Paul Brumfield took over organization of Sandy Lane that same year.

I wasn't particularly crazy about Sandy Lane when I first rode it in 1957, and I never did develop a real liking for it. I would often jokingly tell Paul Brumfield when I arrived at the Pic-a-Lilly that I hated his run, to which he would answer, "So what did you come for, Boonstra." He could care less!

They had a huge box trailer parked at the site, in which they would disappear after the run to figure the scores; and I for one believed they were all inside getting "crocked" while we riders suffered through many long hours of waiting for the bitter end, when the scores were finally posted. Sometimes it was almost midnight before they came out.

I didn't really hate that or any other endurance run, and theirs met most of the qualifications I thought a run should have, especially the endurance part, and its almost continuous toughness, which was in fact what I did come for, but it wasn't my kind of terrain, especially for making up time; and I never did well there, although I placed high a few times.

Its continuous toughness, as well as the occasional bottomless mud bogs and water holes, was what might have given both Gene Esposito and me a slight edge at Sandy Lane; but Gene had something I never had, which was the ability to make up time riding the unstable, sugary sand trails, after having cleared an obstacle. The sand trails would allow him to make up much of his time very quickly, while I usually went along as if it were still tough. Gene won high score at Sandy Lane twice, in 1965 and 1966, which were two of my best years for placing high at other enduros; but I just couldn't do it at Sandy Lane.

Following is a report of the 1965 Sandy Lane that appeared in Leslie Pink's column, *Metropolitan Motorcycling,* in Cycle Sport magazine:

Sandy Lane Swamped with 194 entries

SANDY LANE ENDURO – SEPTEMBER 26, 1965: *For a change of pace, we decided to try our hand at an endurance run, so off we went to the 125-Mile National Championship down in Atsion, N.J. It was the 28th annual running of this great enduro. A record of 194 riders staggered the officials, and they had to scrape in all the corners for more route sheets. They had run out of number plates, souvenir wagon wheels and route cards; but everyone was taken care of with a little stretching.*

All the top enduro riders in this area were on hand. Bill Baird from Illinois was here to try to win the Grand National Championship Award for the 5th year in a row. He and Bill Decker of Butler, N.J. are running about tied, and the Sandy Lane event and the Jamestown, N.Y. event are the remaining two runs in which each can rack up some more points. It's a close battle this year.

To say that enduro riders are an enthusiastic group is borne out by the fact that with an 8:00 AM starting time, he has to drag his weary bones out of bed at 4:00 AM and drive several hundred miles to get to the start. Many of the out-of-town riders arrived on Saturday and stayed overnight at area motels. Riders came from Illinois, Ohio, Delaware, Maryland, New York, New Jersey, Mass., Conn., Penna., and probably several other states that I missed seeing.

The riders were started two on a minute, and first men were out at 8:01 AM. The run was an excellent combination of steady woods going. Very little paved road was used at all. They just put you on the sand lanes and you can go hundreds of miles without seeing a car or blacktop road. From my personal experience, I can only tell you about the first 21.2 miles, as that was as far as I got. All I saw in those miles was sand – and that varied only in depth – sometimes it was 6 inches deep and sometimes up to a foot deep. It was loads of fun, but very tiring on this little gal. There was one other girl entered and we cried on each other's shoulders along the sand trails. The noon control was in Manahawkin, N.J., and the riders were given an hour to eat, repair and rest up for the afternoon section. Quite a few riders were out by lunchtime with machine breakdowns. Several had lost more points than they should have due to getting lost. It isn't hard to get lost in this type of going. Generally speaking, the markers were very good. However, some of the intersections on these sand trails have at least 6 trails branching off in all directions. Just one snap decision can take you up a wrong trail and you can go for miles before discovering you are wrong – and then you have a job remembering which direction you came from. There are tire tracks going in all directions and it is just a gamble as to which is the right way.

Some of the early riders lost very few precious points up to noon check, and their spirits were high. Sal Scirpo got off to a very late start due to electrical problems, but had made up most of his lost time by lunch check.

The afternoon section was a little tougher than the morning, with a lot tighter and slower riding, including the infamous stump fields. A group of the early riders missed some arrows and got very lost. However, the later riders had more tracks to follow and fared a little better. The finish back at the Pic-a-Lilly Restaurant was at 2:37, and the riders rolled in pretty much on time.

I think the promoters of this event deserve a big round of applause for putting on a truly championship event. The course was excellent, the markers were good, checker's watches were right on the nose, the checking teams very efficient, and results were ready that evening; and the awards given out to those riders that were able to stay. They had the C.A.P. at the checks radioing the times into the finish where the results were being figured as the run was still in progress. A sheet was printed up for the spectators giving several spots where the riders could be observed with directions on how to get there. This is a very helpful guide to wives and families that want to observe their riders in action.

In addition to the usual high score, and the three trophies in each class, there were a dozen special trophies. The high score winner also has the honor of having his name engraved on the perpetual Wagon Wheel trophy.

Congratulations to all the winners – you did a terrific job. And Congratulations to the Meteor Motorcycle Club – you also did a terrific job.

As I mentioned previously, Gene Esposito won that event with a score of 990. Bill Baird finished a close second with

989. I finished 7th overall and 3rd in Class A Light Heavyweight behind Bill Baird and Charlie Stapleford, who rode a 500 Matchless. He was also very good in the sand. Bill Decker, in contention for the national championship at the time, finished 5th overall and first in Class A Medium Weight with a 250 Greeves.

Among the many obstacles at Sandy Lane were the infamous stump fields, where many years ago forest fires had razed all of the low brush, bushes and small trees, leaving only roots and stumps. Years of re-growth obscured most of the stumps; but they were high enough to catch toes, and would sometimes reach up and hook the foot pegs. Every stump was an obstruction that you didn't want to hit with your toe, the foot peg, or the front wheel; and there were millions of them hidden in hundreds of acres of low shrubbery. A few of the experts were able to maintain the 24 mph average speed through the stump fields. I would sometimes get zigzagging through the maze as fast as I could go, and then suddenly I'd hit one of those big stumps head-on, which would totally break my concentration, especially if I was trying to figure out my time when I hit it.

I recall once in the late sixties when I was headed for Sandy Lane very early in the morning on the day of the event: I was alone, driving my Camaro, and hauling my bike trailer along the New Jersey Turnpike a bit faster than the posted speed limit. I was running a little late, as usual. The fog was so thick at the time that I couldn't see for more than a few yards.

I was straddling both lanes so that I would have the ability to veer in either direction if something suddenly loomed out of the fog. I was fighting sleep at the time, when I spotted a string of construction cones separating the lanes. In my groggy state of mind, I didn't know which lane might have been closed as I began to plow through the first of the cones. I quickly chose to go right, and I yanked the wheel in that direction; but the road was very slick and the car went into a full broad-slide, at 70 mph – with the trailer attached.

I glanced in the rearview mirror as I slid, and couldn't see the bike or the trailer. The second time I glanced, I saw the bike pass across the rear window as the trailer whipped from one side of the car to the other. After finally getting it all under control without crashing, I looked again and didn't see the bike at all.

Gene Esposito (left) won
Sandy Lane in 1965 and
1966.

Gene Esposito looks for the trail to get out of this water hole.

Both photos above by Boyd Reynolds

Negotiating the infamous stump fields at Sandy Lane.

Photo by Boyd Reynolds

Riding across a narrow, rickety bridge over a huge watery swamp at Sandy Lane, Many riders walked their machines across. It could certainly appear scary to some.

Photo by Boyd Reynolds

Sal Scirpo at Sandy Lane. Sal rode with a cloth aviator's helmet and pilot's goggles for years before the helmet law required him to wear a hard helmet.

Photo by Boyd Reynolds

My heart dropped. I was sure I had lost it – maybe trailer, bike and all; but as I pulled over to stop, I could see the bike leaning way over on the trailer. I had been using automotive hood springs with the chains for my tie-downs, and one of the springs stretched far beyond its limit. I pulled over and stopped, only to learn that the rim on the bike's back wheel had gotten twisted, from being chained down tight. It pulled the wheel out of alignment when the bike leaned too far. I rode the run with it anyway, and was able to straighten it a little before the next run.

The Corduroy

The Corduroy Enduro, known as "The Cord" for short, was held in Ontario for several years before I first learned about it and became interested. It had already earned a reputation of being an excellent two-day, 350-mile endurance run, better than most of our own national championships, which was attributed to an excellent layout job by Ron Jackson of the British Empire Motor Club. It was run mostly over old abandoned roads and trails in a sparsely populated area of central Ontario. It started in Coboconk, about 100 miles north-northeast of Toronto, in an area known as the Haliburton Highlands.

The total length and toughness of the Cord sounded right to me, the entry was not nearly as crowded as most of our own nationals and it was NOT being held on a holiday weekend. It was about 550 miles from home, which was a little closer than Little Burr and a good deal closer than Jack Pine.

Many well-known New England riders, including Sal Scirpo, Frank DeGray, Phil Bourdon and others, had already competed there and spoke well of it. Ralph and I decided to try it for the first time in 1967, as did my RAMS teammate, Bud Peck. With Bud and Phil Bourdon on a RAMS #1 team, it would give us an excellent shot at the team trophy, if nothing else.

On our way across the border, Ralph and I visited the duty-free liquor store to pick up some blackberry brandy for after the event. We hoped to find *Jezynowka*, pronounced jez-NOFF-ka, which according to Leroux's label is "designed especially for the Polish taste." Bud had already given it the name, "Jezzy," and it had become somewhat of a cult favorite among a few of the RAMS. I think that Christy Scholar actually started the blackberry brandy tradition among RAMS.

No luck finding it at the duty-free shop. The only blackberry brandy they carried was imported from France. It was called Marie Brizzard, which Bud promptly nicknamed Marie's Gizzard. He could usually come up with a nickname for just about everything and everyone. His name for me as best I could determine was "The Big Boon," although he had several more characteristic names for other riders, many of which I wouldn't repeat here. He might even have had another more characteristic name for me that he would use when I wasn't around.

There wasn't enough motel space in the entire area in 1967 to house as many people as were being drawn to the Cord, so many townspeople offered sleeping accommodations in their homes and summer homes at reasonable prices, similar to West Branch with the Jack Pine. Ralph and I had reservations at someone's summer home that first year.

The event started and ended at the Gold Rock Lodge in Coboconk. The lodge was owned and operated by "Les" North. Several cottages and "cottagettes" were available there, some with up to three bedrooms; but they were all booked by the time we signed up for the run. The cottages were fully equipped with modern toilet conveniences, running water, refrigerators, and electric or propane stoves for cooking.

I heard that at least one of John Penton's older brothers was there, but not John. I also heard that his brother didn't come to ride, but only to party, and that Gold Rock was known for the partying that took place there during that weekend. I don't know how anyone got any sleep because the partying went on most of the night, with a huge bonfire in the open area.

There was a Finnish steam bath available at Gold Rock where some of the partygoers could sweat out their party juices the morning after, followed by a plunge in the ice-cold lake! I heard that Les North used this sauna practically every day and also swam in the icy water every day after emerging from his sauna. There were hot showers available after the run, which many riders availed themselves of.

I recognized many New England faces in the starting lineup on Saturday morning, as well as names that were familiar to me from the Midwest, including Marv Cutler, Dick DeGraw, Paul Goulet and the Kussmaul brothers, all from Michigan. I also recognized Walt Lohrer from PA, Charlie Stapleford from Delaware, and Frank Piasecki and others from Ohio. With a total entry of 230, they started three riders on a minute.

My first year at the Corduroy, 1967, was the last year that they ran the event under AMA rules, which required everyone to keep time. Starting in 1968 the Cord would be run under their own variation of international rules, which virtually eliminated the time keeping aspect of the game, and it became much more like a cross-country race. I'm glad I got to run it under the AMA rules at least once. The British Empire Motor Club, who organized the Corduroy, later described the 1967 event as being, "run in fine weather, with a record entry and 350 miles of rugged trail riding."

Reports of the 1966 event noted that Bill Sharpless of Ontario had demolished the field. He didn't quite demolish the field in 1967, but he did manage to outpoint everyone to win his third Corduroy in 12 attempts. By that time the Cord had been run for 15 years.

A total of 230 entries, which included six solo classes and four sidecars, were signed up. The first bikes left the starting area Saturday morning at 8:01. The field included Canada's best, plus a group of accomplished U.S. enthusiasts from 14 states. Saturday's route covered more than 200 miles, with a 50-minute lunch break in Bancroft. The schedule was set at 24-mph, except for two short 30-mph sections of gravel roads.

Paul Goulet from Lansing lost only 2 points by the Saturday morning gas stop, compared with 3 for Sharpless and Phil Bourdon. Being usually a slow starter, I dropped 4. The rest of Saturday morning's course became exceptionally tough, and cost some of the top contenders several points. Dick DeGraw of Michigan on a Triumph Cub was fastest through the morning section, with a loss 9, while I lost 10. Both Walt Lohrer of PA on a Greeves and Bill Sharpless on a Bultaco lost 12 points apiece.

I managed to pass Bill Sharpless and several others in the toughest part of the morning section, along a rocky uphill on an old abandoned woods road in a section known as the Peterson Trail. I didn't know at the time who the rider was, but it was obvious that he was one of the top experts, and his bike had an Ontario plate. Bill approached me later at lunch with a friendly smile as I sat eating at the counter. His first words were, "You must be Piet Boonstra."

After answering in the affirmative, he introduced himself and said that he had heard I was there, and he knew it was I who had passed him on the Peterson Trail. He said he had never seen a 500 Triumph go quite that fast over the rocks. He offered his hand, which of course I shook, and introduced Ralph and Bud. Bill Sharpless is a fine competitor.

Immediately after lunch, the Irondale River, swollen by recent summer rains, killed the hopes of many, by putting several riders over their hour. Only about half of the original field reached the first check after lunch. During the return trip from Bancroft to Gold Rock in the afternoon, Bill Sharpless lost only five points to wind up his first day with a total loss of 20. Dick DeGraw lost 21, while Walt Lohrer and I both dropped 25. The total retirement toll for Saturday was very high.

Sunday morning was clear and cool, making it a perfect day for a ride in the woods. Of the 94 who finished the first day's strenuous course, only 88 were willing and able to make the starting line on Sunday morning. The short field afforded us the luxury of a 9 a.m. start. The first 73 miles retraced a portion of Saturday's course, although there was a higher loss of marks the second time around, as the checks had been relocated.

At the lunch stop on Sunday, Sharpless still led the field with a total of 29 points lost, Dick DeGraw was second with 31, and I stood third with 32. Walt Lohrer had dropped 33, while Paul Goulet lost 38. The only remaining sidecar outfit made it to lunch, but no farther. Mechanical problems prevented them from continuing, but the sidecar trophy was theirs, as they had covered more ground than all of their competitors.

The final 55-mile leg from Haliburton to Gold Rock was where I had an exceptionally good ride, zeroing most of the checks. Less than 15 miles from the end I felt that I had the run in the bag, having made up most of the deficiency I had at noon, and picking up at least a few more points on Sharpless. I was quite sure I was leading the pack at that point.

I was only about ten miles from the end when I came to a wide plank with wood strips along the edges, which were designed to keep the tires from slipping off. It was called a monorail, and I had heard about them. They were designed to be a bridge over bottomless peat bogs. Several planks were attached end-to-end to reach for more than a hundred feet across the bog. I had also heard that you should always use them and never try to go alongside.

But this one was totally blocked with riders, and a guy with a 650 Triumph was stuck sideways on the plank halfway across. I figured the score was so close at that point that if I waited for the plank to clear I would certainly lose the high score there, but if I was able to go straight through, without stopping, the overall win was mine.

I took a quick look at the clearing alongside the plank and it didn't look too difficult or ominous, especially if I crossed it at speed. So I grabbed a big handful of throttle and went for it. I hit the bog at more than 30 mph and got at least a third of the way across before it even started to sink. But it quickly sunk deeper and deeper as I went; and by the time I was two-thirds of the way across, I was totally "bogged" down and stopped. I was 10 feet past the guy stuck on the plank, but I was still more than 20 feet from the other end of the peat bog.

I tried to drag it over to the plank before the guy could get his 650 straightened out, but my wheels were so deep in the muck that it created a suction, which held it there. I couldn't even tip it sideways very far, due to the strong suction. I made several trips into the woods to find branches and heavy sticks to make a bed for the sides, to help me to break the suction, and so I could eventually leverage it out. I worked at it for at least ten minutes just to get it into a position to drag it over to the plank.

Meanwhile, with some help, the guy with the 650 had gotten his bike to face in the right direction and he was long gone. The plank was then clear, but I was still stuck in the mud trying to get the Triumph loose. It took all of my strength to finally free it from the mud, and to get it to face in the right direction on the plank. By the time I finally got moving again, I had lost a lot of time. I arrived at the final check late, in spite of making up much of it.

The final scores were Bill Sharpless, 957; Dick DeGraw, 956; and I finished with a 951, for third overall. I was named the "Best Opposite Champion," since both Bill Sharpless and Dick DeGraw were on lightweights, while I was riding a heavyweight. The next highest expert heavyweights were Paul Goulet with a score of 950 and Phil Bourdon with a 938. The RAMS #1 team easily won the team trophy.

I returned in 1968, although the event was run under international rules, and the things I remember most about it were actually peripheral to the run itself. I had done very well during the spring season with several high scores and I enjoyed a healthy lead in the standings for the New England Enduro Championship, before I decided to retire the 1966 Triumph. It was the best Triumph I had ever owned and it served me well throughout 1966 and 1967, but it began to show a good deal of wear from hard use. I had gotten into the practice of replacing it every two years anyway, so I bought the 1968 model.

My job was also getting very demanding of my time, so I took a hiatus from riding for the entire summer. As of the end of August my score in the overall standings for the New England championship stood at 948, while the next five places were: Ron Webster 896, Bill Perry 884, Bud Peck 838, Ron Commo 568, and Dave Latham 550. I had thought that Dave was devoting most of his time to his studies, as he was working toward his doctorate, but unbeknownst to me, he and Bud were practicing.

I skipped Jack Pine because I was far too busy at my job. The first run of the fall season for me would be the Corduroy, although I still wasn't sure I could make it. The entry blank arrived in the mail a month before the run, and I didn't get around to returning it until late in August, just before the deadline for mail entries. Before I did, I got a call from Bud Peck. He suggested that when I send in the entry, I request the same number as he and Dave Latham. I didn't like the idea at first, mainly because we all had our individual riding styles and skills, and I thought we would be getting into each other's way.

But he reminded me that we were in it mainly for the fun, and that it should be a lot of fun for the famed RAMS #1 team to line up together on the same number at the starting line and ride together all day. Oh well, why not? We were assigned #9, which was in our favor, and we looked great as the three of us headed out at 8:09 a.m. Saturday morning.

There were about 5 miles of tarmac before turning into the first woods section, and I was bringing up the rear as we neared the first turn into the woods. I figuring it might be a tight section, and I thought it would be best if I passed them and entered the woods first, so they wouldn't be getting in my way.

I made the turn and began to set a fast pace on the narrow trail; but when I got to the speed that I thought was right for the trail, I heard the blat-blat of Dave's Greeves close behind. I stepped up the pace and still heard him there. He even blipped the throttle a few times, which is a subtle signal of wanting to pass. I figured I'd let him go by because it's a long run; and why go that fast when we're already running so early. When I got to the first wide spot in the trail I pulled over a few feet and Dave flew by. As I was about to drop back to the center of the trail, Bud also flew by. In less than 10 seconds they were both out of sight. I could hardly believe it.

I got to the first check plenty early and they were there, standing beside their bikes with big grins as I pulled up. Some of my thoughts at the time were that my new Triumph wasn't handling quite right, that I was out of shape from having taken off all summer, that I'm usually a slow starter, and several other excuses; but I also felt that we had a long, 2-day ride ahead of us and it would be a different story later.

But it didn't change much during the next two days, as the run turned out to be much more of a high-speed event than the previous year. High-speed trails were more in their range of abilities. There were times during the two days that we were pretty evenly matched, and Bud and I would ride together for long distances. We would often pass other riders with one of us flying by each side of the guy at the same time. I'm sure our big Triumphs startled them when we went by. We certainly did have a lot of fun that day!

By the end of the first day, I was already worn down to a frazzle, and the two of them were still full of energy and hopping up and down. By the end of the second day, I had to admit that I was getting old. Dave took the picture of me collapsed against a picket fence, with an apple in my hand and a bottle of "Marie's Gizzard" sitting nearby. The photo appeared in Cycle Sport the following month as it now appears on the next page. I was actually saying at the time, "One of these days I'm going to have to retire!"

For all of the excuses I could come think of, I finished 6th in my class, while Bud won the "Best Opposite Class" trophy with a loss of only 10 points. I used all of the monorails and never got stuck in another peat bog again. Leroy Winters won high score overall with a loss of 9, while Dave took third in the Expert Lightweight class behind John Penton and Bob Maus. They lost 10 points each, while Dave lost 12.

Mostly due to my loss of a whopping 62 points during the two days, our club team finished second to the Penton Imports trade-supported team of Leroy Winters, John and Tom Penton, and Bob Towne. Leroy and John rode 125 cc Pentons, while Tom Penton rode a 100 cc Penton. Bob Towne rode a 250 cc Husqvarna.

We returned to the Cord several times in later years and won the team trophy a few more times. I won the Senior Class in 1970 and 1971. I was still riding the 1968 Triumph for the 1970 win; although in 1971 I did it on a 250 Suzuki.

Taken after the 1968 Corduroy Enduro. I was saying at the time, "One of these days I'm going to have to retire." My teammates Bud Peck and Dave Latham were getting a great deal of enjoyment from having run the "old guy" ragged.

Photo by Dave Latham

Cayuta

The Schuyler County M.C., based in Cayuta, NY, began to host a 150-mile national championship around the beginning of the 1960s. Earlier they hosted a NY State championship. Dave Barnes, who rode a BSA single in many prestigious enduros in the East, and usually finished high in the results, was the driving factor and pathfinder for the event. He did an excellent job of layout and administration of the run, which had a lot of great off-road riding, and he used very few roads. It was far-and-away my favorite national.

I rode Cayuta for the first time in 1961 and finished first in Class A Lightweight on a 250 cc DMW. What can I say – it was my type of run. It was the first time I had ever ridden in a national championship and my final score ranked in the top ten overall. John Penton won that first event on a BMW 250. Only about one-third of the 73 entries went the entire distance, which can usually be attributed to the toughness of the course, although it was ride-able all the way.

Cayuta was the place where I first met Bill and Millie Baird. Ralph and I usually stayed at a motel in Horseheads, NY, about 12 miles from the start of the run. We used a restaurant across the street for our breakfast and dinner. One evening in the early sixties, we entered the restaurant while Bill and Millie were there. As soon as we came through the door, they invited us to join them at their table.

I had never met Bill Baird and didn't recognize him at first. I found them to be one of the most affable couples I have ever met. We immediately became friends and have retained that friendship for more than 40 years. It's one that I've cherished over the years, as they are always a joy to be with. Even to this day, if they get to an AMA dinner before I do, they'll always save a seat for me.

Besides having won the national enduro championship seven consecutive years during the 1960s, Bill Baird was a true sportsman who exhibited as much or more sportsmanship at our game than anyone I know. During a time when other top riders would bend the rules to gain an advantage, Bill always played the game aboveboard, and he still emerged the champion. He was a fine example of an enduro rider from the golden age.

In the late 1960s, when it became common knowledge that a few of the well-known national riders were making a regular practice of bending the rules to gain an advantage, Bill Baird quietly, but permanently, hung up his leathers and retired.

One of the problems in our sport was that not everyone played the game at the same level of sportsmanship. It seemed that when the stakes were high enough, like when competing for the national championship, there were some who would go to great lengths to win. It was common knowledge that the practice was rampant at the ISDT in Europe, but not here.

Riding the course, or having it scouted before the day of the event, was one of the things forbidden by our rules, as was cutting the course to avoid an obstacle. I had heard that Cayuta was one of several places where these practices had been detected. I always knew it went on regularly at Jack Pine, but having it happen at Cayuta, my favorite national, where I was able to do well, was upsetting to me too.

Seven times national champion Bill Baird setting up his route sheet holder before one of the national events, under Millie's affectionate supervision. I found them to be one of the most affable couples I have ever met. Note the lack of a six-figure support vehicle, or any factory or trade support of any kind. Bill competed totally at his own expense, and rode with the machine as it came out of the crate, except for a few minor personal modifications. Bill once passed me at Sandy Lane; after which he calmly returned a wave and a smile to a child spectator, while I struggled to maintain control on the rough trail.

Photo by Boyd Reynolds

A few of the better performances I put in at nationals were at Cayuta. This was taken in 1966, the year I also won the championship in New England at age 41. I got the 4th highest score overall that day at Cayuta, riding in the Senior Class.

Photo by Boyd Reynolds

Bill Baird looked the same as any other enduro rider out there on the trail. If it weren't for the icon of the State of Illinois on the side of his helmet, and the fact that he was moving a bit faster than just about everyone else, one might never recognize him. Here, with Millie looking on, he splashes through a mud hole the same way I might do. They always came to the events in their private vehicle, just like all of the other independent riders.

Bill Baird would have been the quintessential enduro rider, except that he usually won so much more than anyone else. He kept his equipment in good condition; never received any factory support; and he rode with the same time keeping equipment as anyone else. I figured he must have been a master at not only time keeping, but also concentration, riding fast in the tight stuff, riding fast on the third-gear trails, and figuring out from his route sheet where the next check might be located. He must have also had a cool enough head to ride slower when his watch told him he was about to run early.

As many years as he tried, and I think it was around 13 times, he only won Jack Pine once, and that was in 1968, the last year that he rode. If I were to broach the subject of Jack Pine in his presence, Millie would usually nudge me and shake her head, like, "Let's not bring up that subject." Knowing about some of the things that went on at Jack Pine, it wasn't hard to understand that he might be sensitive about it.

Photo by Boyd Reynolds

This photo was taken at the 1967 150-mile national at Cayuta, when I finished 4th overall for the second consecutive year. It appears from my expression that I was having fun splashing around in the water, which I was.

Photo by Boyd Reynolds

Receiving the award for the New England Enduro Grand Championship from Al Eames, at the conclusion of the 1966 enduro season.

I also won the Woods Class Championship in Metropolitan Sports Committee competition in 1966. Ralph Spencer (center) was 2nd, and Bob Maus (left) was 3rd. Bob also won a 3rd in the Road Class that year – hence the two trophies.

This photo was taken at the Tompkins County 90-Mile National Championship in Newfield, NY, near Ithaca. It was run on a totally miserable day in April 1968, when it rained all day. Only about 33 riders finished the entire course. I finished 3rd in Class A Medium Weight. Our RAMS #1 team took 2nd place in the team competition, as all three members of our team finished. Bill Baird won high score in the event, riding with a brand new suit of leathers, with the word, TRIUMPH across the front of it. When I asked Millie if he was really planning on riding with those beautiful leathers, she said, "It's the only thing Triumph ever gave him, since he started riding; so yes, he does intend to wear them."

Photo by Boyd Reynolds

Using the legitimate method of skirting the edge of a "bottomless" mud hole at the 1969 90-mile national at Newfield, NY, although it's occasionally gotten me into even more difficult situations – like at Sandy Lane, for example.

He often went unrecognized at the national events, but his name was well known to the entire enduro community; Al Sedusky (left) was the inventor and supplier of AlJo brake linings that would work when totally waterlogged. It was rare that even purpose-built enduro bikes of the mid sixties were equipped with waterproof brakes. Enduro riders from all over the country would send their brake shoes to Al to be relined. Here he is waiting to start with Gene Esposito.

Both photos by Boyd Reynolds

Riding in the 1969 Curly Fern, a 95-mile national. Following me into a swampy area is Buck Walsworth, riding an Ossa Pioneer. He was an up-and-coming rider at this point. He returned to win high score at the 1970 Curly Fern the following year, while I won a first in Class A Heavyweight. Buck Walsworth was an excellent enduro rider who would often go unnoticed.

Photo by Boyd Reynolds

From the time I first started riding enduros, I had thought about how great it would be if manufacturers would come up with a good lightweight four-stroke motorcycle, built for the enduros. The machines that came the closest in the early days to being enduro bikes were a few English two-strokes, like the Villiers-powered DMW and DOT. But each left a lot to be desired in dependability and reliability; and they weren't always easy to start. Power was also lacking, but power wasn't always as important as a few other factors.

Most manufacturers were more concerned with their ability to market the product, and at that time there weren't enough enduro riders around to constitute a real market. It was commonplace to see only 35 and 40 riders show up for a local event in the late fifties and early sixties, whereas in 1970, one RAMS enduro in New Hampshire drew almost 400 entries, and about 85% of them were purpose-built lightweight two-strokes.

Toward the end of the 1960s, John Penton, John Taylor and a few others began to introduce new purpose-built machines that were designed and manufactured to withstand the abuse that they were being subjected to. Although most of those were two-strokes, the new designs incorporated many features that made them tougher, more reliable, and much better machines.

In hindsight, when I went looking for a motorcycle in 1970 to replace my aging 1968 Triumph, I probably should have switched to the Ossa. It was obvious that the Ossa Pioneer was doing well, as was the Husqvarna and the Bultaco, although all were two-strokes and I was looking for a good four-stroke with a local dealer.

Of the 500 Triumph riders from the 60s, Gene Esposito went first to Bultaco and then to Husqvarna, Don Cutler switched to the Ossa, Bill Baird seemed to have given up riding enduros altogether and Bud Peck tried a Ducati, a big Suzuki and a few others, but nothing brought back the thrill and pleasure of riding the old 500 T100C Triumph. I switched temporarily to a 250 Suzuki. It wasn't until 1979 that I was able to acquire a decent four-stroke single, purposely built for enduros, the Honda XR500. But by that time I was 54 years old.

Chapter Ten

The Berkshire Trials

Organizing and promoting long, challenging endurance runs and making them happen has always been a huge task, even for an energetic club with many members and help from other clubs. It requires a knowledge of countless miles of abandoned roads and trails on which to lay out the course, the time and manpower to do it, measuring distances between the turns, recording them, preparing the route sheets and tacking up the arrows. There's also a huge amount of logistics involved with planning a run, obtaining permission from landowners, talking with police departments and village officials, planning and setting up the checkpoints, finding people to man them, ordering the trophies, preparing all of the paperwork involved, and many other chores, before, during, and after the event.

As soon as the run is over, the task of figuring out the scores begins, followed by the presentation of trophies and awards, additional mailings, announcements and publications. The longer the run, the more work it involves. And too often when it's all over, riders who have had a bad day will blame everything that happened to them on the organizers; and much too seldom would anyone take the time, effort and courtesy to thank the club, or complement them for a great event.

New England has always had enough motorcycle clubs to put on endurance runs, but by the mid-1960s most of those clubs had either lost territory or lost interest in organizing runs of 100 miles and longer; especially when so many of the contestants of that era preferred riding shorter runs, for a number of reasons. I would have loved to see runs of 200 miles and longer. I preferred riding enduros to either scrambles or trials in the first place because it provided a full day of riding in the woods, in a highly competitive and mind-challenging game. The longer the run, the more worthwhile it was for me to travel the distance, especially for the good ones.

The Pioneer Valley Motorcycle Club organized long runs in the Berkshires for years, culminating in their successful 1961 Covered Wagon 200-mile National Championship; but they were no longer putting on any runs by the mid-sixties. The Meriden Motorcycle Club, one of the oldest in the country, had also given up running the Great Eastern Championship due to a loss of many of the trails and woods roads in the area, either due to the state closing the forests to motorcycles, or from the population explosion in that part of Connecticut.

They did, however, continue to put on a much shorter closed-course enduro, in what they called their "Boneyard," which was the rocky, hilly piece of land adjacent to and immediately behind their clubhouse. Most other clubs were doing well to put on and successfully run any enduros of 100 miles or more; and it was becoming commonplace to see 70 to 90-mile open-course runs, and 20 to 30-mile closed-course runs.

A few of the larger clubs still organizing enduros in the New England hill country during the mid-sixties were the RAMS and the Connecticut Ramblers. Of note among the others were the Greylock Riders, Rifle City Riders, Springfield M.C. and New London M.C. A few other clubs would occasionally put on enduros, but most of those were rare, or were run in less hilly terrain. The RAMS sponsored an average of two to three runs a year and sometimes more, as did the Ramblers, but neither had the capability, manpower or territory to organize an event of 150 to 200 miles, and certainly not one longer than that.

Soon after the Pioneer Valley Club ran their last Covered Wagon, Al Eames of Pittsfield, along with his club the Greylock Riders, began to organize a few excellent short runs called the Sugar Loaf and Greylock Enduros. Buoyed by the success of these shorter runs, Al began to work on what later became known as the "Berkshire International Trials." He chose to run his new event under international rules similar to those used in the International Six Days Trial (ISDT), which had been run in Europe for more than 40 years.

Al wasn't familiar at the time with enough territory, nor did he have enough manpower to put on a six-day event, so he started with something much smaller, his first attempt being a long one-day event. Whether he believed at that time that he could eventually organize a six-day run in the Berkshires, and seek full international recognition, I don't really know; but with the help of club members, friends from the area, and a few other clubs like the RAMS, he began his untiring efforts toward organizing the first international-style event in New England. I believe it might have been the first-ever in this country.

I was probably in the minority, and maybe I still am, but I had always favored the traditional AMA-style endurance runs, organized and administered under AMA rules, where the brainwork and concentration involved in keeping time on the trails was one of the primary factors. With the international-style event you could leave your watch in the car, and as long as the course was well marked, you could leave the route sheet there too, and just go racing for the day. The primary object under international rules was to get to a series of known checkpoints within a prescribed time limit. It became more like a long cross-country race, with many little rest stops along the way.

The advent of factory support for some of the riders then injected money into our game, which suddenly made the sponsored rider's motivation different from the motivation of the independent riders, who were still competing primarily for the fun of it, and for their personal glory. A significant advantage swung to the side of those with factory support. So, between the international rules and the factory support, I thought at the time that it began to signal the end of the golden age of enduros, as we once knew it.

Although I loved riding in the Berkshires and probably would have ridden Al's first event in 1965 if I had the time and a good running machine, I didn't have either. I had just run the 250-Mile Little Burr the previous weekend, where I not only had problems with the Triumph, but I also missed our family's Memorial Day picnic; not to mention Lillian being eight months pregnant with our fifth child. So I chose to skip his event in favor of spending time with my family, and using some of that time to get my equipment back into working order. Apparently my presence was missed at the run and many thought that I was deliberately snubbing the event.

That first Berkshire Trials was held on June 6, 1965, using two laps of slightly less than 90 miles each and starting at Happyland Ski Area on US Route 20 in Becket, Mass. The international rules called for special tests along the way, so Al included a timed hill-climb test in the morning and a timed cross-country test in the afternoon.

I think the reason Al originally chose June 6th was because it was well after the spring thaw and the worst of the

1964 New England Grand Champion Bill Perry won a silver medal in the 1965 Berkshire International Trials.

Al Eames front-running the course on his DOT

Photos scanned from Cycle Sport Magazine

heavy spring rains in the Berkshires. For my own partiality to long, wet-and-sloppy runs, I would have preferred mid-May, which was the time he eventually chose for subsequent Berkshire Trials events after experiencing excessive heat during that first one. Weather has always been a major factor in planning endurance runs in the northern Berkshires, where the woods can often become totally impassable in the early spring – first from the heavy snow on the trails, and later from the deep mud created by the spring thaw and the almost continuous rains.

The Pioneer Valley club ran their Covered Wagon in the fall, after most of the heat was gone and before the fall foliage season, when the woods are much drier. Although being more fun to ride, the dry trails are less challenging for the "endurance" part of the game. Another deterrent in the fall is the increased number of hikers in the woods.

The time schedule was set at 24 mph throughout, with no penalty for early arrival at the checks, per the international rules. At noon, two riders remained without penalty, Sal Scirpo and Paul Cramer. Twelve others were still eligible for silver medals with less than 25 points lost.

It wasn't long before the top runners began to have problems. Sal Scirpo rolled in by mid-afternoon after having gotten lost. Cramer came in on a truck, as his gearbox had packed in. Don Cutler, with only 1 point lost in the morning, came in with a flat, having ridden 35 miles on the run.

Of 70 who started the 1965 Berkshire, 18 completed the entire course, although no one finished with the perfect score needed to earn a gold medal. Chuck Boehler emerged as top man, earning a silver medal. Also earning silver medals were Bill Perry, Veto Bonan and Roger James. Fourteen others took bronze medals. Roger James set the fastest time in both the hill climb and cross-country tests.

The second Berkshire Trials, in 1966, was planned to be a two-day event, held on May 21st and 22nd. I rode it in spite of the 22nd being Lillian's and my wedding anniversary. Al laid out a 180-mile loop, which included twice the number of trails he used in the 1965 event. It started again from the Happyland Ski Area in Becket. The plan was to use the same 180-mile loop on both days, but with a faster 26-mph schedule. Two special tests were scheduled for each day.

All machines entering the event were inspected late Friday afternoon and placed in a locked paddock. All essential components such as the engine, the wheels and the suspension units were marked to ensure that the identical parts were still on the machine at the end of the run.

The event drew 114 riders, an increase of more than 60% from the previous year, which was certainly a credit to Al's organizing, and the word was getting around that it was a premier event. It was the first time that a run of that length, 350 miles, had ever been held in New England. Al used many of the trails that would later become known to many, like Torrey Mountain Road, the rough trail leading to and over Petersburg Mountain, as well as the deep water and mud of the infamous Sucker Pond. He also included a few unpredictable beaver dams, where the conditions can change overnight.

Al spent several months laying out the course, using primarily old town roads and rights-of-way that would require steady hard riding from the contestants to maintain the faster, 26-mph schedule. The choice of checkpoint locations and the proper mix of rugged terrain and decent roads were vital to the success of the event. Deep spring mud in the mountains would introduce an unexpected additional obstacle for the second day.

Many riders easily ran ahead of schedule early in the run and enjoyed the scenic Berkshire mountain country, but as the day progressed, more and more of the less-experienced riders dropped behind. Some of the two-stroke machines ran out of gas in the first 60 miles, even before the first planned gas stop.

A 15-minute noon layover was planned in the town of Readsboro, VT. Up to that point, which was about 95 miles out, the run had included several tough mountain roads with mud and rocks; and also some easier going on woods roads and improved dirt roads. The toughest test came right after lunch, in the form of nine miles of old stage road across Woodford Mountain, in the Green Mountain National Forest in Vermont. The road was arduous due to the spring mud, sinkholes and beaver dams that flooded much of it under a foot or more of water. About 10 miles of good road lay beyond, and then into a check at the foot of Petersburg Mountain in Pownal, VT.

The top riders made it into the check with very little time to spare and were immediately faced with the hill-climb test, a 1½-mile climb over the muddy abandoned dirt road to the top of Petersburg Mountain. It was unrelentingly steep the entire distance, with several switchbacks, turns, and alternate dry spots and mud; and many water bars, which are diagonal dams a foot or more high built across the roadway to run off water, and cut down on erosion. Many riders had problems, but the successful ones were making it up the hill in the 5-to-6-minute range. Don Cutler and I set the fastest times on the hill, and we received 60 bonus points each for our efforts.

From the top of the hill, the course ran for about a mile along a hiking trail that was more than a thousand feet above the valley; then down the New York side, along another steep logging road and back to good dirt; and then we had some pavement that led us into a checkpoint at New Ashford, Mass., after which the course entered the Mt. Greylock reservation.

From there to the finish the course used portions of the Appalachian Trail, followed by more abandoned town roads. One section ran directly through the center of the town of Cheshire, where Al had done a lot of public relations work. The police didn't bother us at all. Some residents even sat at the roadside to watch us come through, en route to the Cheshire Harbor Trail.

Late in the day, and with only about 10 miles to go, we arrived at the acceleration-brake test on a section of dirt road in Washington, Mass. The town had graded the road for the event. Each rider had to make a standing-start, followed by a 100-yard dash, and he had to stop in a small area 10 feet beyond the finish line; that is, if he wished to remain without penalty. Some went way too far, sliding and spilling to a stop beyond the line, while others, like myself, slowed down too soon and had to gas it again to make it to the stopping area.

Don Cutler turned in the fastest time at 7.8 seconds, as he slid sideways to a stop in the 10-foot stopping zone, which earned him another 60 bonus points. Several riders endured wild gyrations trying to stop with waterlogged brakes.

On Saturday night, 49 of the original 114 starters parked their machines in the locked paddock, of which 20, including myself, were "still in the gold," meaning no points lost on the trail. Parking the machines in the paddock overnight is another integral part of the international rules. It is designed to prevent working on the machines after the start of the run. Riders are granted 15 minutes to service the bikes Sunday morning, just before starting out on the second day.

Al Eames was discouraged as he came in. He had ridden the course ahead of the riders to check arrows, and later he rode

Myron Hooker   John Taylor   Bill Moss
Larry Browe   ·Bill Dutcher   Bud Peck   Sal Scirpo   Piet Boonstra   Phil Bourdon
                                                                                              Bob Maus
        Ron Moon   Gary Nelson   Don Cutler   Dick Vittone   Jim Moroney   Jess Thomas

Most of the gold medal winners from the 1966 Berkshire International Trials

RAMS #1 was the winning team in the 1966 Berkshire International Trials

1966 silver medal winners, from left: Timmy Sochia, Jack Sartorius, Harold Ward, Dick Heins and Bob Wagner.

Most of the 1966 bronze medal winners are -- in front, from left: Jim Helliwell, Ed Chartier, Bill Fitzgibbons, Dick Thayer, (?), and Bob Hogan.

Standing, from left are: Pete Niemi, Dick Hall, Henry Royce, Ken Gardner, Charlie Coles, Jacques Cadgene, Dale Schmutzler, Dick March, (?), (?), David "Pop" Moody and Manny Swass.   (Sorry I couldn't recognize everyone.)

Photo from Cycle Sport

behind them to recheck the course. The conditions of a few of the sections were so bad that he was determined to get out on the trail at first-light on Sunday and reroute some 20 miles that he judged to be virtually impassable. The original plan was to run the first day's course in reverse on Sunday.

Several of the riders still in the event were totally exhausted after the first day, and many would have been just as happy to skip the second day, as the course would become badly churned up, with even deeper mud; and it would become almost impassable. Most of the riders seemed to have had enough; although I, for one, was actually looking forward to riding on Sunday, as it would become an extreme test of riding through deep mud and over slippery rocks, roots and ruts for the entire day, and regardless of the AMA rules or international rules, very few would survive.

Dawn on Sunday found heavy rains pouring down, which had been falling since 1 a.m. The prospects of trying to reroute large portions of the course in the downpour were appalling to Al. So, at 6 a.m. the decision to cancel was made. I was hoping to go, but there were others who said, "If you say we go, we go, but I won't be happy about it." I learned that Don Cutler wouldn't have been able to ride the Sunday portion because his shoulder was acting up. The awards were given out Sunday morning at 8 a.m., an odd time for an awards ceremony.

The final tally of the 47 medal winners, those who completed the entire course within the one-hour-late limit, was: 20 gold medals, 5 silver (less than 25 points lost), and 22 bronze medals (finishers). The RAMS #1 team of Bud Peck, Ken Gardner, Pete Niemi and I was the only team to finish all 4 men. Bud and I earned gold medals, while Ken and Pete took bronze. The Cemoto East trade team of John Taylor, Bill Dutcher, Jess Thomas, and Nolan Hill was second, with Taylor, Dutcher, and Thomas all finishing with gold medals. That's the same Bill Dutcher who became founder and director of the Americade Rally held every year at Lake George in Upstate New York.

It required a tremendous effort on the part of Al Eames to set up the Berkshire. He racked up over a thousand miles on his woods bike that year, laying out the course and doing the public relations work. All of the property owners along the route were visited, all of the towns passed through were alerted to the event, and he saw to it that all of the area newspapers carried advance articles of a favorable nature. He also persuaded many of his friends and relatives to work the checks. His goal was to have the run become a major motorcycle event, as well as one that would be accepted by the general public.

In 1967, the third year of it's running, the Berkshire finally attained two-day status, as well as becoming a true international event, in the persons of Arthur Browning and Bill Brooker of England, Oriol Bulto of Spain, and the Canadian team of Carl and Larry Bastedo, Rudi Marczi, and George Kirkpatrick. A record entry of 168 starters represented yet another increase of almost 50% over 1966.

The event also attracted several Midwestern riders, including John Penton, who rode a 360 Husqvarna, a purpose-built motorcycle that was gaining popularity as a true enduro competition machine. The last time I remembered seeing John ride in New England was six years earlier, in 1961, with a 250 cc BMW, when we rode two minutes apart in the 200-mile Covered Wagon. Speaking of the Covered Wagon, I noticed that Coleman Mitchell was also there. He had come out of retirement to ride the old stagecoach trails he knew so well from laying out the Covered Wagon many years earlier.

Mid-May was becoming the traditional date for the running of the event. Al laid out a figure-eight route for 1967, with two laps around an easy 99-mile circuit on Saturday, and two laps around a much tougher 89-mile loop on Sunday. Hot dry winds the week before had dried up much of the mud that is so prevalent in the Berkshires at that time of year.

In spite of it being run as an international-style event, which precludes the time keeping, I thoroughly enjoyed the 1966 Berkshire event, and was looking forward to another great ride. The Berkshire never had trail marker problems or errors in the mileages, or problems with the law, for the entire distance, which could be attributed directly to Al's great organizing efforts and public relations.

On Friday evening I had the opportunity to talk briefly with Arthur Browning and his riding buddy Bill Brooker. Arthur was a top English scrambles rider and a well-known mud expert. I got so busy socializing on Friday night, that I didn't get a chance to look over the entry list to see whom else was there, and who might be riding near me on the trail.

Saturday morning as we lined up for the start, I looked for familiar faces with numbers near mine. I was riding #105, scheduled to leave at 9:05, which I figured would be to my advantage, with very little traffic to contend with and a minimum of churned-up trails. The numbers were assigned by an earlier drawing. In later years they started the lightweights first, giving them the course advantage of riding up front. I noticed that Bob Maus from the Crotona club was three minutes in front of me and Bud Peck, my RAMS teammate, was two minutes behind. Most other top riders seemed to be much farther back.

The first few miles out took us west on the tarmac, up a long, steep grade towards Lee. I picked up a few minutes with the Triumph as I rode slightly above the posted speed limit, since there was no penalty for running early. I carried my watch, although there seemed very little need for it. It said that I entered the first woods section several minutes early. I was riding behind someone I didn't recognize at first on a 250 Greeves with a Pennsylvania plate. I could tell that he wasn't a novice.

I was trying to adjust my thinking to the international rules as we rode. At first I had the urge to go by the Greeves, but since I was already well ahead of schedule, there seemed no need for it, so I settled in behind the guy as he began to set a fairly fast pace. With almost 400 miles to go, it was too early for going much faster. I figured out from watching him ride that it had to be Walt Lohrer from Erie.

Passing someone under AMA rules was different from passing under international rules, particularly the incentive to pass. Riding an AMA event, one would usually pass because he had a definite need to pass, due to his time schedule. Under the international rules, as long as he is early – and he should always be running early – there seemed no critical need to pass, without making it appear like it's a race. My psyche was not tuned to racing, but rather to competing in a timed event.

When we got to the first slippery trail, Lohrer gradually moved away and out of sight. I didn't see a need for going much faster, and I never traveled that fast on high-speed slippery trails anyway. About 5 miles out we went through a deep water hole, followed by an even slipperier trail.

I was going about as fast as I cared to go on the slick surface when I got my first glimpse of this little guy on a Bultaco. My first thought as he flew by was, "Wow, some people have no fear at all," and I began to wonder who that was. I didn't get a good look at the guy, because he passed me and disappeared so fast. I began to realize there were a few more experts out there than I had first thought.

Bud Peck came alongside about 20 miles out and we rode into the first checkpoint together, almost 15 minutes early. I asked Bud if he recognized the little guy on the Bultaco, but he said he didn't. I adjusted some of the slack out of my worn chain, and sat and watched about 20 other riders come in – most running very early. One guy on a heavyweight was hammering out a bent rim with a big rock, while others made minor adjustments, or just sat waiting.

The second section was much like the first. There were a few dry trails, but most were wet, high speed, and very slippery. There were lots of secondary roads thrown in for making up time, if anyone had trouble maintaining the 26 mph schedule. I was on a muddy stagecoach road when my mystery man went by again. This time I thought I was doing pretty good in the deep mud, but he flew by at twice my speed with both feet on the pegs and the back end of the Bultaco whipping from side to side. In a few seconds he was out of sight. I thought about the Road Runner in the TV cartoons, with the "Beep-beep" and he's gone!

A short while later after easing off the speed, since I was already running about 10 minutes early, Bud joined me again and we rode somewhat leisurely up a wet, rock-strewn hill together into the second check. The hill had the potential of becoming a nasty obstacle on the second lap.

The Road Runner was there checking over his Bultaco, while I adjusted my chain for a second time. (Seems as though I always ran with a half-worn chain and tires.) I studied the guy's face, trying to figure out who it might be. He looked older than I, but I couldn't recall ever having seen him. I figured he must be one of the retired New England scramblers, although I couldn't imagine how he could have picked up that kind of woods riding experience merely riding scrambles.

The third and fourth sections were much wetter, and although the water wasn't very deep, the constant spray from the front wheel was finding its way into my air cleaner, where I had jury-rigged a temporary cover. I lost the stock filter cover the previous week in a Connecticut enduro and I didn't have time to get a new one before this run, which was a repeat of one of my main problems. The wire-mesh element I had installed temporarily was not up to the job. It would clear itself in the long dry sections, but it would get wet again in the very next water splash, and then I couldn't get the revs up.

The acceleration and braking test was held at the noon layover, so I removed the filter before entering the test. It made a world of difference with acceleration, but I hit the brakes far too soon again and earned a mediocre score, which proved again that I was an endurance run rider, where I didn't have to do that.

Later, while having lunch at the lodge I watched from a window as Arthur Browning ran the test. He went far beyond the point where I thought he could ever possibly stop in the prescribed area. But he threw the Greeves into a full broad-slide in an instant, with both feet on the pegs. After coming to a stop in the stopping area he turned the bike to an upright position with both feet still glued to the pegs, balancing it there momentarily until his time was recorded; and then he merely let out the clutch and rode away, still standing on the pegs. I wished I hadn't looked! I was already beginning to get a complex from being passed in the woods by some little guy I didn't even recognize.

The afternoon section was a repeat of the morning. The trails were surprisingly easier, after 180 riders had been over them, as most trails had dried up. The edges were worn off most of the ruts and it was easier to spot solid ground; although this time the water holes were deeper, which kept fouling my filter.

We got to the first cross-country speed test soon after lunch. The test consisted of about 3 miles of seldom-used, fairly rough dirt roads with lots of ruts and puddles. I couldn't get the revs I needed out of 2nd gear due to the filter, so I had to use 3rd most of the way, killing my chances for a decent score.

I learned in the next section that my elusive mystery man was indeed fallible. I was in some deep, well-churned mud when he went by me again, in the same way as before – both feet on the pegs and really moving. The mud was fairly deep this time, but he still went by very fast, with the tail end of the Bultaco whipping like an angry cat. Suddenly his front wheel must have struck something in a cross rut, and he took a very spectacular dive over the handlebars and landed in the mud.

I stopped to see if he was OK. He was lying there in the mud laughing! I looked down and said, "Are you all right?" He said while laughing, "Yea, thanks. I'm fine." He was up and away in seconds. I described the incident to Bud at the next check, and Bud said that he had heard at lunch that Dick Mann was somewhere in the starting lineup. I was convinced that this guy on the Bultaco was, in fact, Dick Mann. Putting the name with the face and the riding ability left no doubt.

That night I tried to clean the filter element at the motel, having removed it before putting the bike into the overnight compound. But it was for naught, and the next day it only got worse. My fifteen minutes of free time with the bike was used to put the filter back, gas up, check the oil, oil and readjust the chain, and try to fix the kick-starter. My time ran out, so I finished working on the kick-starter at the first check.

The field of riders on the second day had considerably thinned out, as less than half of the original 168 starters left Becket on Sunday morning, in spite of drier trails. We went east along US 20 toward Chester on about 10 miles of hard-surfaced roads before entering the first woods section. I rode with Walt Lohrer again; and after several miles of dry trail, we crossed the face of the old beaver dam of Covered Wagon days together.

A short while later we turned onto the Knightsville Dam property. I thought we would cross the river with the slippery rocks, and ride up the rough mountain trail on the far side, as we had done so often in the Covered Wagon; but we didn't. I learned later that Al was never able to find the exact spot where the Covered Wagon crossed the river. Instead we followed a dirt road along the riverbank.

On the previous day I had hoped to see Dick Mann on a long dry hill, with lots of rocks firmly hitched to the ground, ruts, and washouts – the kind I usually did well on. It happened in the second section, on just such a hill. I thought I was doing well, but he went by me again with the greatest of ease. It's a good thing I knew who he was, for the sake of my self-respect.

The last 5 miles of that section included a tough swamp. I passed a guy in the middle of it, who had his bike stuck in two feet of mud. I found an easier way to skirt the edge. There was a steep downhill in the last mile of that section with deep water at the bottom, which didn't help my filter much. By the time I arrived at the hill-climb test it was badly clogged again. I wasn't able to use more than a quarter-throttle without flooding the engine. I considered removing it, but not knowing what came afterward, I decided to leave it be.

I sputtered up the hill, which consisted of about a mile of mostly dry, rocky, and rutted trail. The third woods section of the day was tougher, with lots of woods and a long, rough downhill that crossed a stream at the bottom, with huge boulders. I walked the bike across. We continued on a dry trail that was followed by a check on a hardtop road where many spectators had gathered.

On one of the rare occasions that I dropped the bike, Boyd Reynolds was right there to record it. I hit a bare root at the wrong angle. Teammate Bud Peck (right) hung this photo on his office wall, where he kept it for 30 years.

Photo by Boyd Reynolds

The number of riders arriving early at the checks was thinning out, and only Dick Mann and Walt Lohrer were waiting at one of them near the end. I thought Bud might come, but he didn't show before I left the check. I was concerned because he had dropped his bike once while we were running together, and I thought he might have damaged something on it. He did arrive at the check on time though, right after I left.

That afternoon the beaver dam was much easier to cross, and it was no problem to arrive with plenty of time to spare at the second afternoon check. I talked with Dick Mann there and he told me that he was able to lighten big Triumphs like mine considerably by rebuilding the frames. He also mentioned having owned several Greeves.

Other afternoon sections seemed tougher as the mud got deeper. Most of the trails suffered from heavy traffic, after having been used twice. I pulled into the next afternoon check totally beat, and I was beginning to sweat – not only from being overdressed, but also from exhaustion. We had been riding for the better part of two days and I was feeling it.

But familiarity with the sections the second time around helped me to pace myself. After having become familiar with the course, I knew how fast I had to ride to still hit the checks early. The toughest part of the run was over when we got to the river the second time. Bud mentioned that he was also exhausted. I think it was Dick Mann who said, "It makes you feel a little sad that it's almost over, doesn't it?"

Of the 168 entries that left Becket Saturday morning, 41 finished with gold medals. John Penton won overall, for having gotten perfect scores in every special test. Based on those same special test scores, I finished 5th in the heavyweight class. Fifteen riders earned silver medals, while 9 finished with bronze.

I learned later that Dick Mann had gotten a flat tire shortly after the noon control on Saturday. He returned to Becket, repaired the flat, and went back out, arriving at the first afternoon check only 12 minutes late. This ruined his chances for a gold medal, but he was back on time before the second check. He went on to set the second best bonus point score of 497. Only the flat tire kept him from being the top finisher in his class.

Of the 17 teams entered, the RAMS fielded three. Our RAMS #1 team with Bud Peck, Phil Bourdon and Ken Gardner and I won the overall team trophy for the second consecutive year. Only two other teams finished all four riders: the Penton trade-supported team and the RAMS #2 club team.

The next Berkshire, in 1968, was later described as "tougher than intended." Saturday was planned to be relatively easy, but turned out to be a devastating experience for many of the newer riders, as well as for several unprepared experienced riders; as three-quarters of the 240 starters failed to make it through the 187-mile first day. It would have been tough enough dry, but the rains came late on Saturday and finished off most of those still on the trail, as it turned steep hills into mudslides and made the deeper mud holes far too much for many.

I had gotten my new 1968 Triumph earlier in the spring and it handled a little differently than my '66 model, but I had gotten used to it by then, and I had been doing well with it. I thought when I entered the event that having a new machine would be to my advantage, especially since most of my previous problems were due to maintenance and preparation.

The 5-mile cross-country and hill climb test was staged about 30 miles out from the Saturday lunch stop. It was laid out over the same rough, muddy woods road that leads to Petersburg Mountain, followed by the steep, rocky climb up side of the mountain. Don Cutler and I had set the fastest times there in 1966. This time Ron Jeckel and I tied for the fastest time, – he on a Greeves and I with my new Triumph. I began to feel that I "owned" the mountain. Ron and I were awarded Barbour enduro jackets at the trophy presentation for it.

Only 58 riders were still running after the first day. The heavy rains continued to fall all night, adding to the already mushy going, so Al Eames cut the Sunday route to one lap. After having left the bikes in a closed, outdoor compound overnight in the continuous heavy rain, the dead-motor start concerned many, as no one was allowed to start his bike until his moment to leave. Many riders, upon pushing their bikes to the starting line, had to kick several times to get them started. I pushed the trusty Triumph out, and when I got the signal to go, it started with one soft kick, bringing cheers from several of the spectators.

About 80 miles into the Sunday route, I set the 2nd fastest heavyweight time in the hill climb test. It was a steep gas-line hill with many huge water bars, which had to be approached through a patch of deep mud and water. John Penton turned in the fastest time on his Husqvarna.

The air filter on my new machine began to cause the same problems as with my other bike, and consequently knocked me out of the gold on Sunday. I should have removed the stock filter element and replaced it with an aftermarket unit, as the one that came with it was made from some kind of tightly packed fabric that clogged as soon as it became soaked with water.

I lost my gold in one of the wettest and muddiest sections, in the pouring rain, when I couldn't get enough rpm from the engine to make up the time I had lost in a long, tough, watery section. In spite of being concerned that I might destroy the new engine, I stopped along the road in the heavy rain, knelt beside it, and stabbed many holes through the element with a screwdriver to try and relieve it, but I still arrived at the next check six minutes late, which cost me the gold.

The final tally of scores proved how much tougher the 1968 Berkshire was than in 1967. Instead of 41 gold medals, only one was earned in 1968, as only John Penton made it through without trail penalty. Ten riders finished with silver.

Along a sloppy power line in the 1968 Berkshire.

There was plenty of water and sogginess along all of the power lines in 1968.

Photos by Boyd Reynolds

RAMS #1 won the team trophy for the third consecutive year.

Of those, Leroy Winters, on a 125 Penton, was best with 3 points lost, while I was 2nd with six. Only 35 riders completed the entire course to earn bronze medals. In view of the severity of the event, earning a bronze was still quite an achievement.

Team trophies were awarded to the top scoring AMA club team, and also to the top-scoring trade team. Of the 17 club teams entered, only RAMS #1 finished all four riders. Bud Peck, Phil Bourdon, Dave Latham and I took the award for the third straight year, losing 259 trail points and earning 944 bonus points. The Penton Imports team was the top-scoring trade team, as John Penton, Leroy Winters, and Al Born finished with 149 marks lost, but with only 763 bonus points. Tom Penton failed to sign in at the end of the speed test, so he got no score, and was not credited with finishing. The RAMS #1 was the best overall team in the Berkshires for the third consecutive year.

The 5th Annual Berkshire in 1969 was a 330-mile event, starting from the Middlefield Fairgrounds. Saturday morning's course took us north, while we went south from there in the afternoon. The morning included a 3-mile, timed speed test over an eroded stage road, with rocks, mud, and deep ruts. RAMS #1 teammate Dave Latham set the absolute fastest time through it on his 250 Greeves. On Sunday, in the hill-climb test, Dave tied with Ron Jeckel for the fastest time in that test as well.

About half of the 312 starters completed the 188-mile first day, of which 46 were still in the gold. Sunday's course was easier, so the average speed was increased to 26 mph. But the change proved to be an undoing for most riders still in the gold, as the 142-mile loop went east and north into new territory. About midway through the morning, we faced 26 miles of continuous woods roads, tight trails, a few dirt roads, and a 7-mile cross-country speed test, where only 16 riders emerged with their gold medals intact. Of the heavyweights, I scored 5th fastest time through the cross-country test.

Soon after the noon control, where Leroy Winters changed a flat tire that he had run the morning speed test with, we faced a one-mile hill-climb up an old woods road. The hill had at least 25 huge water-bars, which hurled riders far into the air, making it a popular spot for more than 300 spectators.

The 26 mph average was particularly tough to maintain in the final 35 miles on Sunday afternoon. I arrived at the river crossing near the final check with very little time to spare. Eighty-nine riders finished, of which 16 earned gold medals, of 312 who started. I won my third Berkshire gold medal, giving me a total of three gold and one silver since the trials began in 1965, which was the best aggregate performance of anyone. Thirty-three riders earned silver in 1969, and the other 40 finishers were awarded bronze medals.

Two RAMS #1 team riders failed to finish, so we lost the team trophy for the first time in four years, leaving John Penton's Ohio teams to win both team trophies. The Amherst Meadowlarks dropped only 5 enduro marks to take the club team trophy, while Penton Imports dropped 149 enduro marks for the best trade team, as the purpose-built enduro bikes reigned.

Jeff Penton on a 250 Husky was best overall at the special tests, with a gold medal and 386 bonus points. Gordon Razee topped the 125 Class on a Penton with a gold medal and 374 bonus points. Best Open Class rider was Ron Bohn on a 360 Husky, taking a gold and earning 382 bonus points. The newer technology seemed to dominate the event. I managed to finish 2nd in the open class on my Triumph, with 354 bonus points.

Ron Jeckel on a Bultaco 250 set the best aggregate performance across all of the special tests with 393 bonus points, although a broken chain cost him 40 trail marks, which dropped him to a bronze medal.

On May 16, 1970, the earliest date ever for the running of the Berkshire Trials, yet another record entry left Middlefield. After 180 miles of easy going, most of the 370 starters were still in the running Saturday night; but on Sunday morning we faced a challenge of pouring rain at a time when the spring thaw had barely ended in the northern Berkshires. I was one of 80 still in the gold after the first day, of which only 9 would survive the next 150 miles of unrelenting water and deep mud.

A California team, all riding delicate-looking Harley-Davidson Baja 100 cc bikes, and led by none other than Dave Ekins, drew a huge crowd of curious spectators and riders to watch them start. Ekins, who had previously won both the Catalina and Greenhorn enduros, as well as the Baja 1000, was also part of the first American Vase team to compete in the International Six Days Trials in 1964. In all, he took part in five ISDTs and ISDEs, earning two gold medals and one bronze. The team ran only the Saturday course. One member didn't finish the first day, and I have no idea why the rest didn't ride on Sunday.

The wave of heavyweights left Middlefield a full hour after the first of the lightweights started on Sunday. We faced extremely churned-up conditions all day, as the mud on the trails got deeper and soggier as the day wore on. The Colrain power line became like a nightmare to the heavyweights, and it took its toll on almost all of the remaining gold medals, including mine, as torrential rains continued to fall all day.

Bud Peck, riding the same 1966 Triumph that he rode in four previous Berkshire Trials, earned the only heavyweight gold medal in 1970. His Triumph had several thousand enduro miles already logged on it. The other top heavyweight riders, riding trade-supported, hi-tech Husqvarna, a specialized enduro motorcycle, all lost their gold medals during that torturous day. Bud later proudly proclaimed this ride to be his "finest hour."

My problem was caused by my failure to mount a new chain before the event. I had ridden the entire spring enduro season with that same chain, and unfortunately it reached its maximum wear limit along the muddiest part of the Colrain power line, where it flew off several times, as I tried desperately to keep it going and finish within my hour. I had already scored the third fastest time at the Saturday hill-climb test behind Gunnar Lindstrom and Ron Bohn, both riding Husqvarna.

In 1970, Saturday was a good day as many spectators lined the route.

Photo by Boyd Reynolds

But the rains came on Sunday, and combined with the spring thaw, the trails became a total mess. Here a few unidentified 250 cc riders struggle through the mud.

Photo by Marcia MacDonald

Bud Peck and I, with Bud's son George at the start of the 1970 Berkshire.

Photo by Marcia MacDonald

Since Bud's riding position was only five minutes ahead of mine (his number was 69 and mine was 74), I gladly agreed to share my "pit man," Ralph Spencer, with him. It worked out fine until Sunday afternoon, after my problems began. I entered the Colrain power line running almost a half-hour late, with the chain already stretched far beyond its wear limit. I tried to skirt the edges of the deepest mud holes on the power line because every time I got into the deep mud, I'd throw the chain again.

Coming off the power line in the pouring rain, along the steep, narrow downhill trail, I was literally surrounded by a river of mud. The mud flowed down faster than I was going, which was a weird feeling, as I couldn't see solid ground under me. I was clocked into the check 42 minutes late, but still within my

Bud Peck beginning to show extreme fatigue while crossing one of the power lines late in the day on Sunday. By this time, just about everyone else from the heavyweight class were left far behind, and Bud was riding alone.

Photo by Marcia MacDonald

Bud stands alone at a checkpoint, on Sunday afternoon, soaking wet from the torrential rains, and wondering if anyone else is still out there somewhere

Photo by Marcia MacDonald.

Leroy Winters won a gold medal in the 125cc class.

Photo by Boyd Reynolds

There are plenty of rocks to be found in New England. Here the author, once known as the "Master of New England Rockery," goes by two other riders in a rock pile, during the 1970 Berkshire.

Photo by Marcia MacDonald

hour, with a few ounces of strength left. Most of the gas crews and spectators had already left. I looked for my pit crew, but Ralph was also gone. Someone offered to fill me up, so I took on gas and headed for the next section.

  Ralph had been forced to make the difficult decision that a multi-rider pit crew hopes he'll never have to make – to wait for a late rider, who might never show, or to leave and be there for his other rider, who might still be going and doing well. It was even tougher for Ralph because we came to the runs together for years, and he had always been there when I needed him. He hated to pick up and leave, because he knew that if I finally arrived late, I might not be able to find gas; but gas was the least of my problems at the time. I went over my hour in the very next section after the chain flew off a few more times.

Twice New England Grand Champion Frank DeGray along the power line, riding his "Grumph." He built a machine that had a Triumph 500 engine mounted into a Greeves frame.

Photo by Boyd Reynolds

Bob Maus, riding a Bultaco 250, goes around riders stuck in the mud. Bob won a bronze medal, having lost 27 enduro marks, only 2 points out of the silver.

Photo by Marcia MacDonald

Once again the Penton teams took both team awards. Their two lightweight trade teams alone finished five of the total ten gold medallists. No other team came close. Penton-supported riders earned the top special test scores too, as Tom Penton topped the 125 cc Class and Jeff Penton topped the 250 Class. Jeff was also the overall top scoring gold medal winner, taking a first and three 2nd spots in the four special tests.

The Swedish heavyweight riders, Gunnar Lindstrom and Lars Larson, both riding for Husqvarna, were the top scorers at the Sunday cross-country test, but both suffered mechanical problems that cost them trail marks, dropping them to silver. Larson lost 7 points on Saturday, while Lindstrom was stopped on the Colrain power line on Sunday with a broken chain and no repair link. He had to wait for another rider to come along with the correct size link, which cost him four trail marks.

Five of the ten gold medals went to 125 cc class riders, all of whom were on trade-supported teams: Tom Penton, Jack Penton, Doug Wilford, Dave Mungenast, and Leroy Winters. Four 250 cc Class riders also won gold medals: Jeff Penton, Don Cutler, Dave Latham and Chuck Boehler. Chuck had also won the first Berkshire in 1965.

By then Triumph had stopped making the T100C, so when my 1968 reached a point where it was no longer reliable without having to do too much work to it, I bought a 250 Suzuki. It didn't fit me well, nor did it have the power I needed. It even died once near the top of a mountain in a Vermont enduro when it overheated the piston. It would go no farther until I was able to cool it down. The combination of my weight, how I was using it, and what I expected from it was far more than it was capable of giving. It also did not handle as well as the Triumph.

I was able to win high score with it in a few local runs, and I entered and competed in the Senior Class at several national championships with it, usually finishing 1st or 2nd in the class, but it was not nearly as satisfying as competing in the expert heavyweight class. I borrowed a 400 Husqvarna from Jack Nash for a weekend, but it was far too much in the other direction, where I didn't like the wild torque. It would rear up every time I twisted the throttle a little for power. In hindsight, I should have switched to Ossa, like Don Cutler, Dave Latham, Ron Webster and many others did at the time.

I rode the Suzuki in the 1971 Berkshire Trials, and halfway through the first day I lost the front fender. I finished the day with a steady spray of water and mud in my face. I rode without glasses after the mud covered the glasses over so fast that I couldn't see. Riding with bare eyes was OK sometimes, but with a steady spray of mud it gets annoying after a while.

I tried to find a replacement fender for the Suzuki Saturday night, but had no luck, so I decided after hearing the weather forecast of steady rain on Sunday, that it just wouldn't be fun anymore, and it wasn't worth the grief, especially when I believed the Suzuki wasn't up to the task in the first place.

Finally, in late 1972, Triumph came out with the 500 Trophy Trail. I immediately bought one. I was able to go fast through the woods with it, and it would climb the mountains just like before, so I began to get myself back into shape, winning a few enduros with it.

Early in 1973 I got a call from California, from a guy named Foster. He said he was the ISDT team manager for Triumph USA, and he was putting together a Triumph team to ride the six-day ISDT in the Berkshires, which was scheduled to take place in September of that year. He said he had been "talking with Towson," who told him that I was the Triumph rider from the East Coast best qualified to ride in the Berkshires. Towson, MD is where the East Coast distributor was located.

We talked for several minutes, during which time he asked many questions, including, "Could I get the time off from work to ride the qualifiers?" I answered that I would have to check with my employer, since it would probably amount to far more than I had vacation time for. Toward the end of his questioning, he said, "How tall are you?" and, "How much do you weigh?" When I answered 6-foot-4 and 230 pounds, he said, "Oh, Big fellow, eh?" I said, yes, it takes a big fellow to ride a Triumph in the Berkshires. I wondered why he was asking those kinds of questions. The next question was, "How old are you?" I thought to myself, that's what he wanted to know all along!

When I answered 48, there was a long pause on the line. I said, "Are you still there?" He said, "Do you have a son that rides?" I said, "Yes, I've got three of them, but they're not the ones Towson told you about."

The next question rang in my ears for years, "Can you still ride six days?" and then, "Do you think you can win us a gold in Texas next week?" and "Can you be in Oregon the week after and give us gold there too?"

"Look," I said, "I can't promise you anything about Texas or Oregon because I've never ridden there, and I'm a little out of shape from not riding as much lately, to talk about next week, but I'll come up with a gold in the Berkshires for you when the time comes." He asked me to see if I could get the time off, and we would talk again.

I got the OK from my job before his call the following night. After telling him I was cleared by my employer to take as much time as I needed, based on a seldom-used "once-in-a-lifetime opportunity" practice at work, he began diplomatically to tell me that they had made up their minds. He said they have already decided on their team, and he mentioned the names Bud Ekins and Feets Minert.

I knew they were both legends, and I knew a little about each, but I considered them to be primarily West Coast desert riders. I also knew that Bud Ekins actually pioneered off-road motorcycle competition in this country and won several gold medals in ISDTs. He also did a lot of stunt work for the movies, including the famous jump over the fence for Steve McQueen in the *Great Escape*. I wouldn't stand a chance against him.

Feets Minert was also a legendary off-road rider from the 1950s, mostly in desert competition. I even thought he might be older than I was. I wished Fisher luck and added that there's a difference between desert riding and riding the rocks and mud in the Berkshires. I thought about the Harley Baja team that showed up a few years earlier, with brother Dave Ekins, when the team only completed one day.

I learned later that neither rider was used. Bud Ekins had movie commitments, and I forget what it was with Feets. I heard that Foster had chosen two Midwest riders to replace them, John Greenrose and Dave Mungenast. I remembered John from his riding the Cord in Canada; and although I knew he was an expert motocross rider, I also figured he would find the Berkshires different from any terrain he had ever ridden.

I didn't know Dave Mungenast, but I was aware that he had ridden in the Berkshires in 1970 and that he had earned one of the few gold medals that year. But riding a 125 cc Penton in the front of the pack is a lot different from bringing up the rear on a Triumph, especially in the Berkshires. I predicted, based on my knowledge of the terrain that the Triumph team would not earn a single gold medal, in spite of it being run in the fall when the ground was much drier and the conditions were far easier than in the spring. The prediction was accurate.

My personal satisfaction and some degree of vindication came 22 years later, at age 70, when I was invited by Dave Latham to join him and a group of Europeans that he had invited over, along with a few past New England Grand Champions from the 1960s, for a friendly six-day ride in the Berkshires, which Latham billed as the *1995 GS-USA*.

Seems that Dave had ridden the 1993 Transdanubia ride in Europe, which is a rough six-day dual-sport ride from Munich, Germany to Budapest, Hungary, mostly off-road. Besides having won the Senior Class there, Dave made several new friends, and he convinced a few of them to accept his invitation for a friendly six-day ride in the Berkshires. Dave laid out the entire run using many of the original maps that Al Eames used to lay out the 1973 ISDT, and he used many of the same trails.

Four Germans: Willie, Edwin, Matthais and Ralf; and one Swiss rider, Uli, accepted his invitation. Of the past New England Grand Champions from the 1960s who accepted were Bud Peck, Frank DeGray and myself. RAMS rider Jake Herzog, who rode the 1970 Berkshire, and spent 12 days assisting Dave to confirm his layout, rode along with us, bringing up the rear in the "sweep" position. A few others accompanied us for a day or two along the course.

I needed to get into shape because I hadn't ridden seriously in the woods for several years, so I signed up to ride the Beehive Enduro near Cape May, NJ, the week before our six-day Berkshire ride was scheduled. I had a 1979 Honda XR500 that I had ridden in enduros on and off for fun for about 16 years. I hauled it out of the garage and rode it the 200 miles to the start of the Beehive on the morning of the run.

When I went into the firehouse at the starting point of the run to pick up my "rider's packet," the girl said she needed to check out a few things on my entry blank. First she wanted to know, "Are you really 70 years old?" and then, "Are you really an "A" rider?" I thought, how soon they forget. Yes, I was 70 years old, and yes, I was an A rider – 40 years ago, which was probably long before the young lady was born!

I had a little trouble with the carburetor during the Bee Hive and I had to nurse it through the last 20 miles of trails, but I finished, and I won a 5th place trophy in the "Master's Class" for riders over 60, Since I had to get home before dark, and I had about 200 miles to ride, I left for home right after signing into the final check, and without working on the carburetor first.

The problem was with the float sticking. But I learned that I could run for a minute or so before it totally flooded with gas. Then I'd shut the petcock off and run it for another minute or so until it ran out of gas. That worked fine – for a while. I repeated that cycle hundreds of times as I raced for home. But going through the cycle of running far too rich, and then far too lean, over and over again, eventually caused a problem.

I was more than halfway home, doing about 65 on the highway, when I heard the faintest little squeak. I thought, I hope that wasn't the.... – Suddenly it made a much louder squeak as the piston seized and the engine abruptly stopped running. I quickly pulled the clutch handle and coasted to a stop. I found a motel, pushed it there, and called home. The next morning Lillian and one of my sons came to pick me up.

I was trying to get up the courage to tell Dave that I wouldn't be able to make it, when I walked down to my other garage in the back, and I looked at that old '74 Triumph Trophy sitting there, which hadn't run for years. I wondered if there was a possibility that it might still run. Sure enough – after cleaning the carburetor bowl and filing the points, it started on the 2nd kick. I rode it down through the back yard and it felt like it had no suspension at all, as compared with the newer suspension that I had gotten used to. My old eyeballs wouldn't stay caged as the tires ran over the rough surfaces. Then when I tried to slow it down, I realized that the brake pedal was on the wrong side.

I did a lot of soul-searching in the next few days. I still hadn't cancelled, and I hadn't told Dave that I blew the Honda engine. Foster's question of 22 years earlier rang in my ears, "Can you still ride six days?" I was sure I could with the Honda; but I wasn't too sure with the old Triumph, without suspension and with the brake on the wrong side; and we had both aged considerably. Oh well, let's give it a shot!

I pulled the rusty old trailer out of some bushes and tall grass, only to learn that the wheels barely turned and the tires were flat. I serviced it and hooked it up to the same Camaro that I had traveled to many of the enduros with years earlier. I arrived at Dave's Oak Ridge Farm near the Smithsonian Astrophysical Observatory in Cambridge, Mass. where today he searches for intelligent life in the far galaxies.

A few of the Europeans were already there when I arrived, and before they even greeted me, they stood staring in awe at that 21-year-old Triumph perched proudly on my trailer. I think it was all like a joke to them. "Are you really going to ride that thing?" and "Are you really 70 years old?" The big smiles turned to friendly laughter, something to which I've become accustomed.

Sitting next to the specially prepared BMW R80GSs and R100GSs, my 500 Triumph looked small. I did have a problem during the first few days with the brake pedal and shifter being reversed. Several times I got into tight spots where I instinctively went for the brake, but found that I wasn't stepping on the brake at all, but pressing down on the shifter lever. I didn't feel too bad about my riding, though, because the Europeans weren't used to all those rocks either, which made us even.

One of the BMW R80GS machines riding In the Sucker Pond area.

A pit stop for the Triumph. The BMWs had a much greater range than the Triumph. Here it's getting refueled from Dave's tank using a siphon hose.

By the third day I got more accustomed to the strange controls and I was able to keep up with Dave on the tougher trails; as the two of us would often emerge from a tough woods section several minutes before the Europeans; and we'd have to wait for them to catch up. Dave was riding his highly modified R100GS, which was set up especially for the woods. It got so every time we would stop for gas or for lunch, the cameras would come out again, as the Europeans had to get one more shot of the old guy standing next to his Triumph.

Day 3 was a tough one for me for a number of reasons. It was one of our longest, at 182 miles; and the fatigue from being out of shape was beginning to set in. Every time I got off of the bike I had to be careful my legs didn't give out under me; pains were beginning to be felt in several areas, especially in the morning; and I think Dave decided the Europeans have had enough "practice" in the rocks, so he stepped up the pace.

It rained a little on the fourth day, and Uli dropped his R80GS in one of the covered bridges, where the visibility isn't the greatest. He struck some rain-slicked planking at the wrong angle and dumped the bike in the darkness inside the covered bridge. Neither he nor the bike sustained any real damage.

We had a few mechanical problems, mine being with the Lucas electrics; but with Frank DeGray along, we were able to get the Triumph going again quickly. At one point Matthias had some bearings go out in his rear suspension, which caused him to miss some of the run while repairs were being made.

We traveled over many of the same trails as the ISDT, including the steep, rocky climbs on Tunnel Road and Torrey Mountain Road. Dave even included Sucker Pond, which Al Eames had left out of the ISDT for fear that it would become too tough, and become a serious bottleneck. While coming down Tunnel Road, I got moving much faster than I had intended, and I slightly lost control on the rocky downhill. I was standing on the pegs at the time to ease the discomfort of the seat, when I realized I was going much too fast. I went for the brake, but going for it on the wrong side only got me into more trouble. Uli, who had been following, said later that he had never seen anyone so close to going over the handlebars, and simply refused to go! My thighs were practically against the bars before I finally regained control of the old girl.

We rode almost 900 miles in six days, after which Dave invited us into his home for a dinner of filet mignon and corn on the cob. During the dinner Dave broke out a bottle of Scotch, vintage 1966, which was the year I won the New England Grand Championship. It was also the year of the last really good 500 Triumph. Our after-dinner wine was port, also vintage 1966.

I felt that I was totally vindicated from having been dropped from Triumph's 1973 ISDT team 22 years earlier, for having been too old to ride six days. I held up the glass of port and toasted Dave's 1995 GS-USA, which was a fantastic ride that might even have been my own "finest hour."

This photo was taken in front of a motel in Greenfield, MA, just before starting out on our 5th day. We used this location as a central point for three days of our six-day GS-USA Berkshire ride. I am with the Triumph on the far right, while Dave Latham is in the foreground, second from the right, and Jake Herzog is third from the right, also in the foreground.

Photo courtesy of Jake Herzog

Chapter Eleven

Epilog

I still competed in many enduros throughout the 1970s, especially in the early seventies, but the game was never the same again, after having worn out my last Triumph T100C, and after many changes brought about a virtual end to our golden age of endurance runs.

The changes that most affected the game that I enjoyed so much, were the computers taking over the time keeping, the ever-increasing number of trade-supported riders competing against independent weekend riders, and all of the newer, purpose-built motorcycles that were flooding the market. With reliability being built into the newer machines, it resulted in fewer failures, which in turn resulted in less worry about ever breaking down. The runs got faster and faster and many of the contestants began to refer to our little game as a race, which was a word we just didn't use in the 1950s and 1960s.

In 1980, Bud and I returned to ride the Greylock Rider's 100-mile National Championship in the Berkshires the old-fashioned way – by riding our enduro bikes to the event. Except that this time we rode eight days of trails to get there. Since the New England Trail Rider Association had published a book of maps with dozens of full-day trail rides, we thought we'd link together and ride a series of those trails, some in total, and others using portions of the rides. The national enduro started at the Middlefield Fairgrounds, just like the ISDT and several of the Berkshire Trials did years earlier. I was 55 at the time, and Bud was 50, so we would compete in the Super Senior Class.

Except for a flat tire on my machine on the third day and a deep dunking in a beaver dam with Bud's bike on the seventh day, we had no mechanical problems. Both mishaps were quickly corrected. A rim pinch caused my flat. We repaired it on the spot with a small patch kit and two CO_2 cartridges that Bud carried in his luggage. We rode twin 1979 Honda XR500s.

Good practice to test the depth before diving in. Photo taken in Berkshires.

Note the difference in the amount of luggage carried for a 9-day trip.

Herluf Johnson accompanied us on the first two days, while Ed McIntyre escorted us from Somers, CT to Holland, MA on part of the third day. We rode the entire seventh day in the Berkshires with Jake Herzog. The Berkshire section was the best of more than 20 NETRA trail rides that we rode either all or part of on our trip. We also used 184 miles of Bud's "private stock" on the fourth day, in the Monadnock area of New Hampshire, over trails he had scouted while practicing for the enduros in 1968. We rode much of that in fog and drizzling rain. Our fourth day included an impromptu side trip from our planned course along a continuous series of logging roads and un-maintained woods roads for an additional 83 miles.

The fifth day, which was another of our better days, began in Springfield, Vermont, where the trail enters the woods less than a mile from the center of town where we had a motel. It started right up a challenging rock wash for an early-morning eye-opener and continued over many miles of challenging trails, including some that took us deep into the Green Mountains and ended near Greenfield, MA, where we spent the night.

We encountered a good deal of logging activity along the way, since we traveled during the normal workweek. We saw skidders, logging trucks, and loggers cutting and chopping. We exchanged friendly waves with the loggers as we appeared out of, and quickly disappeared into the timber, so fast that it must have left them wondering what they had just seen.

On the morning of the fifth day I got my foot tangled in some roots in a jeep rut, which twisted my ankle. We were on a rough logging road, going uphill. We stopped in Wilmington, VT to purchase an ankle brace, to keep the swelling down, and we continued on our planned route in spite of the pain. That evening Bud picked up a small bottle of blackberry brandy that he claimed would "heal it from the inside out;" otherwise, he offered very little sympathy. He would just grin and say, "If you'd keep your feet on the pegs, that wouldn't happen."

We had a little rain, mostly light drizzle, on the first, fourth, fifth and seventh days. A steady downpour at the start of the seventh day threatened to dampen our pleasure in the central Berkshires. As we sat eating breakfast near a picture window that morning, I asked Bud, "Do you think it's gonna' rain today, Bud?" It was coming down in torrents at the time. Without even glancing toward the window, he answered loudly and emphatically, "No!" Bud hated pessimism.

After getting out onto the trails, we soon forgot about the weather, although the rain offered many extra thrills as the tires would slide out along fallen branches and roots, which would occasionally send one of us off into the woods. By noon that day the sun came out and we rode an extra 45 miles, which was originally planned for the following morning.

Running ahead of schedule left the entire eighth day for servicing the bikes in preparation for the competition on the ninth day. The service consisted of an oil change, a chain adjustment, a new rear tire and tube on my bike, and a new countershaft sprocket on Bud's. I lost the odometer knob from my speedometer on the seventh day. After a futile search for a new knob around the local dealers, I was finally able to borrow a speedometer from a friend to use for the run.

My luggage for the trip consisted of one change of riding clothes, leisure shoes, a rain suit and a selection of spare parts and tools. Bud carried about 30 pounds on his rear luggage carrier, while my load was considerably lighter. I had only about ten pounds, divided between a small handlebar pack and a fanny-pack. Bud carried many spare parts and tools, while I carried my vitamins. For the most part we slept in motels and ate in diners and restaurants; and we usually stopped for lunch at quaint little general stores along the way.

Rating our daily rides on a scale of one to ten, we concluded with a variety of scores from zero to 9½, but the enduro on Sunday was a perfect ten. We arrived at the finish check knowing that we had ridden faster, harder and with more enthusiasm than we had all week – or for years, for that matter. We vowed to do it again the following year, except that we would also return home via a different 5 to 7 days of trails.

Jake Herzog wrote this article for Trail Rider Magazine about yet another unique adventure we enjoyed, riding our enduro bikes to the Cord in Canada in 1982, and then riding them home after the event:

Boonstra's Last Hurrah

The first sign of a grand finale came in August of 1980, when Bud Peck and Piet Boonstra took their eight-day trail ride, ending with their participation in the Greylock national enduro in Middlefield, MA. Piet wrote an article on those nine days, which subsequently appeared in Trail Rider Magazine.

The 1980 Greylock 100-Mile National Championship took place 7 years after the ISDT in 1973. Bud took a second place in the Super Senior Class, while I took the first. Al Eames is seated between us. Standing behind Bud is RAMS club member Ralph Watson of Bennington, VT. Al's wife, Marie, was inside the camper mixing up some of her famous "peach fuzz" for our victory celebration.

The following year, 1981, Piet and Bud planned a longer, sixteen-day ride with the national enduro falling in the middle. After a fine week's ride prior to the national, Piet was injured during the enduro, and was forced to miss the second week. In 1980 I had the opportunity to ride the last couple of days with these guys, and in 1981 I planned on riding the whole second week with them, but unfortunately Bud and I rode the second week without Piet.

The matter of how to top this was dealt with in 1982 at our annual winter "BS Night" at Tom Brigham's place, when Dave Latham said that he was thinking of making a comeback at the Corduroy enduro in 1982. Although Dave eventually declined, Piet jumped on the idea, saying that he would be happy to do the same, but the only way to go was to ride the woods bikes to and from the event. Although I thought it might have been the party atmosphere of the moment, Bud, Al Eames and I agreed to do it with him.

The next step was an 8-day "shakedown," beginning on the 28th of August at Al Eames' house in Dalton, MA, and ending back there on September 4th. This ride covered most of NETRA's trail system in Massachusetts, New Hampshire and Vermont, with a good bit of Bud's "private stock" in New Hampshire thrown in. Bud always spent a great deal of time laying out these rides, and the result was a daily 100-plus-mile ride over the best terrain this country has to offer.

Piet was the only one to complete the eight days intact. On Tuesday Bud discovered several teeth missing from the countershaft sprocket and was forced to ride from Springfield, VT to a bike shop in Northampton, MA to get a replacement. So Piet and I rode the "Reading Loop" without him. I cut my ride short a day, and had my wife Arlene pick me up in Springfield while the others rode the planned course back to Al's.

We now felt ready for our big event – the trip to the "Cord." At this point, Bud's '79 Honda XR500 had over 5,000 miles on it, Piet's over 3,000 miles and my '81 XR500 Pro-Link over 2,000. None required more than normal maintenance.

On Wednesday September 8th, Bud and Piet arrived at my home near Albany, NY just in time to help me change tires and install my windshield. Bud's bike was stock except for a trials tire on the rear. Piet had installed a small fairing and a road tire on the rear for the trip. I went overboard with a windshield, trials front tire and a K81 rear, plus eight teeth less on the rear sprocket – I think. I was ready for Bonneville!

Thursday morning Al Eames arrived with our support vehicle, the 1973 BMW he received as a gift at the 48th ISDT, pulling a borrowed fiberglass trailer. Into the trailer went most of our gear, enduro tires, etc. Anything that wouldn't fit was lashed to the motorcycles.

The first day consisted of a scenic route through the Adirondack Mountains to Alexandria Bay and the Thousand Island resort area. Friday we arrived in Haliburton, Ontario, in early afternoon, with plenty of time to change tires, register and check the bikes in. Because the motorcycles are impounded at night, we anticipated a transportation problem.

Four adults just don't fit on a BMW, even with a trailer. Fortunately however, our cabin had a kitchen, and it was located within walking distance of the start area. Piet agreed to do the cooking, and Friday night we stocked the cabin with supplies for the weekend, including the mandatory back-bacon and Labatt's.

We were surprised Saturday morning at the lack of New England riders at the event. The last time we had ridden here was 1972, and then there were a large number of familiar Yankee faces, and many were winners.

One really has to ride the Cord to appreciate the terrain, organization and generally great atmosphere that Canada has to offer. The British Empire Motorcycle Club has been putting on this run for a good many years, and the spirit the club gives the event is truly inspiring.

The run began at a resort area near Haliburton, and several members travel from Toronto to spend their summer vacations laying out and working on the event. Canadian spectators and support crews seem to put a lot more enthusiasm into an enduro than I've seen in New England in several years.

This spirit became more evident at the start of the event, as the word spread about the crazy, aging Americans who had ridden their bikes to the event, and worse yet, planned to ride them home. We wore the old RAMS blue-and-white striped vests over old Barbour jackets, just like 10 years earlier, but instead of remembering when the RAMS dominated the teams at the Cord; the Canadians were calling us (jokingly) referees, as in ice hockey. The RAMS vests were recognized, however, and we got several thrills through the spectator points, when the crowds yelled and cheered.

Although enthusiasts might forget competitors of the past, it was obvious they don't forget the organizers. From the time he arrived, friends and well-wishers surrounded Al Eames. Al capitalized on his audience by offering a running critique of the Canadian "Brand X" rules, which differed from both AMA and international rules. Al didn't favor them, and with good reason, for they cut "Boonstra's Last Hurrah" a day short.

Piet, always a precise time keeper, went over his hour on the first day, due primarily to his disinclination to ride early, and build up a huge buffer to be depleted during the rest of the run. One was expected to ride the entire event like it was a long cross-country race.

For variety of terrain it's tough to beat the Cord. There is something for everyone including fast dusty trails, good tight stuff, long runs through water, steep hills, bones, and bottomless peat bogs, which are often crossed by corduroy bridges or their famed "monorail."

Saturday ended with three very tired riders retiring early, while Al socialized at the parc ferme. Late that evening we were awakened by the arrIval of our "host," John Hand, the Canadian guy who had made the arrangements for our cabin, and was our liaison to the Canadian way of life.

John turned out to be quite a charming fellow, giving us tips as to how to blend in with the Canadian way of life. We learned to say "eh" quite frequently, drink Labatt's, eat back-bacon, and put vinegar on our French fries. He even ate his soft-boiled eggs from funny little cups that were in the pantry, something I hadn't seen in 30 years.

Unfortunately, our early retirement to the cabin Saturday evening caused us to miss the old movies, some of which showed riders in old RAMS vests, which were probably Piet and Bud, riding together and going very fast in 1968. Sunday morning Bud and I tried to keep the legend alive.

Saddened by the loss of our teammate, we pressed on through some really slick mud about two miles out; then on to the famous "staircase" at the start of the Petersen Trail, some hand-cut sections after the Petersen, about 20 miles of uninterrupted gravel road following a power line, and finally back through a very deteriorated mud section to the finish. After being separated at the "Staircase," Bud and I joined up for the last 50 miles, and rode into the finish together. Even though we didn't have winning scores, the great reception we received made it all worthwhile.

Piet had planned to make use of his day off by preparing a worthy feast, but his plans went awry by "blue laws," or something like them. The stuff he had planned to buy for our victory supper was nowhere to be found. The stores were all closed. He did a creditable job with spaghetti though; and after a day of enduro riding, ending with a tire-changing session, (we figured on getting it done while dirty), it tasted like dinner at Alfredo's.

At the start of the 1982 Corduroy International in Haliburton Ontario. From left in striped vests, riding on #16, are Bud Peck, Piet Boonstra and Jake Herzog. Between Bud and Piet with the big smile is Al Eames. He came along with us, pulling a trailer behind his BMW road bike, with our enduro clothes, tires and tools, and he served as our pit crew.

Photo courtesy of Jake Herzog

    The return trip was made in two easy days. We crossed into the States at the same point, but took a more direct route home with our Monday night layover in Lowville, NY.

    The warm-up ride in New England and the Canadian trip combined, involved over 2,000 miles of riding. The road ride to and from the Cord accounted for about 930 miles alone. The rest was enduro-type terrain. Mechanical problems were practically nil, amounting to a broken bumper mount on the fiberglass trailer, Bud's sprocket problems in Vermont, a flat rear tire on Bud's bike Saturday at the Cord, and a constant problem with Piet's chain oiler dispensing the required one drip every 30 seconds, or whatever.

    Now comes the sentimental part. A couple of weeks after the Canadian experience, Piet, Bud & I got together at Ed McIntyre's for a fall ride with other over-the-hill RAMS members, Eddie Mac, Joe Eaton, Joe Kuzdal, and Perley Parker. Tom Brigham and Charlie Sibley supplied us at various locations along the route with refreshments from Tom's side-hack. It was a good ride, no one got hurt, no breakdowns, etc., but it bothered me, because I knew it would probably be the last trail ride I'd be on with Piet. This became quite clear at the end of the ride when, instead of partying in his usual boisterous manner, he sat alone and silent.

I have never been a serious competitor, I don't have a house-full of trophies, and so it is difficult for me to understand why someone has to quit riding when they no longer feel they are "competitive." After more than 35 years of enduros, Piet made a decision that many riders make after only 4 or 5 years. I know I feel a personal loss knowing that he won't be woods riding with us anymore.

It seems that as we RAMS "get along in years," (to quote Bob Hicks in the February '83 Trail Rider), we've moved a bit toward road riding, with a definite preference for the poor quality, more adventurous tar and dirt roads, Piet having made two separate trips alone to Alaska already in the past few years. I hope he'll come up with a new challenge soon, and hopefully he may let a couple of old riding buddies be part or it.

Appendix

Selected Result Sheets

The following pages represent a compilation of result sheets from many of the enduros I rode during the golden years. I saved most of the result sheets that were mailed to me, all of which are not shown here. The golden age, as I characterize it, ended for me in 1970, for reasons I described earlier. I competed in many national championships after 1970, although I rode most of those in the Senior Class, as I turned 45 in 1970. From the early sixties to the mid 70s, I rode well over 200 enduros, a few times more than 20 runs per year. I rode my last enduro in 1995 at age 70, a run in which I took a 5th place in a special "Master's Class," for riders over 60.

Yonkers M.C. Turkey Run - November 14, 1948

(96 Total entries)

1 (HS)	Albert Kroeger	Triumph	Rochester, NY	984
2	Don Pink	H.D.	Yonkers, NY	979
3	Sal Scirpo	H.D.	Middletown, CT	976
4	Albert Haessig	Indian	Wallkill, NY	974
5	Julius Kroeger	Triumph	Rochester, NY	971
6	Warren Sherwood	Matchless	Cornwall, NY	970
7	Spike Griffin	Norton	Ninevah, NY	960
8	Dorrance Wood	Triumph	Binghamton, NY	955
9	Rod Coates	AJS	Pluckemin, NJ	944
10	George Farrier	Jawa	Philadelphia, PA	910
11	William Kelly	B.S.A.	Belair, MD	901
12	Randy Bynoe	Matchless	Amityville, NY	885

Novice Class (60)

1	Wm. Mulholland	Matchless	Nyack, NY	963
2	Jack Corriell	Matchless	Roselle, NJ	956
3	Henry Vondermock	Triumph	Nyack, NY	953
4	Gordon Potter	Harley Dav.	Rochester, NY	948
5	Jack Mercer	B.S.A.	Bronx, NY	937
6	Sheldon Unold	Harley Dav.	Tappan, NY	925
7	Drew Smith	Harley Dav.	New York, NY	919
8	Herky Leatherwood	Harley Dav.	Bridgeport, CT	899
9	Duane Wert	Triumph	Bedminster, NJ	866
10	Chris Christenson	B.S.A.	Westfield, NJ	833
11	George Maune	Harley Dav.	Brooklyn, NY	817
12	Robert Crane	Triumph	Clifton, NJ	753
(16th)	Piet Boonstra	Harley Dav.	Buchanan, NY	161 mi.

Sidecar Class (10)

1	Clem Murdaugh	Indian	West Chester, PA	972
	George Graff		Wilmington, DE	
2	I. Charbonneau	Harley Dav.	Newburgh, NY	859
	J.T. Washington		Rock Tavern, NY	
3	Frank Dean	Harley Dav.	Souderton, PA	802
	Ralph Hesmere		Montgomeryville	
4	Louis Yeager	Indian	Feasterville, PA	560
	Clarence Allen		Hatville, PA	
5	Al Weinert	Indian	Newburgh, NY	138 mi.
	Alfred Hein		Newburgh, NY	

Yonkers Turkey Run
Yonkers, NY - November 18, 1956
(47 Total entries)

High Score

Don Pink	HD	975

Class A Light (11)

Joe Kastner	HD	975
Don Whyte	DMW	971
Bob Maus	Tri	966
Drew Smith	DMW	40 mi.
Leslie Pink	HD	30.4 "

Class A Heavy (7)

Jim Fennell	Tri.	955
Gene Esposito	Tri.	890
R. Williamson	HD	100 mi.
Chas. Watson	Tri.	45.2 "
A. Roberts	HD	10.4 "

Class B Light (5)

Piet Boonstra	HD	879
Ralph Spencer	Tri	99 mi.
Nick Tusa	Tri	52 mi.
R. Thompson	Tri	40 "
R. Dannenburg	BSA	10.4 "

Class B Heavy (24)

S. Cardinale	Tri	943
Whitey Loud	AJS	926
John Weigold	Allstate	899
Al Weinert	Tri.	880
Cliff Caswell	AJS	871

Club Team – Crotona M.C.
Pink, Whyte & Fennell

Maple Leaf Enduro
Hoosick Falls, NY – October 6, 1957
(43 total entries)

High Score

Charlie Schumitz	Match.	997

Class A Light (4)

Manfred Schmid	DOT	994
John Miller	Ind.	987
Greg Lipsky	Allstate	976
Les Beach	Adler	948

Class A Heavy (8)

Jim Fennell	Tri.	996
Paul Walton	AJS	994
Richard Chandler	AJS	993
Melvin Kraft	Tri.	992
Coleman Mitchell	Tri.	991

Class B Light (11)

William Rich	Tri.	991
Ralph Spencer	DMW	976
Charles Hebert	Zund.	974
William McDermid	TWN	954
Piet Boonstra	HD	949

Class B Heavy (20)

William Brittain	BSA	990
Bob Hogan	Match.	990
George Ellis	Tri.	988
Wayne Hovey	Tri.	986
Ron Alleman	Tri.	986

Club Team – Milford Riders
Schumitz, Walton & Chandler

Pioneer Valley M.C. Covered Wagon Enduro
Southwick, MA – September 29, 1957
(110 total entries)

High Score

Don Pink	HD	992

Class A Light (9)

Joe Kastner	HD	990
Robert Maus	Tri.	978
Manfred Schmid	DOT	973
John Miller	Indian	963
Drew Smith	DMW	963
Leslie Beach	Adler	938
Henry Zientek	Maico	928
Greg Lipsky	Allstate	878
Leslie Pink	HD	79 mi.

Class A Heavy (12)

Jim Fennell	Tri.	987
Paul Walton	AJS	987
Everett Wright	Tri.	981
Frank Kokoszka	Tri.	970
Gene Esposito	Tri.	948
Chuck Oakes	Tri.	943
Melvin Kraft	Tri.	927
Boyd Reynolds	Tri.	917
Ralph Potter	HD	101 mi.

Class B Bantam <175 cc (8)

Harold LaRose	HD	662
James McCauley	HD	149 mi
Robert Schilling	NSU	140 "
Walt Zientek	BSA	101 "
Piet Boonstra	HD	52 "

Class B Light 176-to-250 (25)

Walt Knights	Tri.	977
Fred DePaso	Tri.	927
Anthony Castanza	Tri.	889
Bob Wagner	Zund.	889

Class B Heavy (50)

George Ellis	Tri.	976
Richard Hansen	BSA	960
Wilfred Chabot	Tri.	955
Charles Harrison	Tri.	952
Seaton Dewey	Tri.	947

Dealers (6)

Bob Hogan	Match.	935
Herb Mogul	Indian	930
Ralph Strong	Indian	883

Club Team – Tri-State Motorcycle Club, Hoosick Falls, NY
Chuck Oakes, Seaton Dewey & Walt Knights

Meteor M.C. Sandy Lane Enduro
Atsion, NJ – October 20, 1957
(148 total entries)

High Score (tie)

Jim Fennell	Tri.	995
Ed Elliott	BSA	995

Class A Light (20)

Joe Kastner	HD	993
Cliff Guild	Tri.	986
Frank Dean	HD	982
D. Rohde	Tri.	967
H. Burton	Jawa	964

Class A Heavy (20)

John Penton	BSA	993
Don Pink	HD	992
C. Stall	HD	992
R. Stall	HD	990
G. Slater	Match.	990

Class B Light (61)

R. Bauman	BSA	984
R. Redden	Tri.	964
R. Wagner	Zund.	963
D. Riegel, Sr.	HD	955
(10th) Piet Boonstra	HD	900

Class B Heavy (47)

D. Wolfe	Ariel	994
Whitey Loud	Tri.	990
T.Grimm	AJS	987
T. Robinson	BSA	987
Sky Ball	Tri.	981

Referee – Pete Epley
Scorer – Bill Wollerton

Crotona Halloween Classic
Yorktown Heights, NY – October 27, 1957
(78 total entries)

High Score

Frank Kokoszka	Tri.	987

Class A Light (14)

Joe Kastner	HD	987
Tom Svack	HD	979
Manfred Schmid	DOT	948
Greg Lipsky	Allstate	858
Joe Denny	HD	857

Class A Heavy (16)

Charlie Schumitz	Match.	971
Paul Walton	AJS	971
Gene Esposito	Tri.	958
Everett Wright	Tri.	949
Coleman Mitchell	Tri.	941
Richard Chandler	AJS	933

Class B Light (24)

Walter Knights	Tri.	975
Bob Redden	Tri.	971
Piet Boonstra	HD	957
Ralph Spencer	DMW	934
Paul Kerr, Jr.	DMW	910

Class B Heavy (23)

Sky Ball	Tri.	978
Whitey Loud	Tri.	971
Sam Cardinale	Tri.	970
Ron Alleman	Tri.	951
William Brittain	BSA	949

Club Team – Milford Riders
Schumitz, Walton & Chandler

Great Eastern Championship Endurance Run
Meriden, CT – November 10, 1957
(47 total entries)

High Score

Coleman Mitchell	Tri.	934

Class A Light (11)

Don Pink	HD	860
John Miller	Ind.	857
Joe Kastner	HD	832
Manfred Schmid	DOT	743
Robert Wagner	Zund.	105.6 mi.

Class A Heavy (7)

Paul Walton	AJS	901
Charlie Schumitz	Match.	891
Jim Fennell	Tri.	886
Don Burnett	Tri.	857
Christy Scholar	BSA	16.8 mi.

Class B Light (13)

James McCauley	HD	904
Douglas Hill	DMW	895
Piet Boonstra	HD	865
Ralph Spencer	DMW	798
Ned Smith	Indian	69.6 mi.

Class B Heavy (16)

Ron Alleman	Tri.	872
Bob Burnett	Tri.	836
Douglas DeCosta	Tri.	808
Frank Held	Nor.	775
Charles Harrison	Tri.	711

Club Team – Conn. Ramblers
DeGray, Alleman & Harrison

Meriden M.C. Endurance Run
Meriden, CT – April 20, 1958
(32 total entries)

High Score

Richard Chandler	Veloc.	998

Combined A & B Light (13)

Joe Kastner	HD	995
Robert Wagner	Zund.	988
Greg Lipsky	Allstate	988
Henry Zientek	Maico	970
Piet Boonstra	HD	967
Ralph Spencer	DMW	965
Douglas Hill	DMW	960
Jim Forbes	DOT	960
Dick Holmander	BSA	944
James McCauley	HD	940
Carl McAllister	HD	937
Patrick Owens	Maico	797
John Miller	Indian	7.5 mi.

Combined A & B Heavy (19)

Jim Fennell	Tri.	997
Charlie Schumitz	Match.	996
Paul Walton	AJS	996
Bob Hogan	Match.	983
Coleman Mitchell	Tri.	969
Gilbert Sarbourin	Tri.	938
John Skopp	Match.	926
Al Samuelman	AJS	911
Herbert Bergere	Match	36.5 Mi
Roger Chase	Tri.	7.5 "
Robert Ronstrom	HD	7.5 "
Terry Barber	BSA	0.0 "
Maynard Ronstrom	BSA	0.0 "

Club Team – Milford Riders
Chandler, Schumitz & Walton

Crotona Observed Trials
Town of Cortlandt, NY – May 18, 1958
(48 total entries)

Class A Light (10)

Tom Svack	HD	952
Joe Kastner	HD	951
John Fennimore	DOT	946
Sam Cardinale	Tri.	897
Drew Smith	DMW	892
Jon Kwoka, Jr.	HD	849
John McLoughlin	DOT	799
John Miller	DMW	785

Class A Heavy (5)

Gay Van Overloop	Match.	905
Charlie Schumitz	Match.	890
Gene Esposito	Tri.	870
Whitey Loud	Tri.	844
H. Birchard	Veloc.	723

Class B Light (27)

Doug Hill	DMW	950
Frank Chromczak	Maico	930
Bob Brizell	Tri.	888
Richard Thompson	Tri.	887
Walt Knights	Tri.	878
Harry Bergen	HD	854
Douglas Ruck	Maico	848
Douglas Pink	HD	821
Ralph Spencer	DMW	818
Piet Boonstra	HD	818

Class B Heavy (6)

John Clayson	Tri.	740
E. Howard	Veloc.	547
Anthony Granone	AJS	511

Great Eastern Championship Endurance Run
Meriden, CT – September 21, 1958
(63 total entries)

High Score

Charlie Schumitz	Match.	979

Class A Light (12)

Manfred Schmid	DOT	896
Joe Kastner	HD	867
G. Frank Dean	HD	855
Henry Zientek	Maico	797
George Whitney	HD	739

Class A Heavy (11)

Coleman Mitchell	Tri.	973
Paul Walton	AJS	966
Dick Chandler	Veloc.	928
Jim Fennell	Tri.	912
Whitey Loud	Tri.	889

Class B Light (28)

Jim McCauley	HD	938
Piet Boonstra	HD	902
Douglas Hill	DMW	869
John Jardin	HD	868
Russell Huber	Tri.	836

Class B Heavy (12)

William Brittain	BSA	917
Ed McIntyre	Tri.	783
Dick Foster	Tri.	107 mi
Earl Darfler	Tri.	75 "
John Giuffre	Tri.	33 "

Club Team – Milford Riders
Schumitz, Chandler & Walton

Pioneer Valley M.C. - Covered Wagon Enduro
Southwick, Mass. – September 28, 1958
(99 total entries)

High Score
Charlie Schumitz

Class A Light (6)

Joe Kastner	HD	916
George Whitney	HD	669
John Miller	DMW	66 mi.
Bill Crowley	DOT	66 "
Drew Smith	DMW	0.0 "
Greg Lipsky	NSU	0.0 "

Class A Heavy (11)

Sal Scirpo	Tri.	968
Jim Fennell	Tri.	957
Paul Walton	AJS	955
Christy Scholar	BSA	947
Everett Wright	Tri.	930
Boyd Reynolds	Tri.	830
Melvin Kraft	Match.	793
Dick Chandler	Veloc.	749
Richard Hansen	BSA	66 mi.
Frank Kokoszka	Tri.	0 "

Dealer Class (4)

Richard Hall	Tri.	869
Ralph Strong	Indian	854
Fred Marsh	Indian	65 mi.
Bob Hogan	Match.	30 "

Girls Class (5)

Leslie Pink	HD	36 mi.
Marlene Wolfe	BSA	36 "
Barbara Hills	Indian	24 "
Mavis Whidden	Indian	5 "
Jean Thibodeau	Indian	0 "

Club Team – Milford Riders
Schumitz, Walton & Chandler

Class B Bantam <175 cc (13)

Jim McCauley	HD	922
Douglas Pink	HD	799
Harold LaRose	HD	66 mi.
Richard Holmander	BSA	52 "
Abe Schilling	NSU	52 "
Robert Schilling	NSU	52 "
Ronald Schneiders	HD	36 "
David McCauley	HD	30 "
Piet Boonstra	HD	14 "

Class B Light 176–250 cc (22)

Walt Knights	Tri.	944
Ralph Spencer	DMW	904
Frank DeGray	Zund.	850
Charles McIntyre	Indian	741
Joseph Rossi	James	134 mi
Norman Morell	Indian	104 "
Fred DePaso	Tri.	104 "
Donald Doukas	Zund.	104 "
Harold Dean	Zund.	79 "
Glen Minnick	BSA	66 "
William Rich	Zund.	52 "

Class B Heavy (38)

William Brittain	BSA	950
Sidney Harlow	Tri.	901
Richard Foster	Tri.	894
William Hogan	Tri.	882
Bren Moran	Tri.	859
Charles Harrison	Match.	715
Ed McIntyre	Tri.	134 mi
Don Pittsley	Tri	114 "
John Skopp	Match.	114 "
Lewis McDaniel	Tri.	104 "
Harry Gagner	BSA	104 "
Gilbert Sabourin	Tri.	104 "
Edward Douty, Jr.	BSA	104 "

Torrington Enduro
Torrington, Conn. – October 19, 1958
(32 total entries)

High Score			Class B Light (9)		
Christy Scholar			Bill Colbert		900
			Jim Forbes		894
Class A Light (3)			Piet Boonstra		845
Greg Lipsky	70 miles		Ralph Spencer	70 miles	
Henry Zientek	56 miles		Bo Corsa	42 miles	
Joe Rossi	42 miles		E. W. Sagan	19 miles	
Class A Heavy (4)			Class B Heavy (13)		
Charlie Schumitz	928		William Brittain		925
Coleman Mitchell	917		Richard Foster		886
Paul Walton	70 miles		Ken Ives		867
			John Sargent	70 miles	
Women's Class (3)			Ned Smith	70 miles	
Marlene Wolfe	30 miles		Frank Herman	70 miles	
Jean Thibodeau	No start		Ralph Strong	56 miles	

Yonkers M.C. Spring Run
Yonkers, NY – April 5, 1959
(51 total entries)

High Score			Class B Light (17)		
Don Pink	HD	912	Piet Boonstra	HD	905
			Jim Forbes	DOT	882
Class A Light (13)			Doug Pink	HD	851
Jim McCauley	HD	889	J. Jardin	HD	846
Charlie Garby	DMW	865	Ralph Spencer	DMW	758
Greg Lipsky	NSU	824			
Sam Cardinale	Tri.	753	Class B Heavy (11)		
			H. Seide	Tri.	7 mi.
Class A Heavy (10)			K. Macri	Ariel	NS
Gene Esposito	Tri.	901	H. Leale	Horex	NS
Jim Fennell	Tri.	890	J. Giuffre	Tri.	NS
Whitey Loud	Tri.	881	Tony Granone	Tri.	NS
Sal Scirpo	Tri.	880			
Charlie Schumitz	Match	843	Club Team – Milford Riders		
Dick Chandler	Match.	841	McCauley, Schumitz, Chandler		

Crotona Halloween Classic
Yorktown Heights, NY – October 25, 1959
(59 total entries)

High Score		
Sal Scirpo	Tri.	953

Class A Light (11)		
James McCauley	HD	942
Tom Svack	HD	940
Joe Kastner	HD	936
Dorney Wood	HD	878
Greg Lipsky	NSU	34 mi.

Class A Heavy (14)		
Gerald Bolt	HD	907
Richard DeBie	Tri.	901
Whitey Loud	Tri.	34 mi.
Boyd Reynolds	Tri.	34 "
John Miller	AJS	34 "

Class B Light (25)		
Douglas Hill	DMW	927
Bill Colbert	DMW	920
Piet Boonstra	HD	910
Ralph Spencer	DMW	910
Doug Pink	HD	34 mi.

Class B Heavy (9)		
Tony Granone	Tri.	34 mi.
Emil Cocce	Tri.	29 "
Ralph Scott	Tri.	22 "
Tony DeMasi	Tri.	12 "
Sid Harlow	Tri.	NS

Club Participation Award
Milford Riders

AMA District #5 Championship Enduro
Northern New Jersey – November 8, 1959
(115 total entries)

High Score		
Dave Barnes	BSA	966

Class A Light (17)		
Piet Boonstra	HD	954
Bob Maus	Tri.	940
Hank Slegers	Tri.	900

Class A Heavy (7)		
Jim Fennell	Tri.	957
Richard Riedel	Tri.	951
Whitey Loud	Tri.	933

Senior Class (15)		
Arthur Auger	BSA	904
Ralph Spencer	DMW	889
Howard Triplett	Indian	789

Class B Light (50)		
Roger Chase	Tri.	933
Max Reams	Tri.	920
George Beauvais	Zund.	915

Class B Heavy (22)		
George Ball	Tri.	931
Joe Sampson	Tri.	908
Paul Riedel	Indian	890

Girl's Class (5)		
Marguerite Biddle	Tri.	NS
Joan Jewell	Tri.	NS
Judith Powell	HD	NS

Club Team – Cycle Alley
P. Riedel, R. Riedel, Bob Brizell

1959 New England Enduro Championship – Final Results

Grand Championship

1 - Charlie Schumitz, Milford, Conn.	MAT 500	64.0
2 - Dick Chandler, Milford, Conn.	MAT 500	63.0
3 – Coleman Mitchell, E. Hartford, Conn.	TRI 500	46.5
4 – Everett Wright, Somers, Conn.	TRI 200	39.5
5 – Frank DeGray, Thompsonville, Conn.	ZUN 250	27.0
6 – Jim McCauley, Bridgeport, Conn.	HD 165	22.0
7 – Harold Dean, Middletown, Conn.	ZUN 250	20.5
8 – Walt Knights, Bennington, VT.	TRI 200	20.0
9 – Sal Scirpo, Middletown, Conn.	TRI 500	16.0
10 – Richard Hansen, Troy, NY	TRI 500	13.0

Class Winners:

Class A Heavy

1 - Dick Chandler, Milford, Conn.	MAT 500	6.5
2 – Coleman Mitchell, E. Hartford, Conn.	TRI 500	5.7
3 – Tinker Foster, Hoosick Falls, NY	TRI 500	3.2

Class A Light

1 – Everett Wright, Somers, Conn.	TRI 200	5.7
2 – Harold Dean, Middletown, Conn.	ZUN 250	5.3
3 – Greg Lipsky, Coventry, Conn.	TRI 200	5.0

Class B Heavy

1 – Larry Browe, Bennington, VT	TRI 500	4.0
2 – Ted Briggs, Bennington, VT	TRI 500	3.1
3 – Myron Hooker, Fiskdale, Mass.	BSA 500	2.4

Class B Light

1 – Frank DeGray, Thompsonville, Conn.	ZUN 250	5.3
2 – Walt Knights, Bennington, VT	TRI 200	4.7
3 – Al Thibodeau, Springfield, Mass.	IND 250	3.3

Girls Class

1 – Marlene Wolfe, Springfield, Mass.	BSA 150	50.0
2 – Mavis Whidden, Springfield, Mass.	IND 150	12.0
3 – Mary Hogan, Springfield, Mass.	YAM 125	11.0
4 – Jean Thibodeau, Springfield, Mass.	IND 150	10.0
5 – Barbara Hills, W. Springfield, Mass.	IND 150	9.0

Pioneer Valley M.C. Covered Wagon Enduro
Southwick, MA – September 25, 1960
(55 total entries)

High Score			Class B Light (21)		
Cliff Guild	Tri.	969	Charles McIntyre	Greev.	956
			Chester Hooker	BSA	942
Class A Light (11)			Francis Turmel	Zund.	941
Walt Knights	Tri.	964			
Bob Maus	Tri.	959	Class B Heavy (17)		
Frank DeGray	Greev.	941	Myron Hooker	BSA	924
Bob Wagner	Zund.	925	Werner Tobler	Tri.	922
Piet Boonstra	Maico	907	Ted Briggs	Tri.	907
Ralph Strong	Tri.	899			
Ralph Spencer	DMW	820	Women's Class (3)		
			Marlene Wolfe	BSA	63 mi.
Class A Heavy (3)			Jean Thibodeau	Greev.	24 "
Bill Brittain	BSA	958			
Carl Wickstrand	Tri.	943	Club Team – Conn. Ramblers		
Richard Foster	Tri.	888	DeGray, Harrison & C. McIntyre		

Passaic Valley Annual Stage Coach Enduro
Passaic Valley, NJ – April 9, 1961
(77 total entries)

High Score			Class B Light (25)		
Jim Fennell	Tri.	913	George Daffin	Zund.	782
			Bruce Triplett	Tri.	759
Class A Light (11)			Anthony Goffredo	Tri.	92 mi.
Bob Maus	Tri.	898			
John Fenimore	DMW	762	Class B Heavy (17)		
Doug Pink	HD	78 mi.	Kenneth Wood	Ariel	92 mi.
George Beaurais	Zund.	78 "	Harry Leale	Tri.	78 "
(8th) Piet Boonstra	DMW	11 mi.	Alfred Nyegaard	Indian	72 "
Class A Heavy (12)			Senior Class (12)		
Dave Barnes	BSA	906	Bill Steele	HD	92 mi.
Sky Ball	Match.	860	Howard Triplett	Indian	78 "
Gene Esposito	Tri.	854	Ralph Spencer	DMW	78 "
Albert Allen	BSA	751			
Bill Decker	AJS	92 mi.	(No team award)		

1960 New England Enduro Championship – Final Results

Grand Championship

1 - Frank DeGray, Thompsonville, Conn.	37/7	5.29
2 – Carl Wickstrand, Yalesville, Conn	30/6	5.00
3 – Coleman Mitchell, E. Hartford, Conn.	29/6	4.83
4 – Walt Knights, Bennington, VT	27/6	4.50
5 – Chet Hooker, Fiskdale, Mass.	27/6	4.50

Class Winners:

Class A Heavy

1 – Billy Brittain, Springfield, Mass.	36/6	6.00
2 – Christy Scholar, Meriden, Conn.	33/7	4.71
3 – Coleman Mitchell, E. Hartford, Conn.	27/6	4.50
4 – Tink Foster, Petersburg, NY	26/6	4.33
5 – Dick Chandler, Milford, Conn.	20/7	2.86

Class A Light

1 – Walt Knights, Bennington, VT	33/6	5.50
2 – Harold Dean, Middletown, Conn.	17/4	4.25
3 – B. Mortensen, Union City, Conn.	24/7	3.43
4 – Greg Lipsky, Coventry, Conn.	21/7	3.00
5 – John Miller, Trumbull, Conn.	18/7	2.57

Class B Heavy

1 – Carl Wickstrand, Yalesville, Conn.	37/6	6.17
2 – Myron Hooker, Fiskdale, Mass.	31/7	4.43
3 – Ted Briggs, Bennington, VT	20/7	2.86
4 – Charlie Coles, Springfield, Mass.	15/6	2.50
5 – Bill Stephenson, Pittsfield, Mass.	17/7	2.43

Class B Light

1 – Chet Hooker, Fiskdale, Mass.	28/6	4.67
2 – Bob Butterfield, Meriden, Conn.	27/6	4.50
3 – Charles MacIntyre, Suffield, Conn.	28/7	4.00
4 – Sonny Turmel, Waterbury, Conn.	32/8	4.00
5 – Dick Turmel, Waterbury, Conn.	24/8	3.00

Westchester M.C. "Closed Course" Enduro
Camp Smith, Peekskill, NY – April 16, 1961
(38 total entries)

High Score

Jim Fennell	Tri.	869

Class A Light (7)

John Wright	DOT	28 mi.
Ralph Spencer	DMW	24 "
Bob Hogan	Yama.	16 "
Piet Boonstra	DMW	12 "
Richard Coriell	DOT	12 "

Class A Heavy (6)

Bill Decker	AJS	28 mi.
Whitey Loud	Tri.	20 "
Gene Esposito	Tri.	NS
Christy Scholar	BSA	NS
Charlie Watson	Tri.	NS

Class B Light (11)

Bob Butterfield	BSA	28 mi.
Bob Moquin	Greev.	24 "
Ken Weinert	Tri.	20 "
Rod Pink	HD	16 "
Al Weinert	Tri.	12 "

Class B Heavy (14)

Roger Chase	AJS	28 mi.
Doug DeCosta	Tri.	24 "
Tony Granone	Tri.	20 "
Whitey Anderson	Tri.	20 "
Dick Heins	Tri.	16 "

No team trophy award
(no team completed course)

Great Eastern Championship Endurance Run
Meriden, CT – September 10, 1961
(38 total entries)

High Score

Christy Scholar	996

Class A Light (8)

Piet Boonstra	992
Frank DeGray	991
Sky Ball	990
Francis Turmel	988
John Fenimore	983

Class A Heavy (6)

Myron Hooker	983
Albert Thibodeau	979
Ed McIntyre	978
Dick Turmel	939
Ted Briggs	64 mi.

Class B Light (16)

Ron Alleman	992
John Jardin	989
Herb Mogul	977
Bob Coriell	962
Charles Baldwin	949

Class B Heavy (6)

Bill Stephenson	982
Werner Tobler	980
Phil Bourdon	979
Don Duchesneau	976
Don Cutler	961

Team Award
R.Turmel, F.Turmel & Jardin

Schuyler County 150-mile National Championship Endurance Run
Cayuta, NY – September 24, 1961
(73 total entries)

High Score
John Penton	BMW	988

Class A 0-200cc (6)
Cliff Guild	Tri.	961
John Fenimore	DMW	948
Harold Kapp	Ducati	146 mi.
Jim Smith	DOT	61 "
Clifford Foss	HD	14 "
John Potter	NSU	NS

Class A 201-400 (10)
Piet Boonstra	DMW	932
Sal Scirpo	HD	922
Tink Foster	Greev.	918
Gerald Bolt	BSA	905
Fred Bourne	BSA	895

Class A 401-600cc (6)
Norm Smith	Tri.	963
Bill Decker	BSA	935
William Monfort	Indian	922
George Peckham	BSA	920
Eugene Esposito	Tri.	32 mi.

Class A 601-up (2)
Robert Cole	HD	953
Bill Horton	Match.	62 mi.

Senior Class (5)
Carl Bergman	Ducati	890
Ralph Spencer	DMW	821
Bill Strickland	DOT	809
John Sorgi	HD	32 mi.
G. Frank Dean	HD	10 "

Girl's Class (1)
Annabelle Smith	BSA	32 mi.

Class B 0-200cc (6)
Bob Coriell	DOT	947
Sliotteo Ruggiero	HD	851
William Sorgi	HD	719
R.B. Rosenberry	HD	702
Howard Campbell	HD	138 mi.

Class B 201-400cc (13)
George Geisinger	BSA	918
Mario R. Ciaudi	BSA	815
Joe Ceci	Greev.	796
Howard Hunter	BSA	146 mi.
Francis Gordon	BSA	130 "

Class B 400-600cc (13)
Arthur Weather	BSA	942
Ted Briggs	Tri.	931
Mal Emsherviller	Tri.	926
Herman Stoeckle	BSA	925
Owen Christman	BSA	916

Class B 601-up (5)
Arthur Forrest, Jr.	BSA	927
George E. Bailey	BSA	906
Howard Smith	BSA	896
John Whitcomb	BSA	92 mi.
Scotty Sarheehi	HD	32 "

Passenger Class (1)
Driv. Jerry Perkins   Tri. 61 mi.
Pass. Bobby Perkins

Side-car Class (4)
Driv. Dick McManamon   HD
Pass. Marshall Rarney   130 mi.

Club Team – Rolling Mohawks
Bergman, Christman, H. Smith

200-Mile National Championship - Covered Wagon Enduro
Southwick, MA – October 8, 1961
(55 total entries)

Grand Champion
Sky Ball	Greev.	975

Class A Champion
John Penton	BMW	973

Class B Champion
Mac Emshwiller	Tri.	963

Class A Light (15)
Piet Boonstra	DMW	966
Harold Dean	Greev.	966
Bob Maus	Tri.	965
Frank DeGray	Greev.	964
Bob Butterfield	BSA	953
Cliff Guild	Tri.	945
Charles Harrison	Greev.	937
Sal Scirpo	HD	926

Class A Heavy (13)
Jim Fennell	Tri.	970
Dave Barnes	BSA	961
Dick Chandler	Match.	956
Norm Smith	Tri.	950
William Thorpe	BSA	946
Robert Miller	BSA	943
Bill Decker	AJS	940
Christy Scholar	BSA	917

Senior Class (10)
G. Frank Dean	HD	940
Ray Goodrich	Tri.	923
Donald Wood	BSA	883
Ralph Strong	Tri.	880
W.S. Chronister	Match.	878
Merritt Smith	Cotton	878
Carl Bergman	Ducati	852
Clifford Foss	HD	743
Ralph Spencer	DMW	173 mi.

Class B Light (21)
John Jardin	HD	957
Edward Douty, Jr.	BSA	942
Herbert Mogul, Jr.	Tri.	918
Charles Baldwin	BSA	895
Robert Moquin	Greev.	874
Francis Kniffin	BSA	762
John Czapor	BSA	628

Class B Heavy (19)
Leslie Palmer	Ariel	952
Owen Christman	BSA	945
Don Duchesneau	BSA	940
Herm Stoeckle	BSA	939
Bill Stephenson	Tri.	934
Werner Tobler	Tri.	931
Howard Smith	BSA	931
Al Thibodeau	Match.	922
Richard Turmel	Match.	917
Ted Briggs	Tri.	910
Charlie Coles	BSA	910
Dick Heins	Tri.	757

"Powder Puff" Class (3)
Marlene Wolfe	BSA	155 mi.
Liz Weldon	Zund.	155 "
Violet Brittain	BSA	24 "

Team Trophy – NJ Riders
S. Ball, Decker & Stoeckle

Pathfinders (Layout crew)
Phil Bourdon
Billy Campbell
Charles Chapman
Coleman Mitchell

100-Mile National Championship - District #5 Enduro
Northern New Jersey – November 12, 1961
(120 total entries)

Grand Champion

Gene Esposito		985

Lightweight Champion

Harold Dean	Greev.	976

Class A Light (21)

Sky Ball	Greev.	971
Don Pink	HD	967
Bob Brizell	Tri.	956
Tom Svack	Tri.	955
Frank DeGray	Greev.	944
Piet Boonstra	DMW	942
Bill Decker	Tri.	932
Jack Wright	Tri.	911
Jim Forbes	DOT	866
Sal Scirpo	HD	861

Class A Mediumweight (15)

Christy Scholar	BSA	968
Dave Barnes	BSA	935
Jim Fennell	Tri.	926
William Thorpe	BSA	892
Myron Hooker	BSA	875
Herm Stoeckle	BSA	70 mi.

Senior Class (12)

Harry Smith	BSA	868
Al Sedusky	Tri.	866
Harry Higgins	BSA	832
Ralph Spencer	DMW	811
Clifford Ross	HD	793
Carl Bergman	Ducati	747

Class A Light Heavyweight (4)

Howard Smith	BSA	874
Mike Gasparovic	Match.	674
Bert Wieland	Match.	42 mi.

Class B Light (40)

John Jardin	HD	952
Carroll Chandler	Zund.	855
Edward Nemec	Tri.	813
Anthony Goffredo	Tri.	800
Kenneth Macri	BSA	790
Donald Bell	Tri.	726
Joseph Wojcik	Tri.	706
Roger Morley	Zund.	663
Bob Wyckoff	Greev.	632
Joe Ceci	Greev.	70 mi.

Class B Mediumweight (18)

Don Duchesneau	BSA	914
Owen Christman	BSA	896
Jim Case	Tri.	802
Phil Bourdon	Tri.	729
Dan Coates	Tri.	723
Ronald Bauman	BSA	674
Max Reams	Tri.	642
Dick Heins	Tri.	99 mi.

Class B Light Heavyweight (4)

Tony Granone	Tri.	753
James Zubritsky	BSA	37 mi.
Gerald Maxwell	Tri.	32 "

"Powder Puff" Class (3)

Gerry Putnam	Tri.	37 mi.
Leslie Pink	HD	32 "
Valerie Eads	Tri.	NS

Passenger Class (4)

Dick/Ruth Walker	BSA	715
Jack/Norma Creelman	"	55 mi.

Team Award – Monmouth SP
Christman, H. Smith, Bergman

Westchester M.C. Closed Course Enduro – Reggie Pink Memorial
Camp Smith, Peekskill, NY – April 15, 1962
(37 total entries)

High Score
Jim Fennell	Tri.	981

Class A Light (8)
Bill Decker	Tri.	953
Bob Maus	Tri.	951
Piet Boonstra	DMW	946
Tom Svack	Tri.	937
Gay Van Overloop	Greev.	900

Class A Heavy (10)
Herm Stoeckle	BSA	951
Gene Esposito	Tri.	943
Dave Barnes	BSA	940
Dick Walker	BSA	915
William Thorpe	BSA	900

Class B Light (17)
Rod Pink	HD	915
Bob Moquin	Greev.	893
Joe Accardi	Tri.	889
Don McShane	Tri.	878
Ed Hoyle	Zund.	876
M. deThomasson	Greev.	871

Class B Heavy (3)
Harry Leale	Tri.	854
Peter Diaz	Tri.	30 mi.
Robert McKay	Tri.	8 "

Club Team – Cycle Alley Riders
Esposito, Decker, Stoeckle

Conn. Ramblers Bushwacker Enduro
Somers, CT – November 4, 1962
(37 total entries)

High Score
Greg Lipsky	Jaw	981

Class A Light
Bob Butterfield	BSA	960
Al Thibodeau	HD	946
Sunny Turmel	Zundapp	935

Class A Heavy
Piet Boonstra	Tri.	979
Chris Scholar	Match	977
Werner Tobler	Tri.	968

Class B Light
Harold Stone	Zundapp	945
D. Ellis	Tri.	942
Ed Hoyle	Zundapp	938

Class B Heavy
Phil Bourdon	Tri.	975
Joe Vittone	Tri.	968
Dick Skinner	Match	934

Team Award – RAMS M.C.
G.Lipsky, C.Scholar, P.Bourdon

Girl Rider
Rusty Brittain	BSA	5.2mi.

Westchester M.C. Closed Course Enduro – Reggie Pink Memorial
Camp Smith, Peekskill, NY – March 24, 1963
(65 total entries)

High Score

Piet Boonstra	Tri.	1000

Class A Light (11)

Tom Svack	Tri.	996
Doug Pink	HD	989
Bill Decker	Tri.	983
Jim Forbes	Greev.	981
Sonny Turmel	Zund.	949

Class A Heavy (8)

Dave Barnes	BSA	985
Whitey Loud	Tri.	984
Jim Fennell	Tri.	982
Mac Emswiller	Tri.	920
Tony Granone	Tri.	844

Class B Light (35)

Zeke Evans	Greev.	980
Kenneth Macri	Greev.	978
Barry Higgins	BSA	977
Merritt Chew	DMW	961
Harold Goemaat	Greev.	947

Class B Heavy (7)

Richard Heins	Tri.	949
Harry Higgins	BSA	949
Walter Durso	Tri.	929
Ronald Baumann	BSA	927
Jim McManus	Match.	838

Team Award – Sport Spot Rdrs.
McManus, Goemaat, Macri

Passaic Valley Annual Stage Coach Enduro
Passaic Valley, NJ – April 21, 1963
(45 total entries)

High Score

Jim Fennell	Tri.	993

Class A Light (9)

Sky Ball	Greev.	990
Greg Lipsky	HD	985
Tom Svack	Tri.	984
Bob Maus	Tri.	979
John Fenimore	DMW	979

Class A Heavy (10)

Gene Esposito	Tri.	990
Dave Barnes	BSA	990
Piet Boonstra	Tri.	984
Dick Walker	BSA	980
Emil Cocci	Tri.	975

Class B Light (9)

Max Reams	Tri.	981
Alfred Nyegaard	Greev.	974
John Larabee	Greev.	972
Joseph Wojcik	Greev.	968
George Daffin, Jr.	Zund.	964

Class B Heavy (2)

Richard Heins	Tri.	961
Jim McManus	Match.	953

Team Award – Sport Spot Rdrs.
Daffin, Higgins, & Macri

Best Represented Club
Cycle Alley Riders

Crotona Split-Rock Enduro
Monterosa Lodge, Fishkill, NY, April 28, 1963
(29 total entries)

High Score
| Bob Maus | Tri. | 998 |

Class A Light (7)
Joe Kastner	HD	971
Tom Svack	Tri.	966
Ralph Spencer	Greev.	944
Gay Van Overloop	BSA	934
Bob Wagner	Zund.	903

Class A Heavy (7)
Don Cutler	Match.	997
Piet Boonstra	Tri.	997
Harry Higgins	BSA	938
Dick Walker	BSA	922
Gene Esposito	Tri.	876

Class B Light (11)
Ralph Durso	Greev.	982
Al Semmelrock	Tri.	980
Harold Steele	HD	920
Frank Hearn	Greev.	886
George Bernzott	HD	24 mi.

Class B Heavy (4)
Richard Heins	Tri.	964
Barry Higgins	BSA	928
Wally Durso	Tri.	12 mi.
James Durso	Tri.	NS

No Team Award

Greylock Riders Sugarloaf Enduro
Pittsfield, Mass., May 19, 1963
(44 total entries)

High Score
| Don Lohnes | Greev. | 969 |

Class A Light (9)
Bob Butterfield	965
Sonny Turmel	945
Sky Ball	942

Class A Heavy (8)
Piet Boonstra	965
Arthur Forrest	964
Bob Hogan	960

Class B Light (16)
John Larabee	968
Veto Bonan	964
Bill Perry	946

Class B Heavy (9)
Don Cole	965
Ronald Ives	923
Charles Baldwin	894

Powder Puff Class (2)
| Marlene Wolfe | 36 mi. |

Team Award – Laurel State Riders – S.Turmel, D.Turmel & E. Hoyle

Little Burr 250-mile National Championship Endurance Run
Columbus, Ohio, May 26, 1963
(253 total entries)

Grand Champion
  Sox Brookhart   Tri. 973
Bantam Weight Champion
  Jim Smith   Tri. 973
Light Weight Champion
  Bert Wieland   Match. 981
Medium Weight Champion
  Bill Baird   Tri. 970
Light Heavy Weight Champion
  Clarence Wise   BSA   968
Heavy Weight Champion
  Bill Maxey   HD   901
Senior Class Champion
  Leroy Hartman   Match. 890

Class A Bantam (20)
  Charles Thiakos   Tri. 958
  Jim White   HD   951
  Kenneth Hardin   Tri. 935

Class A Light (43)
  John Penton   BMW   980
  Bud Wilson   HD   964
  Dave Barnes   BSA   934

Class A Medium (21)
  Norm Smith   Tri. 964
  Owen Christman BSA   957
  Piet Boonstra   Tri. 956

Class A Light Heavy (11)
  Howard Smith   BSA   931
  Ted Schwartz   Match. 916
  Michael Gasparovic "   699

Class A&B Heavy (9)
  Charles Fischer   HD   804
  Millard Reynolds   HD   672
  James Williams   HD 163 mi.

Class B Bantam (27)
  Norman McClintock Tri. 896
  James McBride   Tri. 869
  Melvin Pond   DKW   856

Class B Light (41)
  Robert Towne   BMW   931
  John Buffaloe Greev. 928
  John Semple   Match. 883

Class B Medium (31)
  Claude Cunningham Tri. 936
  Charles Sheppard   Tri. 923
  Lewis Seibert Match. 901

Class B Light Heavy (7)
  Robert Zinn   BSA   912
  Norris Oelfke Match. 901
  Richard Wibel   Tri. 818

Senior Class (18)
  Carl Bergman   Ducati 890
  Ralph Spencer Greev. 808
  Ellis Clement   Tri. 737

Girl's Class (4)
  Karol Noss   Tri. 845
  Margorie Moreland HD 96 mi.
  Doris Carron   Tri. 65 mi.

Buddy Seat Class (11)
  Hawk/Morrison Honda 736
  Potter/Potter   Tri. 721

Sidecar Class (9)
  Johnson/Simpson   HD 158 mi

Team Award – AB Farrow
  B.Wilson, D.Brown & K.Harden

Jack Pine 500-Mile National Championship Endurance Run
Lansing, Michigan – September 1 & 2, 1963
(462 total entries)

Grand Champion
Bert Wieland   Match. 993
Bantam Weight Champion
Charles Thiakos   Tri. 976
Light Weight Champion
Dave Barnes   BSA 979
Medium Weight Champion
Bill Baird   Tri. 989
Light Heavy Weight Champion
Norris Oelfke   Match. 969
Heavy Weight Champion
Curby Cochran   HD 959

Class A Bantam (21)
Jake Kollassa   Tri. 974
Harold Rohrer   Tri. 961
William Brandon   HD 961

Class A Light (52)
Robert Grinstern   Maico 975
Sal Scirpo   HD 973
Harold Denny   Greev. 973

Class A Medium (34)
Norm Smith   Tri. 978
Meldon Mull   Tri. 974
Herbert Kunze   Match. 970
(11th)Piet Boonstra Tri. 947

Class A Light Heavy (17)
Fred Barber   Match. 961
Dewey Hoffman   Tri. 956
Alan Garrett   Match. 955

Class A Heavy (9)
Rudy Stahl   HD 957

Class B Heavy (8)
Ollie Leigeb   HD 946

Class B Bantam (41)
Melvin Pond   DKW 959
Kenneth Hunt   Tri. 915
J.C. Hardin   Tri. 915

Class B Light (104)
Jim Stone   HD 950
Robert Bodkin   Honda 948
Willard Root   Match. 047

Class B Medium (56)
Paul Goulet   Tri. 953
Donald Nichols   Tri. 944
Charlie Stapleford Match. 943

Class B Light Heavy (32)
Thomas Bartells   Tri. 941
Wayne Witt   Match. 936
John Young   Tri. 878

Senior Class (24)
Joe Gee   Honda 969
Marvin Cutler   Match. 963
Lew Atkinson   Tri. 961

Girl's Class (6)
Karol Noss   Tri. 929
Carol Swim   HD 839

Buddy Seat Class (25)
L.Winters/Winters   Tri. 969
B.Howe/D.Romig   Tri. 914

Sidecar Class (14)
G.Wolfe/D.Wolfe   Tri. 879
D.Wertz/E.Gorsuch   HD 828

Team Award – MW Natl. Endur.
W.Baird, W.Maxey & C.Thiakos

Schuyler County 150-mile National Championship Endurance Run
Cayuta, NY – September 22, 1963
(105 total entries)

Grand Champion
Sal Scirpo   HD   977
Bantam Weight Champion
Jim Smith   Tri.   935
Light Weight Champion
Don Lohnes   Greev. 928
Medium Weight Champion
Arthur Forrest   Match. 925
Heavy Weight Champion
Robert Cole   HD   874

Class A Bantam (5)
Bob Maus   Tri.   908
Jerry Norton   Bultaco 765
Dick Rosenberry   HD 146 mi.

Class A Light (12)
Bert Wieland   Match. 917
Chuck Boehler   Greev. 891
Harold Denny   Greev. 849

Class A Medium (12)
Owen Christman   BSA   916
Norm Smith   Tri.   904
Werner Tobler   Tri.   896
(7th) Piet Boonstra   Tri. 121 mi.

Class A Heavy (4)
Hudson Smith   HD 47 mi.
Dewey Hoffman   Tri. 14 "
Howard Smith   BSA 14 "

Senior Class (9)
Carl Bergman   Ducati 793
G. Frank Dean   HD   783
Ralph Spencer   Greev. 745

Class B Bantam (10)
Roger Jack   HD   678
Andrew Knowland   Tri. 140 mi.
Russell Pearce   Tri. 73 "

Class B Light (23)
Paul Cole   Honda   912
Paul Cramer   Greev. 855
Gary Jones   HD   792

Class B Medium (12)
Charles Stapleford Match. 796
Ronald Wells   Match. 699
Bruce Rogerson   Tri.   636

Class B Heavy (7)
George Bailey   BSA   608
Timmie Scotia   BSA 36 mi.
Sieg Langer   Tri. 29 "

Sidecar Class (4)
McMannon/Gowe   HD 92 mi.
Wheaton/Shoemaker HD 24 "
Cox/Martin   HD   9 "

Buddy Seat Class (4)
Potter/Potter   Tri. 153 mi.
Conger/Buell   Tri. 29 "
Perkins/Hart   Tri. 14 "

Girl's Class (1)
Annabelle Smith Honda 29 mi.

Team Award – USA All Stars
S.Scirpo, N.Smith & A.Garrett

District #5 Championship Enduro
Patterson, NJ – December 1, 1963
(59 total entries)

High Score

Sky Ball	Greeves	992

Class A Light

Whitey Loud	Tri.	983
Bob Maus	Tri.	981
Ralph Scott	Tri.	972
Don Pink	HD	971
Tom Svack	Tri.	966

Class A Heavy

Piet Boonstra	Tri.	988
Jim Fennell	Tri.	986
Wink Butz	Tri.	976
Charlie Stapleford	Match.	970
Dick Walker	BSA	94 mi.

Class B Light

Will Dop	Greev.	974
Rod Pink	HD	971
John Larabee	Greev.	971

Class B Heavy

Barry Higgins	BSA	958
Ray Ohswaldt	Tri.	957
Ken Macri	BSA	957

Senior Class

Bob Wagner	Tri.	984
Ralph Spencer	BSA	979
Gay VanOverloop	BSA	964

Layout – Esposito, Stoeckle,
& E. Cocce

Westchester M.C. Closed Course Enduro
Maybrook, NY – April 12, 1964
(47 total entries)

High Score

Gene Esposito	Tri.	992

Class A Light (6)

Bob Maus	Tri.	974
Tom Svack	Tri.	895
Gay Van Overloop	BSA	852
John Fenimore	DMW	800
Sky Ball	Greev.	12 mi.

Class A Heavy (6)

Piet Boonstra	Tri.	957
Harry Higgins	BSA	941
Ralph Spencer	BSA	899
Dick Heins	Tri.	897
Herman Stoeckle	BSA	9 mi.

Class B Light (28)

Bob Padworski	Greev.	971
Donald Bell	Tri.	966
Tom Eaton	DOT	922
Sal DiBiassi	DMW	911
Matthew Petrone	Tri.	878

Class B Heavy (7)

John Lunney	BSA	806
Robert Fletcher	Match.	18 mi
Robert Raymond	Match.	6 "
Clifton Hoke	HD	6 "
Clem Healy	BSA	3 "

Club Team – Morris County M.C.
Fenimore, T.Eaton, DiBiasse

Battle of Monmouth
Belmar, NJ – May 3, 1964
(51 total entries)

High Score (Cannon)

Piet Boonstra	Tri.	992

Class A Light (8)

Bill Brandenstein	Tri.	983
Jim Smith	Tri.	978
Bob Wagner	Tri.	923
Bruce Tripplett	HD	915
Tom Bird	Tri.	838
John Fenimore	DMW	11 mi.

Class A Heavy (5)

Emil Cocci	Tri.	965
Mac Emschwiller	Tri.	939
H. Tripplett	Indian	133 mi.
Ralph Spencer	BSA	59 "

Class B Light (27)

Bill Bitter	Ducati	970
R. Austin	Tri.	943
R.P.Martin	BSA	938
Charles Palmer	Tri.	936
Charles DeBiasse	Greev.	927

Class B Heavy (11)

Ken Macri	BSA	987
D. VanBuren	BSA	981
Edgar Smith	AJS	956
R. Sorenson	Tri.	949
Jack Hallow	Ariel	899

Best Represented Club
Morris County M.C.

Greylock Riders Annual "Sugarloaf Enduro"
Pittsfield, Mass. – May 10, 1964
(34 total entries)

High Score

Don Lohnes	Greev.	984

Class A Light (6)

Sal Scirpo	HD	977
Bill Perry	Greev.	971
Vito Bonan	Greev.	912
Bob Butterfield	BSA	907
Bob Lappie	Match.	5th ck.

Class A Heavy (7)

Piet Boonstra	Tri.	982
Don Cutler	Tri.	971
Tink Foster	Tri.	964
Phil Bourdon	Tri.	958
Frank DeGray	Tri.	948
Jim Stebbins	Match.	917

Class B Light (11)

L. Stewart	Yam.	934
Manny Swass	Greev.	917
Ted Latrell	BSA	916
Bill Doherty	Greev.	916

Class B Heavy (9)

Warren Wolfe	BSA	961
Perly Parker	Tri.	952
G Leeman	Tri.	904
Maynard Ronstrom	BSA	6th ck

Powder Puff Class (1)

Marlene Wolfe		NS

Club Team – RAMS M.C.
Stebbins, Foster & Bourdon

Greylock Riders M.C. "Fall Enduro"
Pittsfield, Mass. – October 4, 1964
(55 total entries)

High Score
Bill Perry	Greev.	967

Class A Light (5)
Vito Bonan	Greev.	966
Sal Scirpo	HD	965
Paul Larabee	Greev.	933
Henry Royce	Greev.	1st ck
Ron Alleman	Greev.	1st ck

Class A Heavy (12)
Piet Boonstra	Tri.	966
Don Cutler	Tri.	961
Frank DeGray	Tri.	957
Al Semmelrock	BSA	953
Bill Decker	BSA	946

Class B Light (23)
Rod Morningstar	BSA	938
Manny Swass	Greev.	919
Ed Provin	Tri.	912
Jim Moroney	HD	881
Al Devereaul	Bultaco	841

Class B Heavy (14)
Tom Blindloss	BSA	937
Fran Nasse	BSA	928
Dave Sime	Tri.	927
Ed Cartier	BSA	821
John Miller	Jawa	9th ck

Team Award – New London M.C.
Cutler, Perry & Semmelrock

Meteor M.C. Sandy Lane Enduro
Atsion, NJ – September 27, 1964
(117 total entries)

High Score
John Penton	BMW	998

Class A Bantam (13)
Cliff Guild	Tri.	997
Wm. Brandenstein	Tri.	993
Bob Maus	Tri.	983

Class A Light (14)
George Talcott	BSA	993
Sal Scirpo	HD	991
Herm Stoeckle	BSA	979

Class A Heavy (13)
Bill Baird	Tri.	998
Piet Boonstra	Tri.	988
Chas. Stapleford	Match.	982

Class B Bantam (22)
Richard Austin	Bultaco	978
John Morgan	Bultaco	961
Cliff Ferris	Tri.	960

Class B Light (33)
George Ellis	BSA	965
Tim Bindloss	BSA	962
Carlton Seward	Match.	962

Class B Heavy (18)
Richard Bender	Tri.	987
Rich Stapleford	Match.	973
Tom Garrett	Tri.	965

Team Award – Midwest Enduro
Penton, Baird & Schwartz

Connecticut Ramblers "Bushwacker" Enduro
Somers, CT – October 25, 1964
(39 total entries)

High Score

Piet Boonstra	Tri.	984

Class A Light (7)

Bill Perry	Greev.	981
Bob Hogan	Bultaco	972
Bob Butterfield	Bultaco	963
Joe Kastner	HD	943
Gus Cornelis	Sprint	908

Class A Heavy (8)

Don Cutler	Tri.	980
Werner Tobler	Tri.	965
Al Semmelrock	BSA	959
Myron Hooker	Match.	956
Joe Vittone	Tri.	941

Class B Light (11)

Al Devereaux	Bultaco	962
Al Eames	DOT	936
Al Gendreau	Greev.	930
Gordon Leeman	Sprint	916
Dick Pearson	Bultaco	888

Class B Heavy (12)

Perley Parker	Tri.	970
Ken Gardner	BSA	934
Tom Bindloss	BSA	922
Bruce Rogerson	Tri.	911
Ed Chartier	BSA	903

Team Award – New London M.C.
Cutler, Perry & Semmelrock

AMA District #5 Enduro
Northern NJ – November 8, 1964
(80 total entries)

High Score

Bob Maus	Tri.	992

Class A Light (11)

Sherm Cooper	Bultaco	987
John Fenimore	DMW	986
Max Reams	Tri.	985
Don Pink	HD	985
Joe Kastner	HD	979

Class A Heavy (8)

Piet Boonstra	Tri.	992
Chas. Stapleford	Match	978
Gerald Maxwell	Tri.	968
Dick Heins	Tri.	NS
Herm Stoeckle	BSA	NS

Class B Light (13)

George Ellis	BSA	991
Bob Coriell	DMW	987
John Sortorius	Honda	986

Class B Heavy (9)

Ken Macri	BSA	976
Ernest Muller	Tri.	929
Art Fletcher	Match	47 mi.

Senior Class (12)

Ralph Spencer	BSA	980
Bill Steele	HD	977
Art Tramontin	HD	976
John Colfax	BSA	976
Clarence Hyde	Tri.	936

Chatauqua Lake Cyclists Little Bone 100-Mi. National Championship
Busti, NY – October 18, 1964
(106 total entries)

Grand Champion
Dave Barnes	BSA	992

Seneca Highlands Trophy
Bob Fusan	Tri.	988

Class A Flyweight (2)
Paul Cole	Honda	978
Walter Kohl	Yamaha	NS

Class A Bantam (7)
Bob Maus	Tri.	983
Jerry Pacholke	Tri.	974
Donald Bailey	Bultaco	974
Lester Cornwell	Bultaco	972
Dick Walker	Bultaco	970

Class A Light (8)
Walt Lohrer	Greev.	991
Sal Scirpo	HD	990
Paul Larabee	Greev.	988
John Penton	BMW	985
Howard Smith	BSA	984

Class A Medium (8)
Bill Baird	Tri.	989
Bob Fusan	Tri.	988
Leonard Claridie	Tri.	986
David McCall	Tri.	965
Piet Boonstra	Tri.	952

Class A Heavy (2)
Sox Brookhart	Tri.	981
Donald Eaken	Tri.	970

Class B Flyweight (9)
Michael Shinners	Yama.	75 mi
Bob Hopfer	Yama.	64 "
Melvin Bohn	Yama.	64 "

Class B Bantam (10)
Fred DeSantis	Bultaco	977
David Reid	HD	976
Walter Miller	Bultaco	965

Class B Light (35)
Rod Morningstar	BSA	987
Ray Holloway	BSA	971
Wesley Price	Jawa	971
Donald Little	Greev.	971
Blaine Miller	Greev.	955

Class B Medium (13)
Ron Bohn	Tri.	968
Merritt Babcock	BSA	962
Jon Wiedmaier	Tri.	957
Louis Lappa	BSA	938
Robert Hayes	BSA	937

Class B Heavy (3)
James Keefe	BSA	42 mi
William Shurtz	Norton	35 "
Ronald Morton	BSA	13 "

Senior Class (9)
Donald Martin	BSA	978
Carl Bergman	Ducati	971
Al Sedusky	Greev.	970

Monmouth Shore Points Scottish Trials
Belmar, NJ – November 15, 1964
(56 total entries)

High Score (Turkey Award)
Bill Decker	Greev.	966

Class A Light (9)
John Fenimore	DMW	958
Gene Esposito	Greev.	953
Pete LeoGrande	HD	925
Al Sedusky	Greev.	903
A. Sabo	Maico	826

Class A Heavy (7)
Chas. Stapleford	Match	962
Piet Boonstra	Tri.	958
Herm Stoeckle	BSA	952
Emil Cocce	Tri.	935
T. Bird	Tri.	825

Class B Light (26)
Bob Coriell	DMW	961
John Boone	HD	936
H. LeTourette	Bultaco	930
S. Hutchinson	Tri.	917
R. Austin	Bultaco	911

Class B Heavy (14)
M. Strong	BSA	933
Rich. Stapleford	Match.	924
G. Cox	Tri.	915
B. Palmer	Honda	878
L. Robacker	Tri.	863

RAMS "Salmon River Ramble" Enduro
East Hampton, CT – December 13, 1964
(38 total entries)

High Score
Piet Boonstra	Tri.	979

Class A Light (9)
Sal Scirpo	961
Bob Butterfield	955
Bob Hogan	918
Tink Foster	915
Al Eames	901
Don Lohnes	7th ck.

Class A Heavy (5)
Werner Tobler	941
Don Cutler	858
Myron Hooker	749
Al Semmelrock	NS

Class B Light (12)
Pete Niemi	770
Manny Swass	734
Bud Peck	721

Class B Heavy (11)
R. Sorenson	923
Perley Parker	881
Ken Gardner	749

Powder Puff Class (1)
Sally Raley	4th ck.

Team Award – Greylock Riders
Eames, Tobler, Vittone

Layout – G. Cornelis, P. Bourdon

Connecticut Ramblers Snow Run
Warehouse Point, CT – February 14, 1965
(53 total entries)

High Score			Class B Light	
Sal Scirpo	HD	981	Dave Kimbal	959
			Bob Moquin	958
Class A Light			Al Gendreau	942
Bob Butterfield	BSA	980		
Bill Perry	Greeves	976	Class B Heavy	
Al Eames	DOT	972	Lewis Whittum	954
			Maynard Ronstrom	953
Class A Heavy			Francis Masse	948
Piet Boonstra	Tri.	977		
Al Semmelrock	BSA	976	Team Award – New London M.C.	
Chris Scholar	Match	975	Semmelrock, Perry, Cutler	

Monmouth Shore Points M.C. Snow Fun Run
Belmar, NJ – February 21, 1965
(65 total entries)

Class A (15)			Class B (50)		
Wm. Brandenstein	Tri.	1000	Cliff Ferris	Tri.	1000
R. Redden	Greev.	996	Rich Stapleford	Tri.	996
Gene Esposito	Tri.	996	R. Austin	Bultaco	995
Piet Boonstra	Tri.	994	J.C. Boone	HD	993
Sam Cardinale	Tri.	993	E.G. Smith	Match.	991
J. Creelman	Tri.	992	Ken Macri	BSA	987
John Fenimore	DMW	992	R. LeTourette	Bultaco	985
Herm Stoeckle	BSA	988	D.T. VanBuren	BSA	984
Bill Decker	Greev.	988	M. Strong	BSA	983
Emil Cocce	Tri.	982	C. O'Neill	Tri.	982
W. Steele	HD	981	W. Gaponouich	Greev.	982
Rod Rosenberry	HD	964	G. Cox Jr.	Tri.	981
Sherm Cooper	Tri.	957	T. Eaton	DMW	980
G. Maxwell	Tri.	930	B. Saporito	HD	978

RAMS Spring Enduro
Ellington, CT – April 25, 1965
(44 total entries)

High Score			Class B Light (18)	
Don Cutler	Tri.	970	J. Veal	959
			Bud Peck	944
Class A Light (8)			J. Bonan	937
Vito Bonan		967	Pete Niemi	934
Bob Hogan		966	Art Milliken	927
Bob Butterfield		961		
Bill Perry		960	Class B Heavy (10)	
Sal Scirpo		958	George Ellis	957
			J. Henri	954
Class A Heavy (8)			Ed Chartier	943
Piet Boonstra		969	F. Nasse	940
R. Bindloss		959	Dick March	904
Werner Tobler		958		
Al Semmelrock		958	Team Award – New London M.C.	
B. Rogerson		953	Cutler, Perry & Semmelrock	

17th Battle of Monmouth
Belmar, NJ – May 1965
(71 total entries)

High Score			Class B Light (29)		
Wm Brandenstein	Tri.	983	C. Riley	Bultaco	975
			C. Seward	Match.	971
Class A Light (16)			John Boone	HD	968
Bob Maus	Tri.	977	J. Cadgene	Bultaco	964
Emil Cocce	Greev.	973	C.F. Scutt, Jr.	Bultaco	962
Bill Decker	Greev.	969			
John Fenimore	DMW	965	Class B Heavy (19)		
F. Chromczak	Honda	964	E. Smith	Match.	971
			M. Strong	BSA	971
Class A Heavy (7)			C. Reed	AJS	969
Piet Boonstra	Tri.	983	G.W. Cox, Jr.	Tri.	964
Chas. Stapleford	Match.	979	S. Debiasse	Greev.	964
G. Maxwell	Tri.	959			
Harry Higgins	BSA	948	Team Award – Blue Hen Ramb.		

Burr Oak – 175-Mile National Enduro
Indiana – May 2, 1965
(286 total entries)

Grand Champion
Bill Baird	Tri.	969

Light Weight Champion
John Buffaloe	Tri.	928

Medium Weight Champion
Harold Denny	Greev.	908

Lt. Heavy Weight Champion
George Ellis	Tri.	887

Heavy Weight Champion
Norris Oelfke	Match.	799

Class A Light (34)
Leroy Winters	Honda	888
Jerry Norton	Bultaco	877
Kenneth Hunt	Tri.	870
Bud Green	Tri.	838

Class A Medium (51)
John Penton	BMW	905
Bill Decker	Greev.	892
Curby Cochran	HD	843
Deloss Aldrich	Greev.	838

Class A Light Heavy (19)
Paul Goulet	Tri.	865
Lynn Tucker	Tri.	861
Piet Boonstra	Tri.	855
Charles Calkins	Tri.	852

Class A Heavy (17)
Fred Barber	Match.	145 mi.
Fred Pease	Tri.	145 "
Robert Stanton	Tri.	96 "
Sox Brookhart	Tri.	82 "

Class B Light (44)
Ray Kussmaul	NSU	860
Donald Bingham	Bultaco	734
Peter Kennedy	Yamaha	710

Class B Medium (61)
Jack LaMastus	Greev.	877
Doug Bories	Match.	545
James Price	BSA	345

Class B Light Heavy (32)
Tom Stratton	Tri.	855
John Hays	Tri.	681
Jim Misunas	Tri.	677
Tom Garrett	Tri.	156 mi

Class B Heavy (8)
Will Guy	Tri.	129 mi
Kenneth Thomas	Tri.	124 "
Clifford Newlin	Tri.	124 "

Sidecar Class (6)
Johnson/Pumfrey	HD	82 mi.
Ludwig/Drouillard	Zund.	68 "
Wertz/Wertz	HD	68 "

Girl's Class (4)
Lucy Stratton	Tri.	77 mi.
Karol Kay Noss	Tri	63 "
Lynn Stump	Yamaha	42 "

Senior Class (9)
Marv Cutler	Match.	861
G. Frank Dean	HD	798
Ernest Maxwell	Tri.	749
Frank Graves	HD	508

Greylock Riders Annual "Sugarloaf Enduro"
Pittsfield, Mass. – May 16, 1965
(43 total entries)

High Score
Bill Perry	Greev.	970

Class A Light
Frank DeGray	Greev.	968
Vito Bonan		957
Bob Hogan		5 ck.

Class A Heavy
Piet Boonstra	969
George Ellis	966
Don Cutler	959

Class B Light
Jim Moroney	961
Joe Bonan	946
Al Gendreau	945

Class B Heavy
Ken Gardner	943
Francis Nasse	907
Ed Chartier	905

Team Award – New London M.C.
Semmelrock, Perry, Cutler

Greylock Riders Fall Enduro
Pittsfield, MA – September 12, 1965
(50 total entries)

High Score
Don Lohnes	991

Class A Light (10)
Bill Perry	988
Veto Bonan	986
Frank DeGray	985
Mac Emshwiller	985
Bob Hogan	984

Class A Heavy (7)
Piet Boonstra	988
Don Cutler	985
Tom Blindloss	983
Al Semmelrock	983
Richard Heins	957

Class B Light (28)
Paul Winters	985
Ken Gardner	982
Michael Waite	976
Joe Veal	975
Al Gendreau	972

Class B Heavy (5)
Robert Collio	903
Fred Moore	811
Bill Fitzgibbons	5th ck.
Joe Henri	5th ck.
Earnest LaFerte	1st ck.

Team Award – New London M.C.
Semmelrock, Cutler, & Perry

Little Burr 250-mile National Championship Endurance Run

Columbus, Ohio, May 30, 1965

(243 total entries)

Grand Champion
Robert Fusan   Tri.   988

Bantam Weight Champion
Robert Freig   Honda   879

Light Weight Champion
Roger Kussmaul   Tri.   986

Light Medium Weight Champion
Sal Scirpo   HD   979

Medium Weight Champion
Bill Baird   Tri.   984

Heavy Weight Champion
Jack Wooten   Tri.   983

Senior Class Champion
Mike VanDamme   BSA   938

Class A/B Bantam (16)
Jim Lytell   Suzuki   684
Leroy Winters   Honda 220 mi.
Paul Cole   Honda 202 "

Class A Light (20)
Bud Green   Tri.   982
Larry Sells   Tri.   972
Kenneth Hunt   Tri.   966

Class A Light Medium (35)
Bill Decker   Greev. 973
George Talcott   BSA   970
J.M. Allen   HD   968

Class A Medium (26)
Chas. Stapleford   Match. 973
Wayne Tingley   Match. 972
(7th)Piet Boonstra Tri.   962

Class A Heavy (10)
Kenneth Harden   Tri.   971
Bill Maxey   Tri.   963
Trevor Bauman   Tri.   949

Class B Light (30)
Ray Kussmaul   Tri.   967
B.R. Huston   Tri.   961
Peter Reynolds   Tri.   951

Class B Light Medium (43)
Bob Coriel   DMW   955
Donald Mapes   Honda   953
Jack LaMastus   Greev. 947

Class B Medium (27)
Ronald Bohn   Tri.   959
Darrell Frick   Match. 942
Wesley Pierce   Tri.   940

Class B Heavy (10)
Glen Arden   Norton   926
Richard Main   Match. 909
Melvin Bohn   Tri.   802

Senior Class (18)
Ellis Clement   Tri.   936
G.Frank Dean   HD   934
Wendell Hicks   Tri.   912

Girl's Class (4)
Doris Carron   Tri. 165 mi
Lucy Stratton   Tri. 165 "
Doris Carron   Tri. 165 "

Buddy Seat Class (3)
Babcock/Babcock Honda 846
Howe/Howe   Tri. 210 mi

Sidecar Class (3)
Johnson/Simpson   HD 158 mi

Team Award – Esler's M/C
Goulet, Kussmaul & Kussmaul

Jack Pine 500-Mile National Championship Endurance Run
Lansing, Michigan – September 5 & 6, 1965
(700 total entries)

Grand Champion
Bill Decker   Greev. 976

Class A Fly Weight (13)
Leroy Winters[CC] Honda   962
Dave Mungenast   "   248 mi.

Class A Bantam Weight (24)
Roger Kussmaul[CAC] Tri. 974
Robert Grinstern[CC] Honda 938
Bob Maus[1st]   Tri. 916

Class A Light Weight (52)
Bud Wilson[CC]   HD   955
Curby Cochrane[1st]   HD   939

Class A Light Medium (21)
John Penton[CC]   BMW   969
Joseph Charlie[1st] Match. 956

Class A Medium (42)
Gene Esposito[CC]   Tri. 974
Bill Baird[1st]   Tri. 973
(10th)Piet Boonstra   Tri. 902

Class A Light Heavy (16)
Fred Barber[CC]   Match. 964
Paul Kiger   Tri. 813

Class A Heavy (13)
Marvin Church[CC]   HD 131 mi.
Dean Potter[1st]   HD 108 "

Senior Class (25)
Marvin Cutler   Match. 901
G. Frank Dean   HD   770

Dealer Team – Eslers M/C

Class B Fly Weight (52)
Wallace Weir   Honda   701
Bob Maiers   Honda   677

Class B Bantam (78)
Doug Wilford   Honda   935
Ray Kussmaul   Tri. 896

Class B Light (112)
John Buffaloe[CBC] Greev. 949
John Taylor[1st]   Bultaco 852

Class B Light Medium (34)
Jack McLane   Honda   907
Bill Sharp   Match. 881

Class B Medium (70)
Russ Wieferich   Tri. 917
Francis Honeck   Tri. 892

Class B Light Heavy (47)
Eddie Brummette   Tri. 778
William Anger   Match. 725

Class B Heavy (13)
Jack Harkness   HD 131 mi
Clare Walters   HD 108 "

Girl's Class (8)
Karol Noss   Tri. 793
Glenda Moreland   Tri. 108 mi

Buddy Class (27)
Howe/Howe   Tri. 913
Dunphy/Dunphy Honda   854

Sidecar Class (15)
Cross/Whitney   Tri. 227 mi

Schuyler County 150-mile National Championship Endurance Run
Cayuta, NY – September 19, 1965
(155 total entries)

Grand Champion
  Bill Baird   Tri.   971
Light Weight Champion
  Gerald Pacholke Honda 935
Medium Weight Champion
  Bill Decker   Greev. 960
Light Heavy Weight Champion
  Gene Esposito   Tri.   958
Heavy Weight Champion
  Robert Cole   HD   940

 Class A Light (11)
Roger Kussmaul   Tri.   907
Bob Maus   Tri.   904
Mac Emschwiller   Bultaco 860

Class A Medium (24)
Sal Scirpo   HD   958
Jim Smith   DMW   950
Paul Cramer   Greev. 945

Class A Light Heavy (9)
Norm Smith   Tri.   955
Bud Green   Tri.   952
Piet Boonstra   Tri.   919

Class A Heavy (5)
George Talcott   Tri.   880
Wm. Montford   Match. 877
Sox Brookhart   Tri. 112 mi.

Senior Class (15)
Carl Bergman   Ducati 829
Ralph Spencer   Greev. 820
G. Frank Dean   HD   768

Class B Light (29)
Clint Riley   Bultaco 790
Frank Dillman   Greev. 781
Michael Waite   Suzuki 760

Class B Medium (41)
William Erwin   BSA   936
Dave Comstock   Greev. 922
David Redman   BSA   895

Class B Light Heavy (10)
John Sartorius   Tri.   871
Donald Moody   Match. 852
Albert Miller   Tri.   845

Class B Heavy (6)
Norm Ford   Tri.   877
Fred Ford   Tri.   871
Will Guy   Tri.   795

Sidecar Class (2)
Wheaton/Guchone   HD 80 mi.
McManamon/McGrew " 52 "

Buddy Seat Class (1)
Grover/Brown   Tri.   744

Girl's Class (1)
Pat Ward   Tri. 80 mi.

Team Award – Bob's Cycle
Forrest, Redman, & Erwin

Sandy Lane 125-mile National Championship Endurance Run
Atsion, NJ – September 26, 1965
(193 total entries)

Grand Champion
Gene Esposito	Tri.	990

Class A Light (11)
Bob Maus	Tri.	977
Wm. Brandenstein	Tri.	970
Gerry Pacholke	Honda	956
Mac Emschwiller	Bultaco	944

Class A Medium (21)
Bill Decker	Greeves	976
James Smith	DMW	975
Don Pink	HD	976
Tink Foster	Puch	965
Don Lohnes	Greev.	962

Class A Light Heavy (15)
Bill Baird	Tri.	989
Chas. Stapleford	Match.	981
Piet Boonstra	Tri.	969
George Ellis	Tri.	965
Don Cutler	Tri.	944

Class A Heavy (3)
George Talcott	BSA	756
Gerald Maxwell	Tri.	51 mi.
Jay Garrison	BMW	DNS

Team Award – Crotona M.C.
Boonstra, Pink, & Maus

Class A&B Bantam (14)
Michael White	Suzuki	456
R.B. Sehorn	Yamaha	425
Everett Laning	Yamaha	417
Mike Gida	Suzuki	395

Class B Light (45)
Clint Riley	Bultaco	936
K. Rosengren	Tri.	933
Louis Russo	Tri.	930
John Boone	HD	927
Bud Peck	Greev.	920

Class B Medium (50)
Al Gendreau	Greev.	947
Cliff Ferris	Greev.	939
Francis Guchone	Honda	927
Joe Henri	BSA	926
Caronton Seward	Match.	915

Class B Light Heavy (24)
Rich Sorenson	Tri.	947
Edgar Smith	Match.	938
Clarence Hyde	Tri.	935
Ray Oswaldt	Tri.	933
Bill Bitter	Tri.	925

Class B Heavy (9)
Will Guy	Tri.	899
Walt Wendel	Tri.	824
Hoss Maybury	Tri.	130 mi

Chatauqua Lake Cyclists Little Bone 100-Mi. National Championship
Busti, NY – October 3, 1965
(137 total entries)

Grand Champion
| Bob Fusan | Tri. | 998 |

Seneca Highlands Trophy
| Bob Fusan | Tri. | 998 |

Class A Flyweight (2)
| Ted Schwartz | Honda | 985 |
| Lester Peckham | Honda | 54 mi. |

Class A Bantam (7)
Gerald Pacholke	Honda	995
John Young	Bultaco	994
Bill Sharpless	Tri.	986
Lester Cornwell	Bultaco	983
Bob Kilbarger	Tri.	979

Class A Light (19)
Walt Lohrer	Greev.	997
Bill Decker	Greev.	996
Dave Barnes	BSA	994
George Talcott	BSA	990
Jack Dunphy	Honda	989

Class A Medium (11)
Bill Baird	Tri.	995
Gene Esposito	Tri.	994
Bud Green	Tri.	988
Don Nichols	Tri.	987
Piet Boonstra	Tri.	982

Class A Heavy (5)
Ron Bohn	Tri.	993
Sox Brookhart	Tri.	983
Bill Maxey	Tri.	976
Bob Cole	HD	963

Class B Flyweight (7)
Clayton Hayward	Honda	862
John Campbell	Honda	75 mi.
Dane Hogan	Honda.	75 "

Class B Bantam (25)
Rudi Marczi	Bultaco	991
Jim Bucks	Bultaco	951
Elmek Morra	Tri.	926

Class B Light (30)
David Redman	BSA	989
David Reid	HD	985
Dave Comstock	Greev.	983
William Ervin	BSA	982
Robert Nadon	HD	969

Class B Medium (13)
John Sartorius	Tri.	976
Dale Claridge	Tri.	874
Albert Miller	Tri.	839
Dennis Feltenberger	Tri.	836
Don Rosenthal	Match.	85 mi.

Class B Heavy (4)
Fred Ford, Jr.	Tri.	988
Norm Ford	Tri.	978
Will Guy	Tri.	46 mi.

Senior Class (8)
Marv Cutler	Match.	981
Carl Bergman	Ducati	970
Al Sedusky	Greev.	941
Ellis Clement	Ducati	916
Ralph Spencer	BSA	75 mi.

Buddy Class (3)
| Pattorence/Shimer | Honda | 918 |

Connecticut Ramblers Closed Course Enduro
Ellington, CT – November 28, 1965

High Score
Piet Boonstra   Tri. 1000

Class A Light
Bill Perry   Greev. 1000
Bob Hogan   Bultaco 999
Bruce Rogerson   Greev. 997

Class B Heavy
Don Cutler   Tri. 999
Myron Hooker   Match. 993
Tom Bindloss   BSA 893

Class B Light
Al Gendreau   Greev. 996
Bob Hicks   Bultaco 994
Pete Niemi   Greev. 987

Class B Heavy
Ed Chartier   BSA 821
Ken Arnold   Tri. 666
John Soltoys   BSA 3 laps

Connecticut Ramblers "Bushwacker" Enduro
Somers, CT – October 10, 1965
(42 total entries)
(Scores not available)

High Score
Bill Perry

Class A Light
Tink Foster
Mac Emshwiller
Bruce Rogerson

Class A Heavy
Don Cutler
Piet Boonstra
Richard Heins

Class B Light
Ken Gardner
Tom Campbell
Ron Webster

Class B Heavy
Ed Chartier
Ed McIntyre
Bill Fitzgibbons

Team Award – New London M.C.
Perry, Cutler, Bindloss

RAMS Team Challenge – Enduro/Trials
Middletown, CT – October 24, 1965
(30 total entries)

Best Overall			Class B Light (12)		
Bill Perry	959/986	1945	Pete Niemi	934/991	1925
High Score Trials			Al Gendreau	940/984	1924
Bud Peck	939/994	1933	Fred Bliven	933/969	1902
High Score Enduro			Joe Veal	940/955	1895
Don Cutler	964/971	1935	Jim Moroney	928/946	1874
Class A Light (6)					
Veto Bonan	946/993	1939	Class B Heavy (6)		
Bob Hogan	951/981	1932	Ed Chartier	898/936	1834
Bruce Rogerson	894/965	1859	Marcel Sabourin	856/954	1810
			Pete Sullivan	848/934	1783
Class A Heavy (5)			Ken Arnold	2nd ck/954	954
Al Semmelrock	947/972	1919	Bill Fitzgibbons	" /945	945
Tom Blindloss	933/961	1894			
Piet Boonstra	943/941	1884	Team Award – New London M.C.		
Dick Heins	846/968	1814	Cutler, Perry & Semmelrock		

Nipmuck Enduro
Ellington, CT – November 7, 1965
(61 total entries)

High Score		Class B Light (37)	
Piet Boonstra	999	Joe Veal	998
		Bud Peck	996
Class A Light (9)		Ron Webster	994
Bill Perry	999	Pete Niemi	994
Al Eames	999	Bill Spinney	994
Veto Bonan	999		
Frank DeGray	998	Class B Heavy (9)	
Bruce Rogerson	995	Joe Henri	995
		Ed Chartier	974
Class A Heavy (6)		Fred Moore	972
Don Cutler	999	Ron Martin	972
Al Semmelrock	998	Curtis Gates	930
Jim Stebbins	997	Ken Arnold	951
Myron Hooker	997		
Christy Scholar	997	Team Award – New London M.C.	
Ralph Spencer	966	Cutler, Perry & Semmelrock	

Monmouth Shore Points M.C. Turkey Run
Belmar, NJ – November 21, 1965
(96 total entries)

High Score			Class B Light (23)		
Piet Boonstra	Tri.	995	Clint Riley	Bultaco	977
			Jacques Cadgene	"	976
Class A Light (14)			Carlton Seward	Match.	958
James Smith	DMW	994			
Mort Stang	Greev.	986	Class B Heavy (24)		
Joe Kastner	Greev.	986	Don Corson	Tri.	986
Emil Cocce	Greev.	977	R. Sorenson	Tri.	985
Sal Debiassi	Greev.	977	David Meade	Tri.	984
Class A Heavy (8)			0 – 150 Class (4)		
Gene Esposito	Tri.	994	F. Chromzcak	Honda	960
Herm Stoeckle	BSA	983	Fred Kitchen	Honda	939
Ken Macri	BSA	982			
Harry Higgins	BSA	974	Best Represented Club		
Gerald Maxwell	Tri.	958	Blue Hen Ramblers		

RAMS Salmon River Ramble
East Hampton, CT – December 5, 1965
(55 total entries)

High Score			Class B Light (19)		
Sal Scirpo	HD	995	Al Gendreau	Greev.	985
			Bill Moss	HD	981
Class A Light (13)			Bud Peck	Greev.	979
Veto Bonan	Greev.	992	Pete Niemi	Greev.	973
Bob Hogan	Bultaco	989			
Bill Perry	BSA	986	Class B Heavy (9		
Bruce Rogerson	Greev.	981	Joe Henri	BSA	978
Tink Foster	Puch	981	Dick Sorenson	Tri.	951
			Ken Arnold	Tri.	920
Class A Heavy (6)					
Piet Boonstra	Tri.	995	0 – 150 cc Class (8)		
Don Cutler	Tri.	994	Richard Baj	Suzuki	964
George Ellis	Tri.	994	William Johnson	Suzuki	6th ck
Myron Hooker	Match.	988			
Tom Blindloss	BSA	975	Team Award – New London M.C.		
			Cutler, Perry & Blindloss		

Rifle City Riders Enduro
Brimfield, MA – April 3, 1966
(55 total entries)

High Score		Class B Light (26)	
Sal Scirpo	986	D. Ford	979
		Joe Veal	974
Class A Light (10)		J. Helliwell	969
Al Gendreau	981	D. Pittsley	968
Tink Foster	976	Ron Webster	960
Perley Parker	974	F. Bliven	958
Ken Gardner	951		
H. Royce	950	Class B Heavy (11)	
		R. Lucas	966
Class A Heavy (8)		Joe Henri	962
Piet Boonstra	985	F. Nasse	954
Myron Hooker	976	L. Wittum	943
Ed Chartier	960	Charlie Coles	896
Tom Blindloss	960	J. Soltys	ck 5
Frank DeGray	955		

RAMS Paul Revere Enduro
Stow, MA – April 17, 1966
(67 total entries)

High Score			Class B Light (24)		
Sal Scirpo	HD	991	Ron Webster	Greev.	972
			R. Lucier	DOT	970
Class A Light (13)			F. Bliven	Bultaco	939
Bill Perry	Greev.	980	Walt Nye	Greev.	936
Al Gendreau	Greev.	980			
Bruce Rogerson	Greev.	979	Class B Heavy (17)		
Veto Bonan	Greev.	975	L. Whittum	Tri.	979
H. Royce	BSA	936	Dick March	BSA	965
			Charlie Coles	BSA	962
Class A Heavy (6)			F. Nasse	BSA	950
Piet Boonstra	Tri.	986			
Frank DeGray	Grumph	976	Bantamweight Class (7)		
Tom Blindloss	BSA	952	Ralph Spencer	Hercules	944
Jim Stebbins	Match.	941	T. Kosewski	Honda	5th ck.
John Larabee	Maico	2nd ck.			

Passaic Valley M.C. Stage Coach Enduro
Northern New Jersey – May 1, 1966
(56 total entries)

High Score

Bob Maus	Tri.	1000

Class A Light (7)

Sky Ball	Greev.	1000
Mac Emschwiller	Bultaco	994
Emil Cocce	Greev.	947
Richard Hall	Bultaco	864
Jim Smith	James	17 mi.

Class A Heavy (5)

Dick Heins	Tri.	995
Ken Macri	BSA	994
Bill Ervin	BSA	989
Thomas Bird	Tri.	17 mi.
Piet Boonstra	Tri.	8.6 "

Class B Light (29)

Jacq. Codyene	Bultaco	995
Jim Hollenbeck	Greev.	994
Tom Diamond	Greev.	993
Bill Hollenbeck	Greev.	991

Class B Heavy (10)

John Bosolt	BSA	997
Herb Walker	BSA	992
Bill Fitzgibbons	BSA	990
Gary Brown	BSA	987

Senior Class (5)

Ralph Spencer	Hercules	990
Merrit Chew	DMW	951
Le Roy Markle	Greev.	916

RAMS Spring Enduro
Somers, CT – May 15, 1966
(40 total entries)

High Score

Sal Scirpo	HD	961

Class A Light (9)

Bill Perry	Greev.	947
Bob Hogan	Bultaco	937
Pete Niemi	Greev.	926
Bud Peck	Greev.	924
Tink Foster	Puch	922

Class A Heavy (3)

Piet Boonstra	Tri.	955
Frank DeGray	Grumph	931
Tom Bindloss	Tri.	914

Class B Light (16)

Ron Webster	Greev.	904
Bill Moss	Bultaco	897
J. Helliwell	Greev.	860
Pop Moody	Bultaco	853
B. Hogan	Bultaco	835

Class B Heavy (12)

Joe Veal	Tri.	910
J. Soltys	BSA	8th ck.
J. Cave	Tri.	8th "
F. Nasse	BSA	7th "
C. Hartmann	Tri.	7th "

Team Award – RAMS #1
Boonstra, Peck & Niemi

Berkshire International Trials
Becket, MA – May 21 & 22, 1966

Gold Medals (20)	M/C	Enduro Points	Bonus Ponts Hill Cl.	Acc/Br.	Total
Don Cutler	Triumph. 500	0	60	60	120
Gary Nelson	Honda 90	0	60	57	117
Bill Moss	Bultaco 250	0	59	57	116
Bill Dutcher	Bultaco 250	0	58	58	116
Piet Boonstra	Triumph 500	0	60	55	115
Jim Moroney	Greeves 250	0	59	53	112
Jess Thomas	Bultaco 250	0	55	57	112
Larry Browe	Bultaco 250	0	59	52	111
Sal Scirpo	Harley D. 250	0	53	57	110
Bruce Rogerson	Greev. 250	0	59	50	109
Dick Vittone	Triumph 500	0	50	55	105
Gene Esposito	Triumph 500	0	51	54	105
Ron Moon	Bultaco 250	0	55	50	105
Herm Stoeckle	BSA 350	0	51	53	103
Bob Maus	Triumph 200	0	50	50	100
Phil Bourdon	Triumph 500	0	43	55	98
Ken Macri	BSA 350	0	48	50	98
John Taylor	JAWA 360	0	45	50	95
Bud Peck	Greeves 200	0	51	50	91
Myron Hooker	Matchless 350	0	39	50	89
Silver Medals (5)					
Harold Ward	Greeves 250	3	60	52	112
Richard Heins	Triumph 500	14	9	52	61
Jack Sartorius	Triumph 500	17	45	54	99
Bob Wagner	Greeves 250	17	43	51	94
Tim Sochia	Triumph 650	22	39	48	87
Bronze Medals (22)					
Jacq. Cadgene	Bultaco 200	34	55	56	111
Bob Redden	Greeves 250	37	52	50	102
Britt Palmer	Bultaco 250	50	52	54	106
Pete Niemi	Greeves 250	53	25	52	77
John Spencer	Matchl. 500	62	55	53	108
Larry Bastedo	Bultaco 250	67	28	53	81

Team Award – RAMS #1
Boonstra, Peck & Niemi

Jack Pine 500-Mile National Championship Endurance Run
Lansing, Michigan – Sept. 4th & 5th, 1966
(592 total entries)

Grand Champion
John Penton   Husqva. 987

Class A Fly Weight (11)
Ted Schwartz[CC] Honda   962
Dan Joslyn[1st]   "   878

Class A Bantam Weight (28)
Dick DeGraw[CC]   Tri.   975
Ray Kussmaul[1st] Honda   967
Robt. Towne   Suzuki   957

Class A Light Weight (58)
Lester Peckham[CC] Bultaco 982
Bern. McGovern[1st]   HD   977

Class A Light Medium (14)
Joseph Charlie[CC] Match. 979
George Charlie[1st] Match. 943

Class A Medium (55)
Bill Baird[CAC]   Tri.   985
John Young[CC]   BSA   978
Don Nichols[1st]   Tri.   972
(6th)Piet Boonstra   Tri.   960

Class A Light Heavy (17)
Ron Bohn[CC]   Tri.   967
Fred Leach[1st]   Tri.   954

Class A Heavy (3)
Marvin Church[CC]   HD 254 mi.
Dean Potter[1st]   HD 67 "

Senior Class (25)
Bernard Slack   HD   938
Marvin Cutler   Match. 901

Class B Fly Weight (38)
John Thomas   Honda   828
John Sawdey   Honda   805

Class B Bantam (68)
Bruce Hornbeck   Tri. 920
Roger Bates   Honda   917

Class B Light (88)
Ken Bronson   Bultaco 926
Terry Maier   HD   919

Class B Light Medium (31)
Forest Stahl[CBC] Honda   954
Jack Boegner[1st]   Match. 900

Class B Medium (84)
Glen Arden   Match. 938
Jack Peebles   Maico   936

Class B Light Heavy (34)
Bruce Cornell   Tri.   886
Eddie Brumette   Tri.   884

Class B Heavy (5)
Jerry Harris   HD 254 mi

Girl's Class (6)
Lucy Stratton   Tri.   825
Karol Noss   Tri.   760

Buddy Class (12)
Howe/Romig   Tri.   916
Fischer/Wymore Honda   897

Sidecar Class A&B (18)
Wertz/Wertz   HD   645

Club Team Award – MWERA – Baird, Maxey & Young

Schuyler County 150-mile National Championship Endurance Run
Cayuta, NY – September 18, 1966
(total entries)

Grand Champion
John Young	BSA	983

High Score NY State Rider
Piet Boonstra	Tri.	976

Class A Fly Weight (2)
Frank DeGray	Hercules	109 mi.

Class A Bantam Weight (7)
Paul Cole[CC]	Honda	951
Owen Christman	Montesa	885
Gerry Pacholke	Honda	874

Class A Light Weight (26)
Bill Decker[CC]	James	982
Mac Emschwiller	Bultaco	965
Art Forrest	BSA	956

Class A Medium (20)
Bill Baird[CC]	Tri.	980
Bill Maxey[1st]	Tri.	946
Gene Esposito	Tri.	945

Class A Heavy (4)
Ron Bohn[CC]	Tri.	967
Fred Leach[1st]	Tri.	954

Class A Heavy (3)
Marvin Church[CC]	HD	254 mi.
Dean Potter[1st]	HD	67 "

Senior Class (19)
Piet Boonstra	Tri.	976
Don Nichols	Tri.	915

Club Team – MWERA
Young, Baird & Maxey

Class B Fly Weight (21)
Roy Meeker	Yamaha	584
John Struik	Bultaco	499
Merl Bigelow	Hodaka	477

Class B Bantam (25)
Slotteo Ruggiero[CC]	Hodaka	731
Elmer Morra	Tri.	870
Jack Winters	Bultaco	806

Class B Light (75)
Jim Moroney	Greeves	928
Gary Brown	BSA	914
R.S.Marczi	Bultaco	893

Class B Medium (36)
John Sartorius	Tri.	904
Paul Winters	Tri.	825
Dennis Feltenberger	Tri.	817

Class B Heavy (11)
Richard Hicks	Tri.	763
Lawrence Pieters	Tri.	718
Patrick McCann	Tri.	615

Girl's Class (1)
Patricia Ward	Tri.	92 mi.

Buddy Class (2)
Blood/Hurley	Ducati	46 mi.
Stein/Warner	Bultaco	17 "

Sidecar Class (2)
Wheaton/Damrau	HD	58 mi.
Miller/Marvine	Tri.	6 "

High Score B Rider
Jim Moroney	Greeves	928

Meteor Motorcycle Club Sandy Lane Enduro
Atsion, NJ – September 25, 1966
(240 total entries)

High Score

Gene Esposito	Tri.	989

Class A Light (16)

Clint Riley	Bultaco	961
John Boone	HD	961
Doug Wilford	Honda	958
Sherm. Cooper	Honda	957
Everett Wright	Tri.	952

Class A Medium (23)

Mac Emschwiller	Bultaco	968
Al Gendreau	Greeves	961
Cliff Ferris	Greeves	953
Bill Perry	Greeves	946
Bob Wagner	Greeves	942

Class A Light Heavy (21)

Bill Baird	Tri.	985
George Ellis	Tri.	978
Bill Maxey	Tri.	971
Charlie Stapleford	Tri.	968
Bill Bitter	Tri	957
(21st) Piet Boonstra	Tri.	44 mi.

Class A Heavy (2)

Rich Stapleford	Tri.	952
Will Guy	Tri.	20 mi.

Team Award – So Jersey CR
Forsyth, Brandenstein, Ferris

Class B Bantam (32)

Rick Spangler	Honda	481
Andrew Collison	Hodaka	461
James Foss	Suzuki	429
Thomas Rossi	Honda	422
Tom Clark	Yamaha	385

Class B Light (37)

John Towery	Tri.	936
Larry Manor	Honda	933
James Foster		786
Tom Clark	Yamaha	782
James Varnes		769

Class B Medium (67)

Neil Forsyth	Greeves	971
Jim Moroney	Greeves	968
Britt Palmer	Bultaco	966
Howard Bennett	BSA	963
Forest Stahl	Honda	946

Class B Light Heavy (35)

Norman Ford	Tri.	970
William Height	BSA	960
Maynard Ronstrom	BSA	952
John Sartoriuse	Tri	931
Ed McIntyre	Tri.	913

Class B Heavy (7)

Donald Corson	Tri.	842
Harry Penn	Tri.	78 mi

Greylock Riders Fall Enduro
Pittsfield, MA – October 2, 1966
(108 total entries)

High Score		Class B Light (46)	
Piet Boonstra	988	Jim Moroney	956
		Art Solomon	954
Class A Light (7)		Jim Helliwell	953
Al Gendreau	983		
Dick Turmel	974	Class B Heavy (26)	
Don Lohnes	968	Herb Walker	966
Mac Emschwiller	967	Joe Veal	956
Gus Cornelis	856	Paul Winters	936
Class A Heavy (12)		100 cc Class (17)	
Frank DeGray	979	Dick Baj	902
Phil Bourdon	967	John Taylor	898
Tom Bindloss	943		
Myron Hooker	936	Team Award – RAMS #1	
Ed Chartier	919	Boonstra, Bourdon & Gardner	

Connecticut Ramblers Bushwacker Enduro
Somers, CT – October 23, 1966
(78 total entries)

High Score		Class B Light (34)	
Piet Boonstra	959	Bill Moss	922
		Bob Perry	894
Class A Light (7)		Bill Hollenbeck	845
Bob Hogan	927	Bill Fitzgibbons	835
Bill Perry	902		
Sal Scirpo	892	Class B Heavy (24)	
Al Gendreau	887	Fred Bliven	894
Gus Cornelis	6th Ck.	Bob Fielding	872
		Joe Veal	839
Class A Heavy (11)			
Perley Parker	951	100 cc Class (2)	
George Ellis	946	Richard Baj	5th ck.
Phil Bourdon	889		
Tom Bindloss	889	Team Award – RAMS #1	
Bud Peck	878	Boonstra, Peck & Gardner	

Meriden M.C. Closed Course Enduro
Meriden, CT – October 30, 1966
(45 total entries)

High Score

Al Gendreau	Greev.	1000

Class A Light (5)

Frank DeGray	Hercules	1000
Bob Hogan	Bultaco	991
Dick Turmel	Tri.	969
Al Eames	Bultaco	969
Ron Webster	Greev.	963

Class A Heavy (5)

Piet Boonstra	Tri.	998
Bud Peck	Tri.	985
Dick Heins	Tri.	970
Ken Gardner	Maico	958
Will Guy	Tri.	953

Class B Light (17)

Bill Hollenbeck	Greev.	981
Jim Helliwell	Greev.	962
Andre Girourd	Tri.	939

Class B Heavy (14)

Charlie Coles	BSA	978
Herb Walker	BSA	975
Dave Latham	BSA	961

100 cc Class (4)

Dick Balocki	Hodaka	883
Jim Foss	Suzuki	4 laps

Team Award – RAMS #1
Boonstra, Peck & Ronstrom

Rifle City Riders Nipmuc Enduro
Springfield, MA – November 13, 1966
(71 total entries)

High Score

Al Gendreau	Greeves	985

Class A Light (6)

Bill Perry	Greev.	979
Ron Webster	Greev.	953
Dick Turmel	Tri.	950
Bruce Rogerson	Greev.	933
Manny Swass	Greev.	855

Class A Heavy (11)

Piet Boonstra	Tri.	971
Phil Bourdon	Tri.	961
Christy Scholar	BSA	961
Bud Peck	Tri.	952
Perley Parker	Maico	944

Class B Light (26)

A. Girouard	Tri.	956
Bob Perry	Greev.	950
Jim Helliwell	Greev.	938

Class B Heavy (20)

Dave Latham	BSA	934
Bob Fielding	Honda	918
Maynard Ronstrom	BSA	912

100 cc Class

C. Hartmann	?	932
Dick Baj	Honda	907

Team Award – RAMS #1
Boonstra, Bourdon & Peck

Springfield M.C. Thanksgiving Enduro
Brimfield, MA – November 30, 1966
(80 total entries)

High Score		Class B Light (33)	
Bill Perry	996	Bob Perry	993
		Jim Helliwell	987
Class A Light (16)		Dick Thayer	979
Frank DeGray	993		
Al Gendreau	991	Class B Heavy (18)	
Ron Alleman	990	Paul Liginbuhl	982
Ron Webster	989	Dave Latham	976
Bob Hogan	987	Bob Fielding	974
Class A Heavy (6)		100 cc Class (7)	
Piet Boonstra	993	C. Hartmann	959
John Larabee	986	Rudy Corsini	895
Myron Hooker	984		
Bud Peck	983	Team Award – Conn. Ramblers	
Phil Bourdon	904	DeGray, Alleman & Webster	

RAMS Salmon River Ramble
Cobalt, CT – December 4, 1966
(55 total entries)

High Score			Class B Light (22)		
Piet Boonstra		921	Jim Helliwell	Greev.	7th ck
			Walt Myska	Montesa	5th ck
Class A Light (7)			David Dukette	Ducati	5th ck
Dick Turmel	Tri.	899	William Ness	Bultaco	4th ck
Bill Perry	Greev.	803	Art Peckinoff	Suzuki	4th ck
Ken Gardner	Greev.	798			
Ron Webster	Greev.	742	Class B Heavy (14)		
Al Gendreau	Greev.	8th ck.	John Soltys	BSA	786
			Bob Fielding	Honda	772
Class A Heavy (7)			Babe Mazur	Maico	751
George Ellis	Tri.	911	Paul Liginbuhl	Tri.	8th ck
Bud Peck	Tri.	845	Dave Latham	BSA	8th ck
Tom Bindloss	Tri.	701			
Ray Sievert	Tri.	5th ck.	Team Award – RAMS #1		
Carl Wickstrand	Tri.	3rd ck	Boonstra, Peck & Gardner		
			(only team to finish)		

Westchester M.C. Reggie Pink Memorial Enduro
Maybrook, NY – April 2, 1967
(105 total entries)

High Score

Herm Stoeckle	BSA	967

Class A Light (8)

Dick Turmel	Husq.	963
Bill Decker	James	961
Bob Maus	Bultaco	961
Jim Moroney	Greev.	3 laps
Don Pink	Suzuki	2 "
Gay VanOverloop	Tri.	2 "

Class A Heavy (4)

Piet Boonstra	Tri.	958
Dick Heins	Tri.	3 laps
Ralph Spencer	BSA	2 "

Class B Light (76)

Robert Wartman	Greev.	962
Jacquees Cadgene	Husq.	961
Bill Fitzgibbons	Greev.	950
Barry Higgins	Moto Guzzi	939
John McCormick	Greev.	937

Class B Heavy (17)

John Bosolt	BSA	950
Tom Coranas	BSA	948
Herb Walker	BSA	941
John Dollard	BSA	923
Dick Smith	BSA	890

Team Award – Cycle Alley M.C.
Stoeckle, Decker & Cadgene

RAMS M.C. Paul Revere Enduro
Stow, MA – April 16, 1967
(68 total entries)

High Score

Bill Moss	Bultaco	971

Class A Light (10)

Ron Webster	Greev.	941
Dick Turmel	Husqv.	926
Al Gendreau	Greev.	921
Al Thibodeau	Greev.	852
Manny Swass	Greev.	801

Class A Heavy (8)

Piet Boonstra	Tri.	958
Carl Wickstrand	Tri.	941
Christy Scholar	Match.	920
Phil Bourdon	Tri.	883
Maynard Ronstrom	BSA	766

Class B Light (25)

Joe Henri	Greev.	961
Art Lataille	Greev.	959

Class B Heavy (16)

Bob Fielding	Tri.	959
Norm Owen	BSA	853

Bantamweight Class (7)
Mark Turkington Honda 7th ck.
Pete Johnson Yamaha 4th ck.

Girl – Cathy Holland Hod. NS
Sidecar – B&J Hicks Tri. 1st ck.

Team Award – Meriden M.C.

Cycle Alley M.C. Big Boar Enduro
Stanhope, NJ – April 23, 1967
(89 total entries)

High Score

Gene Esposito	989

Class A Light (10)

Bob Maus	985
John Boone	963
Jim Moroney	959
John Fenimore	937
Bill Steele	920

Class A Heavy (9)

Piet Boonstra	985
Herm Stoeckle	976
Ken Macri	975
Bill Bitter	974
Tom Garrett	953

Class B Light (55)

Bill Fitzgibbons	969
Ray Smalls	952
Ken Earley	942

Class B Heavy (20)

Tom Coranas	967
B. Height	967
Jim Hollenbeck	957

100 cc Class (16)

Russell Pancoast	826
Jim Vreeland	808
Jim Haddon	765
Steve Seaton	763

Monmouth Shore Points M.C. Spring Enduro
Belmar, NJ – April 30, 1967
(78 total entries)

High Score

Bob Maus	Montesa	995

Class A Light (8)

Bill Decker	James	993
Sherm Cooper	Honda	990
John Boone	Greev.	988
Emil Cocce	Greev.	986
Al Sedusky	Greev.	984

Class A Heavy (12)

Bill Bitter	Tri.	993
Charlie Stapleford	Tri.	993
Piet Boonstra	Tri.	986
Phil Bourdon	Tri.	986
Maynard Ronstrom	BSA	985

Class B Light (33)

Neil Forsyth	Greev.	988
Britt Palmer	Bultaco	987
John Baile	Greev.	981

Class B Heavy (19)

Wm. Height	BSA	993
Don Carson	Tri.	991
Rod VanSickle	Tri.	991

0 – 150 Class (8)

(A)F. Chromzcak	Honda	943
(B)James Haddow	Bultaco	852

Best Represented Club
Central Jersey Competition Rdrs.

RAMS Spring Enduro
Somers, CT – May 14, 1967
(65 total entries)

High Score
Piet Boonstra	Tri.	942

Class A Light (6)
Bob Hogan	Bultaco	926
Ron Webster	Greeves	919
Frank DeGray	Greeves	916
Dick Turmel	Husqv.	906
Sal Scirpo	Greeves	4th ck.

Class A Heavy (7)
Phil Bourdon	Tri.	935
Bud Peck	Tri.	919
Carl Wickstrand	Tri.	915
Ron Alleman	Maico	887
Bob Bindloss	Tri.	875

Class B Light (25)
Andre Girouard	Tri.	882
Bob Mancini	Bultaco	875
Walt Hyska	Montesa	842

Class B Heavy (15)
Bob Fielding	Tri.	891
Paul LaForge	Maico	871
Ron Perry	Tri.	774

125 cc Class (12)
Jerry Ladeau	Yamaha	8th ck
Frank Hanson	Yamaha	8th "
Robert Tinker	Yamaha	8th "

Team Award – Conn. Ramblers
Alleman, DeGray & Webster

Greylock Riders Fall Enduro
Dalton, Mass – September, 24, 1967
(191 total entries)

High Score (Tie)
Piet Boonstra	Tri.	986
Bud Peck	Tri.	986

Class A Light (17)
Dave Latham	Greev.	986
Ron Webster	Greev.	983
Frank DeGray	Sachs	983
Al Gendreau	Greev.	983
Jim Moroney	Greev.	975

Class A Heavy (11)
Phil Bourdon	Tri.	982
Myron Hooker	Match.	971
Ron Alleman	Maico	964
Tom Bindloss	Tri.	918
Maynard Ronstrom	Tri.	884

Class B Light (96)
D. Mosher	Bultaco	981
Art Lataille	Greeves	978
Bruce Cadaire	Greeves	976

Class B Heavy (30)
Herb Walker	BSA	970
Tom Coranas, Jr.	BSA	961
Jake Herzog, Jr.	Tri.	951

100 cc Class (35)
K. Wood	Hercules	942
W. Bertrand	Bultaco	918

Girls Class (2)
Cathy Holland	Hodaka	6th ck.

Team Award – RAMS #1
Boonstra, Peck & Latham

Berkshire International Trials
Becket, MA – May 20 & 21, 1967

Gold Medal Winners - Open (14)	M/C	Enduro Points	Bonus Points
John Penton, Amherst, Ohio	Husqv.	0	500
Gene Esposito, Brooklyn, NY	Triumph	0	464
George Talcott, Clyde, NY	BSA	0	463
George Ellis, Cobalt, Conn.	Triumph	0	459
Piet Boonstra, Buchanan, NY	Triumph	0	457
Jack Dunphy, Cincinnati, Ohio	Husqv.	0	450
Dave Snyder, Vineland, NJ	BSA	0	446
Joe Vittone, Pittsfield, Mass.	Triumph	0	442
Bob Fielding, Waterford, Conn.	Triumph	0	441
Ron Alleman, Tolland, Conn.	Maico	0	439
Bud Peck, Stow, Mass.	Triumph	0	438
Tink Foster, Petersburg, NY	Triumph	0	437
Phil Bourdon, East Hampton, Conn.	Triumph	0	423
John Sartorius, Accord, NY	Triumph	0	411

Gold Medal Winners – 250 cc (27)			
Arthur Browning, Thundersley, England	Greeves	0	488
Ron Jeckel, Glens Falls, NY	Bultaco	0	465
Bill Brooker, Thundersley, England	Greeves	0	461
Gerry Pacholke, East Lake, Ohio	Honda	0	457
Dick Turmel, Waterbury, Conn.	Husqv.	0	456
Al Gendreau, Southbridge, Mass.	Greeves	0	456
Gary Anderson, PA	Greeves	0	455
Walt Lohrer, Erie, PA	BSA	0	451
Emil Cocce, New Milford, NJ	Greeves	0	449
Bob Maus, Valhalla, NY	Bultaco	0	448
Bob Hogan, Springfield, Mass.	Bultaco	0	447
Oriol Bulto, Barcelona, Spain	Bultaco	0	442
Dave Latham, Harvard, Mass.	Greeves	0	439
Al Thibodeau, Springfield, Mass.	Greeves	0	437
Gary Nelson, Hanawa Falls, NY	Bultaco	0	431
Jim Corpe, Schenectady, NY	Bultaco	0	431
Dave Comstock, Wesleyville, PA	Greeves	0	430
Bob Wagner, Meadowbrook, PA	Greeves	0	426
Ken Gardner, New Britain, Conn.	Greeves	0	421
Jim Moroney, Newburgh, NY	Greeves	0	420
Ron Webster, Melrose, Conn.	Greeves	0	411

British Empire Motor Club Corduroy Enduro
Coboconk, Ontario – September 9 – 10, 1967
(230 total entries)

Grand Champion (Lightweight)
Bill Sharpless   Bultaco   957

"Best Opposite" Class (HW Champ.)
Piet Boonstra   Tri   951

Expert Lightweight (32)
Dick DeGraw   Tri. Cub 956
Walt Lohrer   Greeves 949
D. Comstock   Greeves 935
Dick Turmel   Husky 919
Sal Scirpo   HD   910
W. Wilsons   Tri. 878

Expert Heavyweight (29)
Paul Goulet   Tri. 950
Phil Bourdon   Tri. 938
F. Piasecki   Honda 935
Bud Peck   Tri. 932
E. Eaken   Tri. 931
C. Stapleford   Tri. 920

Senior Class (5)
Marv Cutler   Match. 868

100 cc Class (24)
Tim Hoffman   Honda   913
Frank DeGray   Sachs   909

Junior (B) Lightweight (80)
L. Grable   Tri   904
Dave Eames   DOT   892
Ron Commo   Greeves 890
J. Hedges   Bultaco 847
K. Bradley   Greeves 838

Junior (B) Heavyweight (38)
J. Evans   Match.   899
B. Canter   Tri.   887
J. Peppel   Tri.   877
J. Harvey   Tri.   870
R. Woodward   Tri.   845

Sidecar Class (4)
Stueck / Malone   Tri. 283 mi
Zoch / Bentley   HD 122 mi

Team Award – RAMS #1
Boonstra, Bourdon, Peck

Schuyler County 150-mile National Championship Endurance Run
Cayuta, NY – September 17, 1967
(233 total entries)

Grand Champion
Bill Baird   Tri.   918

Class A Fly Weight (2)
Fred Ford, Jr.^{CC} Yamaha   751
Slotteo Ruggiero   Hodaka   629

Class A Bantam Weight (4)
Paul Cole^{CC} Honda   882
J. Shem Cooper   Bultaco   686
Lester Cornwell   Bultaco   661

Class A Light Weight (25)
Jack McLane^{CC} Honda   912
Sal Scirpo   HD   890
Art Forrest, Jr.   Bultaco   853

Class A Medium (22)
Norm Ford$^{Class\ Champ.}$ Tri.   895
Piet Boonstra 1st   Tri.   894
John Young   BSA   889

Class A Heavy (2)
Harold Ward^{CC} Tri.   803
Robert Cole   HD   61 mi.

Senior Class (9)
Cecil Marcom^{CC} BSA   639
John Sorgi, Sr.   Bultaco   80 mi.
Al Sedusky   Greeves   71 "
Bob Wagner   Greeves   61 "

Club Team – MWERA
Baird, Young & Maxey

Class B Fly Weight (35)
Slotteo Ruggiero   Hodaka   629
Thomas Wright   Hodaka   624
David Tuxil   Honda   614

Class B Bantam (36)
Richard Bean   Bultaco   750
James Foster, Jr.   Tri.   747
Francis Guchone   Honda   742

Class B Light (70)
Bill Hollenbeck   Greeves   829
George Westley   Greeves   814
Martin Westley   Greeves   808

Class B Medium (23)
Craig Tabat   Tri.   869
Andy Girouard   Tri.   96 mi.
James Johnston   BSA   80 "

Class B Heavy (2)
George Bailey   Tri.   742
Richard Hicks   Tri.   165 mi

Girl's Class (1)
Shirley Renckert Yamaha   Start

Buddy Class (1)
Goehner/Senne   Tri. 49 mi

High Score B Rider
Craig Tabat   Tri.   869

Meteor Motorcycle Club Sandy Lane Enduro
Atsion, NJ – October 1, 1967
244 total entries
(38 Finishers)

High Score
Jack McLane   Honda   980

Class A Light (11)
J. Sherm Cooper Bultaco 920
Bill Decker   Sachs   879
Rolla Adams   Honda   747
Bob Agans   Triumph 94 mi.
Ed Chartier   Triumph 89 "

Class A Medium (25)
Dave Latham   Greeves 946
Jake Turmel   Husqv. 943
Gerry Pacholke   Bultaco 941
Neil Forsyth   Greeves 937
John Boone   Greeves 926
Sal Scirpo   HD   884

Class A Lightheavy (26)
John Penton   Husqv. 955
Bill Baird   Triumph 949
John Young   BSA   948
Norm Ford   Triumph 937
Gene Esposito   Triumph 922
Piet Boonstra   Triumph 899

No Team Award

Class B Bantam (53)
Ben Trimble   Sachs   473
Tom Chaney   Yamaha 468
Lou Smith   Yamaha 459
Larry Ackley   Yamaha 458
Earl Chilcote   Honda   420

Class B Light (45)
Larry Manor   Honda   874
Rick Spangler   Honda   854
J.C. Foster   Triumph 848
Allan Adams   Honda   769
Warren Kleis   Tri.   105 mi.

Class B Medium (86)
William Height   Bultaco 903
Jack Winters   Bultaco 878
Forest Stahl   Honda   856
Mike Willis   Greeves 855
John Bailey   Bultaco 845

Class B Lightheavy (45)
Dave Snyder   BSA   930
Rod VanSickle   Triumph 905
Herb Walker   BSA   903
Jim Leepeer   BSA   868

Class B Heavy (6)
Don Corson   Triumph 100 mi.
Russell Pancoast Tri.   77   "

Connecticut Ramblers Bushwacker Enduro
Somers, CT – October 22, 1967
(65 total entries)

High Score			Class B Light (25)		
Dave Latham		987	Bruce Gadaire		978
			Dick Thayer		971
Class A Light (7)			Bill Hollenbeck		960
Dick Turmel		986	Bob McKelvey		955
Bill Perry		970			
Ken Gardner		968	Class B Heavy (11)		
Bob Hogan		954	Andy Girouard		969
Dick Heins		953	Don Porter		969
			Ken Ives		913
Class A Heavy (10)			Bill Ives		864
Piet Boonstra		985			
Bud Peck		984	125 cc Class (12)		
Tink Foster		975	Pete Johnson		893
Phil Bourdon		974	Gerry Ladeau		880
Herb Walker		953	John Jacobson		822

Springfield M.C. Enduro
Holland, MA -- November 19, 1967
(75 entries)

High Score			Class B Light (27)		
Paul Luginoul	Sachs	908	Dick Thayer	Greeves	880
			Ron Commo	Greeves	817
Class A Light (5)			Chas. Hildebrand	Bultaco	792
Ron Webster	Greeves	904			
Dave Latham	Greeves	901	Class B Heavy (10)		
Frank DeGray	Sachs	896	Babe Mazur	Maico	810
Dick Turmel	Husqv.	891	Burn Morrell	BSA	23 mi.
Bob Hogan	Kawas.	864	Ken Arnold	Triumph	23 "
Class A Heavy (8)			125 cc Class (24)		
Piet Boonstra	Triumph	878	Mark Tarkington	Honda	37 mi.
Andy Girouard	Triumph	37 mi.	John Soltyx	Sachs	37 "
Bill Brittain	Match.	37 "	John Dennerly	Bultaco	37 "
Bud Peck	Triumph	23 "			
Ralph Spencer	Match.	23 "	Girls Class (1)		
			Gracie Hanson	Yamaha	23 mi.

RAMS Salmon River Ramble
East Hampton, CT – December 6, 1967
(52 total entries)

High Score
Ron Webster   Greeves   954

Class A Light (6)
Frank DeGray   Zundapp   922
Dick Turmel   Husqv.   905
Dave Latham   Greeves   890
Henry Royce   BSA   2nd ck.
Robert Redden Greeves 2nd ck.

Class A Heavy (3)
Piet Boonstra   Triumph   945
Ron Alleman   Maico   907
Maynard Ronstrom   Tri. 2nd ck.

Class B Light (17)
Dick Thayer   Greeves   942
Bruce Gadaire   Greeves   931
Bob Owen   Bultaco   926

Class B Heavy (12)
Bob Fielding   Triumph   877
Don Porter   Triumph 5th ck.
Ken Arnold   Triumph 5th ck.

0 – 125 cc Class (14)
Paul Liginbuhl   Sachs   952
John Soltys, Jr.   Sachs   5th ck.
Kenneth Wood Hercules 5th ck.

Connecticut Ramblers Snow Run
Warehouse Point, CT – February 25, 1968
(89 total entries)

High Score
Bill Perry   993

Class A Light (14)
Dick Thayer   987
Sal Scirpo   985
Bruce Gadaire   979
P. Boonstra (9th) Greeves 916

Class A 125cc (2)
John Soltys   883
Pete Johnson   7th ck

Class A Heavy (12)
George Ellis   992
Perlin Parker   983
Dick Turmel   982

Class B Light (27)
David Eames   942
Rod DeFord   979
Bob McKelvey   970

Class B 125cc (17)
Jim Nash   926
John Burgess   878
Jerry Ladeau   7th ck

Class B Heavy (16)
Ronald Gluck   977
Smiley Hulbert   972
John Lave   944

Team Award -- RAMS #2
Turmel, Gardner, Ronstrom

Meriden M.C. Closed Course Enduro
Meriden, CT – March 31, 1968
(82 total entries)

High Score
Bud Peck   Tri.   887

Class A Light (16)
Frank DeGray   Greev.   876
Ron Webster   Greev.   833
Bruce Gadaire   Greev.   801
Dave Latham   Greev.   800

Class A Heavy (10)
Piet Boonstra   Tri.   825
Perley Parker   Maico   809
Dick Turmel   Husqv. 4/84

Class A Bantam (4)
Don Pink   HD   3/63
Ken Wood   Hercules   3/120
Paul Liginbuhl   Honda   2/66

Class B Light (20)
A. Solomon   Greev. 5/88
Pete Sullivan   Bultaco 5/99
J. Allen, Jr.   Greev. 5/145

Class B Heavy (15)
Tom Coranas   BSA   3/56
B. Morrell   BSA   3/109
R. Balocki   Tri. 3/153

Class B Bantam (17)
John Percoski   Sachs 6/175
Will Bertand   Zundapp 5/182

Legend: x/x = Laps/Points Lost

Reggie Pink Memorial Closed Course Enduro
Maybrook, NY – April 7, 1968
(120 total entries)

High Score
Jim Moroney   Greev. 998

Class A Light (9)
Bill Hollenbeck   Greev. 982
Richard Heins   Greev. 979
Ed VanOverloop   Tri. 979

Class A Heavy (4)
Herb Walker   BSA   992
Piet Boonstra   Tri. 989
Bill Decker   Tri. 973

Class B Light (93)
Chris Case   Tri. 997
Ralph Durso   Sachs 990
Neil Avery   Husqv. 985
John Lesquereux   Sachs 985

Class B Heavy (14)
John McCormick   Husqv. 995
Tom Coranas III   BSA   984
Jake Herzog   Tri. 979
Peter Zloch   BSA   945

Paul Revere Enduro
Sterling, MA – April 21, 1968
(116 total entries)

High Score

Piet Boonstra	Tri.	996

Class A Light (10)

Bill Perry	Greev.	990
Ron Webster	Greev.	988
Ron Commo	Greev.	986

Class A Heavy (9)

Andy Girouard	Tri.	983
Ron Alleman	Maico	981
Frank DeGray	Tri. 650	978

Class A Bantam (4)

Sal Scirpo	Penton	976
John Soltys	Sachs	884

Girls (3)

Katy Holland	Ck 5

Class B Light (47)

Dave Eames	Ossa	983
Bob Perry	Greev.	981
Pete Sullivan	Bultaco	980

Class B Bantam (27)

Karl Schlotter	Sachs	952
Walt Nye	Sachs	919

Class B Heavy (12)

Lee Estabrooks	Tri.	949
Dick Balocki	Tri.	937
Don Blakesley	Honda	928

Sidecars (4)

Art Stuek & friend	Ck 5
Leon Dube & Ray LaJoie	10mi.

Team Award – New London M.C.
Perry, Perry and Manny Swass

Passaic Valley M.C. – Stage Coach Enduro
Northern NJ - May 5, 1968
(77 total entries)

High Score

Gene Esposito	Tri	983

Class A Light (10)

Bill Hollenback	976
Jim Moroney	973
Bob Maus	965

Class A Heavy (5)

Piet Boonstra	974
Herbert Walker	952
Ken Macri	927

Class B Light (32)

Thomas Stuart	963
Chester Puchalski	959
Fred McClernon, Jr.	943

Class B Heavy (6)

James Hollenback	944
James Hoare	942
Doug Bard	907

Under 100cc (20)

John Lesquereax	958
James Haddon	941

Tompkins County 90-Mile National Championship Enduro
Newfield, NY – April 28, 1968
(196 total entries)

High Score
Bill Baird   Tri.   974

Flyweight Champion
Ray Terwilliger   Honda   676

Bantam Champion
Leroy Winters   Penton   861

Class A Bantam (3)
Richard Bean   Bultaco   786

Lightweight Champion
Robert Fusan   Yamaha   963

Class A Light (27)
Fred C. Ford   Husqv.   945
Ron Bohn   Yamaha   940
Dave Barnes   BSA   922
Allen Weir   Bultaco   902

Medium-Weight Champion
John Penton   Husqv.   953

Class A Medium (13)
Charles Stapleford   Tri.   890
Gary Brown   Tri.   850
Piet Boonstra   Tri.   795

Heavyweight Champion
Gordon Potter   Tri.   798

Club Teams (20)
R.J. Bohn Cycle
   R.Fusan, R.Bohn, D.Nichols
RAMS #1
   Boonstra, Peck & Latham

Class B Bantam (23)
John Arnesen   Kaw.   661
Orville Green   Bultaco   80mi.
Thom. Saunders   Bultaco   68mi.

Class B Light (67)
Buck Wallsworth   Bultaco   886
Steven Satll   Yamaha   775
Rob't Berthelot   Bultaco   733

Class B Medium (22)
Richard Roberts   BSA   691
William Williams   BSA   94mi.
Paul Rinck   Tri.   80mi.

Class B Heavy (2)
John Harvey   Tri.   80mi.

Senior Champion
Harold Ward   Tri.   827

Senior Class (9)
Sal Scirpo   Penton   683
Don Nichols   Tri.   682
Carl Bergman   Ducati   65 mi.
Al Seduski   Ducati   42 mi.

Girl's Class (2)
Jackie Cook, Mary Perry   NS

Buddy Class (1)
J Campbell, K.Bechtel   26 mi.

High Score B Rider
Buck Walsworth   886

RAMS Spring Enduro
Somers, CT – May 12, 1968
(70 total entries)

High Score

Piet Boonstra	Tri	936

Class A Light (7)

Dave Latham	Greeves	927
Ron Webster	Greeves	911
Bruce Gadaire	Greeves	853

Class A Heavy (4)

Bud Peck	Tri.	895
Ron Alleman	Maico	878
Frank DeGray	Tri.	Ck11

Class A Bantam (10)

Paul Luginbuhl	Sachs	860
John Soltys	Sachs	746

Class B Light (33)

Dick McKinstry	Bultaco	848
Ron Johnson	Greeves	798
Pete Franklin	Bultaco	707

Class B Heavy (10)

John Clark		Tri. Ck11

Class B Bantam (12)

Karl Schlotter	Sachs	927
Tom Cook	Yamaha	860
John Donnerly	Bultaco	824

Team Award – RAMS #1
Boonstra, Peck & Latham

Green Mountain Riders Spring Enduro
Bennington, VT - May 26, 1968
(108 Total Entries)

High Score

Piet Boonstra	Tri.	938

Class A Light (9)

Ron Commo	Greev.	932
Frank DeGray	Greev.	916
Bill Perry	Greev.	905

Class A Heavy (8)

Bud Peck	Tri.	937
George Talcott	BSA	885
Perlin Parker	Maico	847

Class B Light (54)

Neil Hoag	Yam	898
David Eames	Bultaco	863
Dick McKinstry	Bultaco	850

Class B Heavy (14)

Francis Guchone	Honda	Ck4
Fred Douglas	BSA	Ck4
Bob Hicks	Tri.	Ck4

Bantam (Combined)

Paul Luginbuhl (A)	Sachs	858
Dick Aube (B)	Sachs	Ck4

Berkshire International Trials
Becket, MA – May 20 & 21, 1968

Gold Medal Winners - (1)

John Penton	Husqvarna	291

Silver Medal Winners – (10)

Leroy Winters	3	300
Piet Boonstra	6	275
George Ellis	6	253
Gerry Pacholke	8	291
Ron Webster	9	244
George Bailey	11	238
Ron Jeckel	15	278
Tink Foster	15	251
Bud Peck	15	224
Bob Hermann	16	203

Bronze Medals – (35)

Dick Heins	26	234
George Talcott	36	252
Ron Jackson	40	236
Frank DeGray	42	252
Al Born	46	280
Jim Moroney	46	217
William McPoyle	52	253
John Donnelly	61	183
Phil Bourdon	87	222
John Chicko	90	179
Ed Slegers	92	170
Charlie Vincent	99	242
John Taylor	101	239
George Claiborne	116	208
Art Salomon	132	221
Fran Curro	134	178
Dave Latham	151	223
Roger Lonneville	154	206
Steve Miller	158	234
Jerry Ladeau	166	197
Carl Easton	172	150
Eugene Lauzon	174	162
Larry Bastedo	176	211

Cross Country Test - Open

Piet Boonstra	Triumph	100
John Penton	Husky	94
Paul Cole	Honda	92

Cross Country – 250 class

Ron Jeckel	Greeves	100
Gerry Pacholke	Bultaco	95
Charlie Vincent	Ossa	92

Cross Country – 125 class

Leroy Winters	Penton	100
Al Born	Penton	88
Lee Penton	Sachs	69

Hill Climb Test – Open

John Penton	Husky	100
Piet Boonstra	Triumph	80
Frank DeGray	Triumph	80

Hill Climb Test – 250 Class

Gerry Pacholke	Bultaco	100
Ron Jeckel	Greeves	91
William McPoyle	Bultaco	89

Hill Climb Test – 125 Class

Leroy Winters	Penton	100
Al Born	Penton	100

Acc. & Braking Test – Open

Dave Snyder	Husky	100
Frank DeGray	Triumph	100
Ken Arnold	Triumph	97

Acc. & Braking Test – 250 Class

Jerry Ladeau	Yamaha	100

Acc. & Braking Test – 125 Class

Leroy Winters	Penton	100

Corduroy International Trial
Coboconk, Ont. – September 7 – 8, 1968
(230 Total Entries)

Grand Champion (Lightweight)
Leroy Winters   125 Pen   991

"Best Opposite" Class (HW Champion)
Bud Peck   Triumph   990

Expert Lightweight (38)
John Penton   Penton   990
Bob Maus   Bultaco   990

Expert Heavyweight (22)
J. Mileham   Tri.   989
S. Eaken   Husqvar 971

Senior Class (5)
Sal Scirpo   HD   926

100 cc Class (24)
Tom Penton   Penton   979
J. Sims   Penton   975

Junior (B) Lightweight (102)
M. Shinners   Bultaco   977
Bob Hicks   Bultaco   975

Junior (B) Heavyweight (26)
L. Hunt   Greeves   949
R. Fisher   CZ   949

Sidecar Class (4)
Lucy Stratton   Penton 313 mi.
Team Award – Penton Imports
Winters, Penton, Penton, Towne

Springfield M.C. Maine Enduro
Minot, ME – July 7, 1968
(97 total entries)

High Score
Dave Latham   Greev. 980

Class A Light (8)
Ron Commo   961
Bill Perry   960
Ron Webster   945

Class B Heavy (10)
Bud Peck   897
Piet Boonstra   890
Frank DeGray   872
Andre Giroud   870

Girls (3)
Gracie Hanson   1Ck

Class B Light (36)
David Eames   925
Dick McKinstry   914
Frank Hanson   847

Class B Heavy (21)
Gerry Green   744
Leon Dube   664
James Oxenham   585

Bantam (Combined)
Pete Johnson (A)   NS
Wilfred Bertrand (B)   876
Kall Schlotter   777

Meriden Closed Course Enduro
Meriden, CT – October 13, 1968
(82 total entries)

High Score		
Ron Webster	Greev.	1000
Bud Peck	Triumph	1000

Class A Light (10)	
Pete Sullivan	1000
Dave Latham	999
Bob Fielding	955

Class B Heavy (9)	
Piet Boonstra	1000
Andy Girouard	922
Ed Vanoverloop	6 laps

Class B Light (20)	
Frank Hanson	999.
Ron Johnson	997
W. Muller	975

Class B Heavy (20)	
R. Smith	885
John Liebl	818
Ken Arnold	777

Bantamweight (3)	
Don Pink	882
Bill Decker	4 laps
R. Baj	1 lap

Rifle City Riders Enduro
Becket, MA – November 5, 1968
(84 total entries)

High Score		
Dave Latham	Greeves	990

Class A Light (3)		
Ron Webster	Greeves	985
Dick Turmel	Husqvar	976

Class A Heavy (9)		
Piet Boonstra	Triumph	986
Bud Peck	Triumph	985
Carl Wickstrand	Triumph	920
Gus Cornelis	Triumph	901
M. Ronstrom	Triumph	894

Class B Light (37)		
Bruce Gaudice	Greeves	988
John Lally	Triumph	976
Art Latielle	Greeves	974

Class B Heavy (14)		
Bob Fielding	Honda	924
Andy Girouard	Triumph	926
K. Graham	Triumph	903

Bantamweight (21)		
P. Luginbuhl	Sachs	982
M. Turkington	Kawasaki	970

Team Trophy – RAMS #1
Peck, Boonstra & Latham

Passaic Valley M.C. – Stage Coach Enduro
Northern New Jersey – May 4, 1969
(73 total entries)

High Score
| Gene Esposito | Tri | 996 |

Class A Light (9)
James Smith	991
Bob Maus	976
Ralph Spencer	949

Class A Heavy (9)
Piet Boonstra	995
Bill Fitzgibbons	984
Herb Walker	978

Class B Light (35)
Moncure Corey	976
John Chicko	967
John Lesqueraux	964

Class B Heavy (10)
Arthur Salomon	950
Doug Bard	947
James Slattery	945

Under 100cc (10)
| Nick Irons | 940 |
| Edward Junkett | 918 |

RAMS Soapstone Mountain Enduro
Somers, CT – May 11, 1969
(119 total entries)

High Score
| Piet Boonstra | Tri | 960 |

Class A Light (9)
Dave Latham	Greev.	953
Frank DeGray	Tri.	939
Pete Sullivan	Bultaco	932

Class A Heavy (9)
Andre Girouard	Tri.	870
John Liebl	Tri.	763
Chuck Senecal	Tri.	Ck.6

Class A 100cc (10)
Karl Schlotter	Sachs	Ck.11
Ron Commo	Pen	Ck.10
Peter Cornell	Bultaco	Ck. 1

Class B Light (53)
Brust MacKay	Yam	822
Kenneth Hart	Yam	817
Jim Allen	Ossa	796

Class B Heavy (16)
Brian Inman	Bultaco	831
Art Stueck	Grumph	Ck.11
Hal Wilhelm	Tri.	Ck.10

Class B 100cc (10)
| Richard DeCiero | Yam | Ck.8 |
| John Lisowski | Pen | Ck.8 |

Girl's Class (2)
| Helen Wilhelm | Pen | Ck.2 |
| Diana Johnson | Pen | Ck.2 |

Team Award – RAMS #2
Girouard, Sullivan, Blakesley

Berkshire International Trials
Becket, MA – May 20 & 21, 1969

Gold Medal Winners - (16)

125 cc Class

Gordon Razee	Pen	374
Bud Green	Pen	361
Herm Stoeckle	Sac	359
Al Born	Pen	356

250 cc Class

Jeff Penton	Hus	386
Pete Sullivan	Bul	379
Charlie Vincent	Oss	363
Chuck Boehler	Gre	361
George Bailey	Hus	357
Jerry Lohrer	Gre	352
Jim Allen	Oss	348

Open Class

Ron Bohn	Hus	382
Piet Boonstra	Tri.	354
James Fogle	Hus	344
Tom Janosik	Hus	344
John Liebl	Tri	344

Silver Medal Winners (33)

125 cc Class (6)

Ron Commo	5	359
Leroy Winters	8	378
Tim Hoffman	10	296
D. Rockwell White	15	321

250 Class (18)

Ron Webster	2	346
Bob Fielding	2	345
Jerry Ladeau	2	345
Bob Maus	4	321

Open Class (9)

Jake Herzog	0	311
Bill Perry	2	358
John Penton	5	386
Don Pink	5	344
Glen Jeckel	5	328

Sat. Cross Country - Open

John Penton	100
Paul Cole	97

250 cc Class

Dave Latham	100
Jeff Penton	96

125 cc class

Leroy Winters	100
Ron Commo	91

Sat. Speed Test - Open

Smiley Hulbert	100
John Penton	92

250 cc Class

Jeff Penton	100
Ron Jeckel	99

125 cc Class

Leroy Winters	100
B. Green	95

Sunday Cross Country - Open

Ron Bohn	100

250 cc Class

Ron Jeckel	100
Jeff Penton	97

125 cc Class

Gordon Razee	100
Herm Stoeckle	96

Sunday Speed Test – Open

Ron Bohn	100
John Penton	96

250 cc Class

Dave Latham	100
Ron Jeckel	100

125 cc Class

Leroy Winters	100
Bud Green	96

Pennsylvania State Enduro – 115-Mile National Championship
Dallas, PA – June 8, 1969
(385 total entries)

High Score
Dave Latham	Gre	985

Class A Light (15)
Bruce Sutton	Sachs	945
Lloyd Levinsky	Penton	934
Dave Fisher	Sachs	932
Herm Stoeckle	Sachs	929

Class A Medium (22)
Bob Fusan	Yamaha	978
James Smith	Greeves	977
Jack McLane	Honda	969
Sox Brookhart	Greeves	969

Class A Light Heavy (18)
Dutch Bliss	Triumph	979
Norm Ford	Husky	978
Ron Bohn	Husky	975
John Thomas	Husky	973
John Penton	Husky	968
Bud Peck	Triumph	967
Piet Boonstra	Triumph	964

Class A Heavy (3)
Dave Barnes	BSA	953
Gordon Potter	Triumph	923

Senior Class (9)
Edgar Kauffman	Yama.	868
John Rogers	Bultaco	802
Al Sedusky	Penton	758

Buddy Class (2)
Michael Colligan	Penton	3rd ck.
Susan Richardson (P)		

Class B Bantam 0-100 (52)
Fred Perry	Zundapp	765
George Davidson	Hon	756
Dennis Neubauer	Hon	745
Steve Petty	Penton	735

Class B Light (75)
Dennis Hughes	Penton	896
Michael Curry	Penton	891
Thomas Rossi	Penton	889
Joseph Nash	Yamaha	888

Class B Medium (126)
James Scott	Yamaha	952
Louis Smith	Yamaha	950
William Kain	Yamaha	943
Mike Shinners	Bultaco	941

Class B Light Heavy (54)
Jim Fogle	Husky	953
Joseph Arcosi	Bultaco	939
Harry Lutos	Husky	922
Art Salomon	Husky	914

Class B Heavy (3)
Harry Penn	Triumph	5th ck.
William Sutton	Triumph	2nd ck.

Powder puff Class (5)
Pat Barnes	Bultaco	3rd ck.
Bonnie Elston	Bultaco	2nd ck.

Team Award – RAMS #1
Boonstra, Latham & Peck

RAMS Paul Revere Enduro
Westhampton, MA – June 15, 1969
(176 total entries)

High Score		Class B Bantam	
Dave Latham	958	D. White	870
		A. Hanson	863
Class A Bantam			
K. Schlottler	920	Class B Light	
Ron Commo	863	W. Bailey	945
		J. Allen	934
Class A Light		F. Rice	921
Ron Webster	954		
Pete Sullivan	946		
Will Guy	933	Class B Heavy	
		Don Blakesley	947
		J. Oxenham	883
Class A Heavy		Gerry Green	812
Piet Boonstra	956		
Bud Peck	928	Girls Class	
Phil Bourdon	877	D. Johnson	2nd ck

Team Award – RAMS #1   Buddy Class – A. & M. Eames

Challenger's T-Shirt Enduro
Nashua, NH – June 20, 1969
(180 total entries)

High Score		Class B Bantam	
Frank DeGray	996	Arthur Hart	991
		John Lisowski	991
Class A Bantam			
Peter Cornell	984	Class B Light	
Thomas Cook	978	Tom Grant	995
		Bill Spooner	994
Class A Light		Ronnie King	992
Ron Johnson	994		
Walt Nye	992	Class B Heavy	
Ron Webster	992	Hal Wilhelm	990
		Al Simmons	983
Class A Heavy		Gerry Green	979
Piet Boonstra	989		
John Liebl	988	Girl's Class	
Bud Peck	987	Diana Johnson	878
		Pat Green	858

Curly Fern Enduro – 100-Mile National Championship
Lakehurst, NJ – April 5, 1970
(300 total entries)

High Score
Buck Walsworth

Class A Bantam (11)

Doug Wilford	Penton	975
Gordon Razee	Penton	931
George Cunha	Penton	925
Lloyd Levinsky	Penton	899

Class A Light (32)

Bob Fusan	Husky	985
Bill Osterkamp	Bultaco	984
Dave Eames	Ossa	975
Carl Patterson	Yamaha	966

Class A Medium (14)

Charles Stapleford	Kaw	985
Jack McLane	Honda	982
Norm Ford	Husky	981
Gene Esposito	Husky	968
Paul Cole	Honda	953

Class A Heavy (9)

Piet Boonstra	Triumph	922
Don Corson	Triumph	880
Andre Girouard	Triumph	952
Len Puckett	Triumph	845

Class A Senior (4)

Al Triplett	Kawasaki	846
Sal Scirpo	Harley-Dav.	797
Til Akehurst	Yamaha	779

"Fickle Finger of Fate Award"

John Dyches	Yamaha	693

Class B Bantam (85)

Tom Rossi	Penton	952
James Haddow	Bultaco	909
Sam Estilow	Yamaha	900
Wally Dyer	Penton	873

Class B Light (166)

Phil Ginder	Yamaha	951
Lou Smith	Yamaha	950
Paul Harris	Ossa	935
Bill Pittman	Yamaha	934

Class B Medium (28)

Howard Tomlin	Husky	941
Thomas Michel	Husky	934
Don Moody	Husky	913
Joe Morel	Husky	900

Class B Heavy (19)

Dave Meade	Triumph	923
Bob Evans	BSA	922
Joe DiSimone	BSA	890

Class B Senior (6)

George Wolfe	Bultaco	5th ck
Russ Dunfee	Honda	3rd ck
John Rogers	Bultaco	3rd ck

Powder Puff Class (2)

Cherryl Dunfee	Yamaha	4th ck
Marcia MacDonald	Bul.	2nd ck

Best Represented Club
Delaware Enduro Riders

RAMS Midsummer Special Enduro
Gilmanton, NH – August 9, 1970
(366 total entries)

High Score			Class B Bantam (101)	
Piet Boonstra	990		Thomas Brick	985
			Paul Boisvert	984
Class A Bantam (8)			Richard DeCiero	984
Dick Thayer	988			
Ruane Crummett	980		Class B Light (168)	
Al Simmons	976		Bill VanBuren	987
			Brian Lunt	983
Class A Light (12)			R.H. Youngstrum	983
Frank DeGray	988			
Bob Fielding	988		Class B Heavy (52)	
Dick Aube	985		Jerry Dugan	984
			Jim Hunt	979
Class A Heavy (11)			John Moore	979
Peter Johnson	989			
Maynard Ronstrom	983		Girl's Class (12)	
John Liebl	973		Marcia MacDonald	965
			Gracie Hanson	937
Buddy Class (2)				
Bob & Jane Hicks	919			

Pine Tree State Enduro
Minot, ME – July 5, 1969
(185 total entries)

High Score			Class B Bantam (33)	
Dave Latham	974		Bill Boles	880
			Pete Nielson	849
Class A Bantam (6)				
Ron Commo	958		Class B Light (89)	
Karl Schlottler	913		Frank Rice	923
			Herluf Johnson	915
Class A Light (14)				
Ron Webster	974		Class B Heavy (28)	
David Eames	965		Gerry Green	929
			Jake Herzog	923
Class A Heavy (9)				
Bud Peck	971		Girl's Class (6)	
Piet Boonstra	969		Ellen McDowell	3rd ck

New England Enduro Championship 1959 - 1970

Year	Grand Champion	Heavyweight	Lightweight
1959	Charlie Schumitz	**Dick Chandler**	**Everett Wright**
		Coleman Mitchell	Harold Dean
		Tink Foster	Greg Lipski
1960	Frank DeGray	**Bill Brittain**	**Walt Knights**
		Christy Scholar	Harold Dean
		Coleman Mitchell	B. Mortensen
1961	Bob Butterfield	**Christy Scholar**	**Harold Dean**
		Myron Hooker	Frank DeGray
		Coleman Mitchell	Tink Foster
1962	Frank DeGray	**Phil Bourdon**	**Bob Butterfield**
		Carl Wickstrand	Sonny Turmel
		Dick Turmel	Greg Lipsky
1963	Vito Bonan	**Frank DeGray**	**Bob Butterfield**
		Werner Tobler	Sonny Turmel
		Tink Foster	Don Lappie
1964	Bill Perry	**Don Cutler**	**Vito Bonan**
		Werner Tobler	Bob Butterfield
		Al Semmelrock	Don Lohnes
1965	Don Cutler	**Piet Boonstra**	**Bill Perry**
		Al Semmelrock	Vito Bonan
		Tom Bindloss	Bob Hogan
1966	Piet Boonstra	**Tom Bindloss**	**Al Gendreau**
		Phil Bourdon	Bill Perry
		Bud Peck	Bob Hogan
1967	Dave Latham	**Piet Boonstra**	**Ron Webster**
		Bud Peck	Dick Turmel
		Phil Bourdon	Bob Hogan
1968	Bud Peck	**Piet Boonstra**	**Ron Webster**
		Andre Girouard	Dave Latham
		Maynard Ronstrom	Pete Sullivan
1969	Bud Peck	**Piet Boonstra**	**Ron Webster**
		John Liebl	Pete Sullivan
		Gerry Green	Jerry Ladeau
1970	Don Cutler	**Bud Peck**	**Bob Fielding**
		John Liebl	Ron Webster
		Gerry Green	Ron Alleman
		Piet Boonstra	Dave Latham

Printed in the United States
69917LV00002B/126

9 780971 858923